A World Less Safe

_____

Copyright © 2005 Terrell E. Arnold
All rights reserved.
ISBN: 1-4196-1617-X

To order additional copies, please contact us.
BookSurge, LLC
www.booksurge.com
1-866-308-6235
orders@booksurge.com

A World Less Safe
Essays on Conflict in the 21st Century

Terrell E. Arnold

Booksurge Publishing
2005

A World Less Safe

CONTENTS

Acknowledgments	IX
Part One	**1**
Pre-emptive Regime Change	3
Preventive Strikes A Call To Chaos	15
Us Policy Toward Israel—Stop Pretending	23
Aid To Israel—Time To Set Conditions	27
On The Relevance Of The United Nations	33
Tax Cuts, Food Stamps, And Cost Free War	39
Bush And The Black Box	43
The Outsider Role In Transforming Islam	51
America's Margin For Error	57
We Have Become The Main Problem	71
Where Did You Say The Buck Stopped?	79
Bush Had A Dream During The Convention	83
In Denial On Nuclear Proliferation	89
Deal With American Tyranny First	95
Vindicating American Democracy	101
FEMA Was A Victim Of Terrorism	111
Part Two	**117**
Can We Win The War On Terrorism?	119
Fighting The Real War On Terrorism	123
The Cost Of Becoming Predator	127
Why The War On Terrorism Will Fail	131
Dangerous Imaginings In The War On Terrorism	141
Osama Bin Laden's Cunning Tape Terrorism	145
Terrorism And The Fear Market	149
Terrorism Has Hijacked Our National Priorities	161
Terrorism War Is Main Terrorism Generator	167
Part Three	**173**
Palestine—The Problem And The Prospect	175
The Delusion Of Total Support	184
Palestine's Self Inflicted Wounds	187
The Christian Coalition And Israel	191

Iran—The Next Israeli Domino	195
What's Wrong With Deposing Arafat	199
The Challenge Of Ethnic Cleansing In Israel	207
Against The Law To Criticize Israel	211
The Fallacy Of Even Handedness	215
Making The World Less Safe For Americans	223
An Outrageous Invasion Of American Diplomacy	227
Part Four	**240**
Iraq—The Case Is Still Not Made	241
Saddam's Dilemma—How To Prove A Negative	245
Why Should We Fight Iraq?	249
Democracy On Trial In Iraq	257
Iraq—Dealing With Saddam's Legacy	263
Reforming The Majlis—Iraq's National Assembly	269
Iraq Must Not Become An American Palestine	277
Baghdad And Washington—Iraq's Guerrila Wars	283
Iraq—Deceptions In The War On Terrorism	289
Facing Reality In Iraq	293
Iraq—Past Time To Move On	297
The Enemies In Iraq	301
The Fallacies Of American Democracy For Iraq	307
A Fifty Years War In Iraq	313
Only A Few Bad Apples	317
America's Oil Problem	323
Seeing Our Way Out Of Iraq	335
Part Five	**341**
Another Look At The Black Box	343

ACKNOWLEDGMENTS

Anyone who has ever written a book ends up with spiritual debts he or she can never repay. The money debts get paid, but those people who devote time and mind to reading, editing, and thinking about presentation and the myriad details of publication always do things that money can't buy. I start with Amy Rabas, an intern who just graduated from the University of Wisconsin, Stevens Point, and her mentor, Professor Stuart Morris, of the Department of Art and Design, who developed the cover. They did it under contract and they were paid, but the money really did not cover their fine attention to detail and the times we spent together thinking through the message that finally was given first impact by Amy's cover design. A good part of the credit goes to my wife, Yvonne, who has helped me through one earlier book, three co-authorships, and countless speeches and classroom presentations. Her grammatical and presentational senses are among my most valuable tools. Alexandra Jane Noble, a sharp thinker and graduate of Yale Law School and Stanford University, added her numerous touches to the result.

Retired Ambassador Holsey Gates Handyside, a diplomatic

colleague of nearly 25 years, shared with me his rich background on Iraq and Palestine, and other insights into the Middle East and into the sometimes flaky environment that is our nation's capital. His service in the Middle East, from Libya to Iraq, in the US Department of Energy, and in the State Department as an emergency management trainer—where he and I guided training for much of middle and senior management in the 1980s and early 1990s—provided valuable insights that enriched the book throughout.

Writing today is greatly assisted by the Internet. Especially valuable were the online articles of the New York Times, the Washington Post, the Los Angeles Times, the New Yorker, the Christian Science Monitor, The Cleveland Plain Dealer, and the Guardian, to name a few. Several site managers need to be noted: Jeff Rense at rense.com—where virtually all of the articles in this book were posted, William Rivers Pitt at Truthout.com, Mark Bruzonsky at Mid-East Realities, Amy Goodman at Democracy Now, David Krieger at Nuclear Age Peace Foundation, and a long list of other websites, including US Government departments, all make research and writing richer and more convenient than ever.

All of the articles were written over a period of four years, from 2002 to 2005, and each includes the date written. Since each was written to be free-standing, some repetition of facts and data was inevitable, but wherever possible such points are handled by reference back to the first mention of them. In some instances, thanks to the comments of readers, some information that was available at the time each article was written has been added. Factual errors, where noted or called to my attention, have been corrected. When all of that is said, the contents of this book are my entire responsibility.

Terrell E. Arnold
Plover, Wisconsin

INTRODUCTION

It may be pessimistic to write a book on conflict in the 21st Century when that new era is just getting off the ground. However, our national outlook has changed remarkably and quickly in the five years since President Clinton prematurely announced the new century in his 2000 State of the Union address. He said: "We are fortunate to be alive at this moment in history. Never before has our nation enjoyed, at once, so much prosperity and social progress with so little internal crisis or so few external threats." Actually entering the new century, George W. Bush painted an upbeat picture in his 2001 address, citing (of course without saying so) his inheritances from Clinton: "a balanced budget, big surpluses, a military that is second to none, a country at peace with its neighbors." Clouds had gathered, however, by President Bush's 2002 State of the Union address, delivered only months after the September 11, 2001 attacks. "As we gather tonight," he said, "our nation is at war, our economy is in recession, and the civilized world faces unprecedented dangers."

It is an appalling truth that we entered the 21st century with global conditions as peaceful as they had been at any time in the 20th century, but by the end of the year we were back at war. How we got that way is a striking tale of American leadership, its motives, and its reactions to the challenges facing the United States. The articles in this book, ranging from fairly lengthy essays to brief op-eds, examine numerous decisions, actions, and situations that perturb possible futures, notably political and economic prospects of the United States in the new century.

In the years that followed the 1989 collapse of the Berlin Wall, almost everybody turned off the idea of the Cold War. That essentially bilateral nuclear standoff had dominated global security thinking for almost half a century. America had won with real and divisive costs in blood, but also at the cost of designing, building, and deploying the most powerful military force in history. On the day after, what could one do with such a force?

Former CIA director, James Woolsey, now one of the neo-conservative advisers of the President George W. Bush team, summed up the quandary during his confirmation hearings in a somewhat whimsical way: In his view, we had traded the "Soviet dragon", our singular enemy for decades, for a "pit of poisonous snakes." The reaction was a crashing silence. We, the United States, had multi-billions of dollars in sunk costs and upkeep of a military operating system that had lost its mission. It is impractical and probably not do-able to focus a global military strike force on a snake pit.

From that point to the end of the Clinton administration, the response was military downsizing. Money that might have been spent by the Pentagon was used on social programs and getting rid of budget deficits. The US Government entered 2001 with a budget surplus and a cumulative national debt of $5.77 trillion. The surplus was expected to grow for at least the next decade. For the first time in years officials talked positively about paying off the national debt, hopefully in a decade or less. As seen by most Americans, it was a satisfying end to the 20th century.

As the United States entered the 21st century, in ways that

are most often discussed only among specialists, it was truly a superpower. It enjoyed a gross national product (GNP) of about 10 trillion dollars. The next largest GNP (Japan) was less than half that scale. The US economy produced almost a third of the world gross domestic product (consumption, plus investment, plus exports, minus imports); it was roughly matched by the entire output of the European Community. While still a major world producer of most goods, the United States had entered what some dubbed a "post-industrial" mode that involved diversifying increasingly into service sectors, especially those related to information technologies.

The US occupied an increasingly crowded global living space. While the US had only about 4.6% of the world's people in 2001, senior Americans had witnessed a virtual trebling of world population in their lifetimes. World population had doubled since 1960, reaching more than 6 billion, and was headed toward doubling again by mid-century unless growth rates could be brought under control.

As the leading global model of economic development, the United States faced growing shortages. While its transport systems (air, road, rail, and sea) were almost totally dependent on oil, US oil production had peaked; imports, already more than half of supply, were growing daily. Mexico had larger crude oil reserves. A global peaking of oil output was thought imminent by some analysts, although others were more optimistic. Dependent on coal for the largest share (over 40%) of electricity generation, the US enjoyed coal resources of about 280 billion tons, which, mined at current rates, would last for more than 200 years; but unless the US improved both mining and burning habits, it faced gross environmental damage from coal use. The US had the major natural gas resources of North America, but energy use increasingly exceeded domestic supplies of gas, oil, and coal.

The US had become a net energy importer. A modest percentage of its energy came from renewable sources: wind, sun, water, waste conversions, etc. The US was producing almost one third of world domestic product, while using about a quarter of the world's primary energy (oil, gas, and coal).

Materials markets were being driven by a combination of declining global supplies, explosively expanding competition for available supplies, diversifying uses, and rising prices. The most awkward equations involved (1) increasing human numbers versus decreasing living space, (2) burgeoning demand for material resources versus mostly dwindling supplies, (3) increasing food requirements versus shrinking arable land, (4) rising human expectations versus lagging prospects for satisfaction, and (5) slow development of alternative systems and resources versus rising need for change.

While rocking along for decades at low levels of participation in the global economy, China suddenly took off. With almost 21% of the world's people, China produced less than 4% of world gross domestic product, but it had an asset which seemed hardly noticed at the time: A literacy rate for both men and women of close to 90%; that, with low wages, made China almost ideal as an outsource for consumer manufacturing. India, with a literacy rate of only about 45%, still had a literate population larger than that of the United States and had become a major source of information technology goods and services. Others, such as Brazil, were advancing rapidly.

America was at the pinnacle of a world economic pyramid that was rapidly changing its shape. Rippling peaks were climbing the slopes. The European Community—with about the same number of people—was collectively as productive. In terms of purchasing power parity, China was moving up rapidly. The global battle for resources was rapidly intensifying. While virtually every country had military forces, the competition was not military. It was economic; the competitors were increasingly effective. Staying even had become a chore. Getting bigger was an increasing challenge.

The challenges were real. Not clear was how they were to

be met. As George W. Bush took his seat in the Oval Office, he took the reins of a government that knew all there was to know about virtually anything, except the most secret plans and capabilities of other governments. However, most of the problems he faced were neither about rocket science nor dependent on specific intelligence for basic understanding of what needed to be done. He needed a theory of the problems the country faced; his neo-conservative advisers handed him a set of ideological, unilateral, and warlike choices.

With an occasional backward look, the essays in this book mainly deal with events after the start of the George W. Bush administration. There were significant drivers for coming events. First, the world was not really as peaceful as we seemed to think because some conflicts, especially in West and Central Africa, approached genocide proportions. Second, China, India, and Brazil (in particular) were emerging, both as significant US trading partners and as heavy long-term competitors for shrinking global resources, such as oil, other energy sources, ferrous and non-ferrous metals. Third, the coming competition for access to those resources was ill-defined. Fourth, incoming members of the core Bush team, the larger group of neo-conservatives, and the still larger group of Bush supporters were not pleased with American preparations for that future. The core group had a theory of the problem that was to give us the War on Terrorism, the invasion of Iraq, and moves toward other pre-emptive military strikes. The abrupt ending of our peace-time euphoria and the catalyst for our new war-like posture came with the attacks of September 11, 2001.

The stated goal of the Bush team was to make our country safe. For that purpose, the War on Terrorism was launched with the invasion of Afghanistan. For that purpose, the Bush team invaded Iraq at a cost of hundreds of billions of dollars, thousands of American lives, and tens of thousands of Iraqis killed and wounded. For that purpose, the United States rededicated itself to Israel, while continuing to turn a blind eye to the repression of the Palestinian people. For that purpose, the United States now threatens Iran and fumbles around over threatening North Korea for thinking nuclear, while the United States launches a new effort to design and build new generations of nuclear weapons and deliberately talks about using them.

In their first term, the Bush team assumed a US military posture much like those maintained during the Cold War. It distorted US resource allocation by putting money into military programs, stealing money from social programs, and giving it (through tax cuts) to powerful supporters. But mainly, the Bush team has used extreme US military power to frighten, intimidate, and kill, and create alliances for that purpose, while pre-positioning in the Middle East and elsewhere for the battles that were already underway for control of key resources such as oil. This posture, more aggressively pursued in the second Bush term, announces to everyone that future resource allocations will be militarily competitive, not politically cooperative; it will make the United States the enemy in situations where in the past (at worst) it was neutral.

As several essays point out, we could have made more friends in the Middle East and elsewhere by focusing on programs to end poverty and disease, and by giving proper attention to the rights and needs of the Palestinians and other repressed peoples. On balance Bush/neo-con policies and actions make our situation in the world more difficult to defend. Even more disturbing, they make the world less safe for Americans and everybody else.

For Alfred L. Atherton, Jr.

A brilliant diplomat and tireless advocate
of fairness in American Middle East Policy

PART ONE
US POLICIES AND ACTIONS

PRE-EMPTIVE REGIME CHANGE
August 2002

Talk in Washington for the past several weeks on when and how to take out Saddam Hussein has been conducted at a level of almost childlike faith in the utility of regime change as a way of disposing of the country's enemies and creating friendly governments. In the groups and individuals close around the President, this action has taken on an urgency that is wholly out of step with Washington's willingness for the past several decades to endure and even cultivate Saddam's presence in Baghdad. The premise of promoters in the Project for the New American Century (PNAC), the Defense Policy Board (DPB), and other enthusiasts is that taking out Saddam will usher in a new era of tranquility in the Middle East.

A generous menu of options being considered by the promoters is now public, thanks to a new standard of Washington 'leaking'. It is hard to tell whether the leaks are trial balloons, pre-emptive policy thrusts, power grabs for the promoting groups, or inept official information management. Nonetheless, it is possible to examine in depth the tragic flaws in the idea of a pre-emptive regime change in Iraq, even though any real planning is probably being closely held among true believers.

Why is Saddam still around? The first question—what will be the flavor of Iraqi leadership after Saddam—if raised at all, has gone unanswered. One possible answer is to cobble together a group of exiles that were out of step, out of favor, possibly even threatened, and out of patience enough to leave. The second question—what keeps Saddam in power—if raised, appears to have focused on the wrong answer. Most commonly, one hears that Saddam is a ruthless SOB who permits no opposition and who stifles the fortunes and/or the breath of any promising candidate for succession. That is a cardinal rule for staying on top as a dictator, but Saddam neither created this model nor is he alone or necessarily the worst of those who follow it.

Another answer that needs careful thought is simply that Saddam is still around because he has been able to maintain various coalitions of the elites. Saddam's principal chips for doing that have been money, power, and influence, to say nothing, in some cases, of life itself.

Because their futures are at stake, these elites are likely to lead, or at least finance, a street-by-street battle for Baghdad. Unless they are also removed or leave in any Saddam exodus, any returning cluster of exiles will have to reckon with them. The results of the bargaining will certainly bode ill for the expectations of the regime changers. To know how badly that often works, one needs only to review British experience in Iraq.

One of the problems of Iraq, partly due to Saddam, is that the country is caught in a time warp. Over a long period, rule by fiat creates habits of mind and behavior that do not change quickly or uniformly. While Saddam did not invent the problems of the Sunni and Shi'a Muslims, the Kurds, and the Turkomen in Iraq, he did not try to build cohesion by any means other than brute force. Planting the seed of democracy and throwing water on it won't do much without firm guidance and education, all of which take years of patient effort.

What are the ground rules? The United States is forging new rules by taking out the leadership of a nation merely because US officials do not like it, do not trust it, fear its warlike capabilities, or think it has weapons of mass destruction (WMDs). The roster of countries that have or seek such weapons easily exceeds twenty. Is the plan to go after all of them? Will it make any difference what form of government and leadership they have, or will the sole driver be suspicion of production and/or possession of WMDs?

At the end of World War II, mainly the former colonial powers either revalidated or created our present system of nation states. That system has numerous problems, but it has served the world reasonably well. The system depended heavily on two factors: The first was delineation, codification, and international recognition of boundaries around each state. Much of the world map was already drawn, but during the immediate post-war decades, the bulk of the world's colonial real estate was allotted, mainly to the people who lived in specific pieces of it. Israel was an exception to this rule, because Palestine was already well occupied by the Palestinian people. The territories of nation states that we now know and largely accept emerged from this process. The second factor, an ancient principle of statehood, was general agreement among nations that the people within each nation state had the final word on who ruled them and how. The United States and others have made many attempts to interfere, but the basic rule remains that the choices of form of government and leadership are strictly local options.

The prime sources of trouble – A factor that was not dealt with in post war mapmaking was the rich array of out-groups and ethnic, religious, and cultural enclaves that existed in many of the resultant nation states. It was not likely that these problems could be fixed in any short period, but the disposition, assimilation, exclusion, or otherwise of those groups was left to the leadership of each state. Some pungent liquors, e.g., Afghanistan with at least five contending tribal groups and warlords, remain with us. Bosnia, or the whole remnant of Post-World War II Yugoslavia, is another case in point. A consensus procedure that is well short of democratic has been the rule among these tribal groups and many others for millennia.

The effect of the process has been that although the world is largely free of wars between nations, there are many countries that are not internally at peace. A review of data in the US Department of State annual report, <u>Patterns of Global Terrorism</u>, shows that groups in at least 20 countries seek separation from their parent states. Groups in at least 35-40 additional countries are bent on overthrowing current regimes. That is close to one third of all present nation states. Those countries represent the slow fuse that can explode any plan for pre-emptive regime change. Getting individual tribes or ethnic groups to apply some democratic leadership selection procedure is not nearly as difficult as getting the tribes and factions within present state bounds to work together in some common regime, democratic or not. The recent tendency of Sub-Sahara African countries to break up along tribal lines is one manifestation of the difficulty.

How potentially explosive the situation can be was displayed suddenly and graphically with the fall of the Soviet Union. The nationalities of the former USSR flew the coop as rapidly as possible, and some, such as the Chechens, are still trying.

The need for reform—The widespread tendencies for states to splinter indicate that, globally, the system of nation states is unstable and needs reform. In the late 1950s and 1960s, the United States thought it could deal with the problems of poverty and non-participation, and help bring the out-groups and enclaves into national systems by promoting rapid economic development. That did not work because we had neither good development models nor the will to involve ourselves deeply or long enough to get it done.

Our own transformation as a society had taken almost two centuries, but we expected instant results in any country we assisted. That did not happen. Governments were reluctant to address the out-group problems, and we declined or were unwilling to intervene. Some people got rich, most stayed poor or got poorer, the out-groups barely advanced, and we had inadequate stamina for it. We ended up with our present approach: try to feed the poorest of the poor, ignore development, and don't address the out-group problems.

No better formula has been put forward. We used the Marshall Plan and similar programs to restore Western Europe and Japan, but we were totally at sea on how to promote major social transformations in much of the developing world, and we still are. Part of the problem was that academic political scientists were unable or unwilling (until the last decade) to grapple with the tough questions involved, even though economists such as Walt and Gene Rostow set about doing so with reasonably good results. The UN predicts dire conditions for the planet by mid-century if the wealthy nations do not do a better job in the years ahead, but it will be tough because the population could grow by 5-6 billion people by 2050.

On political reform, we are equally at sea. The best tools we have evolved are evolutionary processes of change, not precipitate transformations of oligarchic nations such as Iraq into modern states. The key task we have been unable to perform well or reliably is selection/identification of the right people. The task is to find/develop capable people who are in for the long haul, have a concept of national interest, genuinely want their nations to grow and prosper, understand their own societies deeply, and are not mere influence peddlers and power seekers. Here, whether we exercised choice directly or indirectly, we repeatedly have used our own criteria of selection, often choosing people with abilities no more critical than English language skill. Few of the regime changes that occurred were to our liking. Some durable ones were anything but likeable.

The US leadership problem—With respect to the pending decisions on Iraq, in the history of the United States it has always been possible that core leadership could operate for indefinite periods without consulting anybody outside the inner circle. In the media rich world of today, one has to be more focused and of stronger will to take that course, because the noise level goes up rapidly, and with the combination of print and electronic media plus the Internet, every corner will be heard from. Thus, several groups are watching and commenting upon the small cluster of Iraq decision makers. The problem is that there appears to exist no counterweight to a group inside and close to the White House who, following the leaders of the Project for the New American Century and the Defense Policy Board, have chosen to carry out a coup and leave the rest of the country, including Congress, on the sidelines while they play out their own scenarios on how the world should be run.

The Iraq take-down promoters cite polls showing wide public interest in Saddam Hussein, but it pays to be skeptical of these polls. The media have made Saddam into a popular villain. That notoriety is enhanced by the attention Washington leaders give him. The concern about Saddam is thus more a reflection of hit count or name drop frequency than it is of any hard knowledge of how real or imminent a threat Saddam may represent to American interests. PNAC and other promoters of a war against Iraq count on this kind of superficial support to justify their venture; their use of such polls misleads residents. The moment enough Americans die in the encounter, however, that support will diminish.

The regime changers around the President, momentarily we hope, also have forgotten the complex, global, interdependent system we thrive on. "Thrive on" is the key term, because our enormous economic power is locked into that system. If it works, we continue to grow and prosper. If it doesn't, we falter. We may not hurt as much as others, but the bloom goes off the rose quickly if the rest of this global system flounders. We can try to tell this system how to behave, but we do not have enough people in enough places with enough experience, judgment, and influence to do that job. We cannot succeed as an island in a sea of hostility.

To our detriment, this group of leaders actually violates a critical, if implicit, principle of American governance: That we will change leadership regularly and introduce new blood. Instead, we are watching a cabal of old blood that is entrenched on a deadly course. Members of this group have been in government so often and at such high levels that they have acquired the arrogance of power that our system was designed to prevent. At one point, with George W. Bush so obviously inexperienced in foreign affairs, it looked comforting to have the old hands on board. On their present courses, we may or may not live to regret it.

Regime change versus terrorism—Meanwhile, the Bush administration is seeking allies to help conduct the War on Terrorism. However, the situation is a Catch-22. In most cases, cooperation with the US on terrorism means not only working against al Qaida, but also against local potential al Qaida recruits. The contribution several countries may make will result in suppressing their out-groups. Thus, as the war on terrorism progresses, out-group resentment and desire to spin off from various parent states is likely to increase.

As discussed below, some out-group problems might be solved in an Iraqi regime change. However, hardly any government in the Middle East is likely to be pleased by deals with Iraqi out-groups that significantly alter the map of two or three countries.

In the fifty or more failed or failing states, each has problems of leadership, and virtually all have out-groups who either have access to or close friends in other countries, including the US and Europe. If the governments of the failed and failing states come down hard on their out-groups in support of the War on Terrorism, the task of controlling outbreaks will grow. Because none of these groups has enough members to take on a government unaided, alliances of the al Qaida type will proliferate. The only weapon readily available to them is some form of terrorism. Unfortunately, the most attention-getting form of terrorism is attacks on civilian targets.

As the Israelis have shown conclusively in the West Bank and Gaza, heavy-handed and powerful military operations cannot prevent the attack of even a 17 year old girl carrying explosives. We are facing similar limitations in Afghanistan. In short, it is not in our interest to continue generating new sources of terrorism by condoning repressive tactics of other governments. We cannot stop all the products of these human failures. That we will fail miserably to stop terrorists everywhere, all the time, is virtually certain. In this environment, the costs of leaving Iraq alone pale by comparison to the potential effects of going ahead.

What about negotiation? Over time, Saddam has been astute about finding the lines he should not cross. If you listen to the Iraqi Ambassador to the UN, the Iraqis are looking and sounding as if they want to talk, perhaps even seriously to negotiate. If that is so, if the hardliners stop now, we can say our bluff worked, that threats sometimes do the trick. No blood has been spilled; inspectors can be put back to work. With their findings, we may move a few millimeters closer to knowing whether Saddam actually has weapons of mass destruction, and we will have avoided turning the region into a quagmire.

Saudi Arabia then takes center stage. A new voice in the person of Crown Prince Abdullah entered the Middle East debate in March, putting on the table a clear proposal for peace in Palestine. However, rather than give the Saudis credit for knowing what their true interests are, our hardliners, apparently led by leaders of the Project for the New American Century, the Defense Policy Board, and the denizens of the Pentagon E Ring have decided that the Saudis must do things our way and give us what we want or they become the enemy. Given what was said earlier about the experience and rank of key players, this outcome makes no sense. It may be exhilarating to take on the center of Islam in a public dispute over intelligence sharing. However, today there are over one billion Muslims, and the policy maker who invites one out of every six people on the planet to become our enemy cannot be our friend.

The law of large numbers intervenes soberly to work against us. There are more than six billion other people out there. They are deeply interested in what we do. They look positively most of the time on relations with us, but they are not wedded to what we do. With 3-5 billion more people on the planet by 2050, the numbers will be even more skewed. We can manage significant parts of our defense problem with high tech, long reach, high performance, and standoff weaponry, but we cannot beat the human numbers problem. In the tense and unfriendly world that will exist after an attack on Iraq, we simply do not have the resources to watch our backs in all the places where they will be exposed.

The Iraqi case model—The case model for unraveling the present nation state system is Iraq itself. It contains the common regional Islamic puzzle of how to sort Sunni and Shi'a Muslims and deal with their respective extremists. Iraq's major ethnic/cultural problems center on the northwestern regions inhabited by Turkomen, Kurds, and Shi'a Muslims. The Shi'a in the northwest are a problem, not because of numbers, but because Saddam implanted them in the region to reduce the number of Shi'a agitators in the southeastern area around Basra. Baghdad, for obvious reasons—oil and national territory—has resisted any concessions to any of these groups for at least half a century. Various political factions in Baghdad may argue over whether a new Iraqi government will be right, center, or left, but the Turkomen and the Kurds want their own separate pieces of territory no matter how things turn out.

As between the Turkomen and the Kurds, the lines are

drawn solidly around the city of Kirkuk, which each wants exclusively for both traditional ethnic reasons and for its location in Iraq's oldest, but still highly productive oil fields. Both Iran and Turkey also get involved in this dispute. Iraqi concessions to the Turkomen may be greeted with favor by Ankara, but not concessions to the Kurds whose people seek both Turkish and Iraqi territory; pressures would mount for separation. Iran will be concerned about what happens to the Shi'a Muslims who are mainly ethnic Iranians. The Kurdish Workers Party, PKK, has been a major terrorist threat to Turkey, but reached an agreement with Ankara after its leader, Ocalan, who was captured in 1999, launched a peace initiative in 2000. Most members of the group are in Iraq. Any peace initiative would come apart if the Iraqi settlement went against the Kurds.

Multiply this model with varying orders of grievance by 40 or so. What happens in each case will be driven by local factors. The world's current hotspots, along with the great majority of its international terrorism-generating disputes, center on areas of the globe where boundary drawing was inept, insensitive, uncaring, complicated by the terrain, or a matter of indifference to the powers whose leaders drew them up. The resulting elites in those countries have done nothing about this problem because the reigning concept of statehood says that there is no give on boundaries or territory. The established rule of statehood literally cements these conflicts in time and place. The unheeded grievances of out-groups make some situations potentially explosive.

The reform of the nation state system is overdue, but little if any thought has been given to how to do it. With respect to Iraq, the problem presents a deal-killing quandary for Washington's regime changers. If they ignore the clamor of the Turkomen and the Kurds, the Iraqi succession outcome will only make Iraq's political situation unstable, even volatile. If the regime changers make territorial concessions to either the Turkomen or the Kurds or both, the stage is set for statehood to unravel anywhere out-groups can make it happen.

What is in it for us? The Iraq road signs caution that we need to weigh carefully what will result from a pre-emptive attack on Iraq versus what we will retain if we desist. If we attack and win, we will have the chance to change the regime, but in what fashion or what degree is presently unclear. Any post-Hussein government has an uncertain future. If installed by us, the new regime's chances are bleak because considerable hostility will go with our involvement. Moreover, it is doubtful we will stick around long enough to assure successful transition. We may be able to terminate an unknown weapons program, but we do not know how important that might be. We can surely alienate significant numbers of people and their governments, including friendly Arab governments. Some of them have power to hurt us, as shown by recent large Saudi withdrawals from US banks.

On the other hand, if we desist, we save enormous resources, starting with a substantial number of American lives. We avoid alienating many friendly governments. We avoid precipitating the decay of the nation state system, but we leave the growing problems of out-groups in failed and failing states unresolved. That demands serious attention for the future, no matter what we do in Iraq. We end up having to put up with Saddam, but it would be best all around for Allah to decide his future, not American hardliners and their supporters among the Israelis and the Christian right.

PREVENTIVE STRIKES A CALL TO CHAOS
October 2002

Appearing before the Senate Foreign Relations Committee last week, Secretary of State Colin Powell stated: "The right to resort to pre-emptive or preventive strikes is inherent in the sovereignty of a nation to protect itself." He went on to state that "The concept of pre-emptive strikes has been included in this year's Strategy Report to alert the public to the fact that (the) terrorist threat is different from other threats." The concept, he said, "could be applied to terrorists or to a country."

In the wake of 9-11, governments generally want to prevent that kind of attack from occurring in their countries. But the statement of the US Secretary of State invites states to use a concept that can wreak fundamental changes in the governments of countries, their relations with neighbors, and probably the map of the world over coming decades. If post-World War II experience is any guide, adopting it as a general right of states would be a clarion call to chaos.

Powell's statement raises many questions: Why would the world's only superpower suddenly abandon foreign policy precepts that have carried it successfully through a century of fundamental and often dangerous changes in the distribution and the scale of world power—with many of the benefits accruing to itself? What could be so prized that its achievement or acquisition would prompt that superpower to abandon or ignore friends, shed alliances, and threaten to proceed alone on a path that has no obvious, profitable, or necessarily successful outcome? What has changed so radically that our leadership feels compelled to adopt a new strategy?

The enemy has changed. We struggled for the past half century under the threat of the Soviet Union, but with the dismemberment of the Berlin Wall and the Union, the evil empire was gone. In its place were many small sources of conflict and potential enemies that were difficult to detect. They lacked the organized structure or territory of states, and that set of conditions imposed brand new requirements on strategy, tactics, equipment, training, and mindset.

We were not ready for this. Our military thinkers and our security professionals have tinkered for years with Low Intensity Conflict (LIC), but it was always considered a small event below the horizon of the larger potential battle. Now it is the potential battle, and the horizon has no other immediate threat promontories.

We are still not ready for this. Our force structure is well-equipped, high tech, resistant to attack, and able to attack in the air, on the ground, and under water, but it is bulky. It can do enormous damage quickly, but it is wasted on small targets. It is designed for battlefield engagement or for standoff destruction, but it is much harder to focus down to the scale of caves, forests, and villages where the rules of guerilla warfare control. That, plus the constant ambiguity of doing battle in a place where most people are not the enemy, is the core problem in Afghanistan.

The search of our leadership is for clarity. Just what specific challenges do these "poisonous snakes" present to us?

Where, when, and how are they likely to attack? When they attack, will we be ready to repel them? Or will our posture be the shocked and reactive one that followed 9-11? Where and how can we station ourselves globally to most effectively defend ourselves? Who can we truly count on? On the scale of terrorist challenges of the past few decades, just how much of our blood and treasure should we plan to devote to this enemy? What is our optimum force structure for this?

We can forgive ourselves if we flounder around in this for a while. In our national interest, however, we must find workable answers and put them in place sooner rather than later.

The questions are good. However, good answers are not easy. The answers we do get begin to shift the moment trouble starts, and any plans we have made become less and less well targeted. The best we can do is plan around as broad a range of plausible scenarios as possible, test capabilities against each of them, and make necessary adjustments. Then we should expect that the next real case will somehow be different but still within our ballpark. Perhaps this quandary prompted Winston Churchill to say: "Plans are useless, but planning is essential."

The change of enemies is not alone responsible for our situation. Uncertainty was there all the time.

Global conditions are the problem. In a world of over six billion people in 192 countries where 50-60 of the countries are variously unstable, just what should we be ready for? The media reporting set of questions—who, what, where, when, why, and how—is the policy starter set. Faced with this order of complexity, it is easy to retreat into fixation on a single enemy, once the Soviet Union, now al Qaida or Iraq. It is also easy to seize on a single answer: pre-emptive or preventive strikes. But who should take such action? Should individual nation states be free to strike, or should the United Nations be the designated actor? How can such a tool be prevented from encouraging random warfare?

Is there, under this convoluted landscape, a pot of gold? There truly isn't. We can assume that with our far superior forces we will surely win, but it would be foolish to consider this an easy campaign. The Gulf War was said to be a slam-dunk, and battlefield casualties numbered less than 800, but in a Veterans Administration report of May 2002, Gulf War casualties were reported to include 8,306 veterans dead and 159,705 veterans injured or ill. When personnel still on active duty are included, the VA indicated in the May 2002 report that a total of 262,586 individuals are "disabled veterans" due to duty in the Gulf and that 10,617 veterans have died of combat related injuries or illnesses since the initiation of the Gulf War. That represents a casualty rate of more than 30% for combat related duties between 1990 and 1991.

If Saddam has only the help of his Republican Guard divisions, estimated at 120,000 strong, and they defend Baghdad as they are setting up to do, our casualties could be far greater than in the Gulf War. If the US uses depleted uranium shells as lavishly as it did during the Gulf War, casualties from radiation alone will be numerous.

What then is the reward? Hardliners may say that we will have had a free hand to clean out a snake pit, that we have shown Saddam and his adherents that they cannot even think about making weapons of mass destruction (WMDs) without our considering it a threat. And that demonstration should be a deterrent to other countries whose leaders have dreams of WMDs, or who already have them. Our "success" in Iraq does not appear, however, to have made much of an impact on Iran or North Korea, but maybe Iraq's lack of WMDs was an object lesson, and that is why they persist.

Pre-emptive and preventive strikes are not a new idea. Strategic or tactical surprise has always been considered advantageous. In the years since its formation over fifty years ago the United Nations, mainly through peacekeeping operations, has had the task of intervening in numerous cases such as East Timor, Kashmir, Cyprus, Bosnia, and the rest of ancient Macedonia, Georgia, the Central African Republic, the Congo, Palestine, and others. Each of these has required extensive, hands-on involvement, sometimes with former colonial powers.

Most of the cases stem from one country or group seeking to take, enlarge, or retrieve a piece of ground and to deal with a population that it would like to acquire, keep, or expel. In many instances, the conflict began with a pre-emptive strike. All of them require detached, third party mediation. Rewards are modest. Successes, such as East Timor, which became independent this year after a 25-year struggle, are not easily come by.

A principal lesson from 50 years of individual state action in this matter is that states that undertake pre-emptive or preventive strikes are unable to clean up their messes without help. Where states do handle these cases themselves, as shown in Palestine, the outcome is hard on the losers. Without third party intervention, the preempting states or groups frequently proceed with heavy costs in casualties and human rights abuses. If third party intervention is long delayed, as in the case of Central Africa, the human costs skyrocket.

The matter of self defense—The principle that one state may attack another to defend itself is well established. Even so, there is much confusion and uncertainty about what constitutes adequate provocation. Thus, the utility, legality, and modality of pre-emptive or preventive strikes are fundamental problems for the nation state system and for the United Nations. The issues are who does the work, what are the rules, and what are minimum acceptable outcomes? The responses to those issues should not enable any nation to garner territory, wealth, influence, or power. An important goal is that the pre-empting state not be allowed to profit from the venture. As a general rule, the United Nations appears to have adhered to such principles in dealing with the many cases since its formation.

It is enlightening to examine the US charges against Iraq

in the light of Secretary Powell's statement. Before the Iran-Iraq War began, the religious leaders of Iran were fomenting the Shi'a Muslims in Iraq to rebel, thereby facilitating Iran's possible capture of a disputed border zone and gain of an ethnic Iranian population. It can reasonably be argued that Iranian actions before the war began were a sufficient threat to Iraqi territorial integrity to provoke a pre-emptive strike. The US seems to have thought so at the time. Under the rules Powell has enunciated, it would have been for Iraq to determine the severity of the threat and to act accordingly.

Before Iraq's invasion of Kuwait began, the Kuwaitis were dumping oil at prices that undermined Iraq's oil income, thereby upsetting the Iraqi economy, which was still in the doldrums from the Iran-Iraq War. Evidently, the Kuwaitis were not listening to the complaints of other oil exporters. The Kuwaiti case is less clear-cut, but Iraq had every reason to consider the Kuwait price-cutting a provocative act, and depending on duration and severity, perhaps cause for a pre-emptive strike. In a future world governed by the rules suggested by Secretary Powell, Saddam could feel free to decide these provocations were harmful enough to attack. Outside consultations before the fact would be nice, but Secretary Powell's statement does not suggest they would be required.

Ironically, under the Powell doctrine, Iraqi leadership could consider the open, frequent, and severe threats US officials have made repeatedly against the country a cause for war. If Saddam were not bright enough to see that, if joined, the battle would surely be lost, a pre-emptive strike might already have been mounted. His best, perhaps his only option in the circumstances is to do nothing, but the provocations are quite real.

A look at the global picture of border disputes, displaced peoples, and discontented ethnic or religious minorities suggests that there are numerous countries or internal country situations today where aggrieved parties could justify pre-emptive or preventive strikes. These could be either against rivals in the next country or in the same country. The United Nations experience in a world where pre-emptive strikes were the unofficial but implicit remedy for an offended party offers more examples than Secretary Powell may wish to elevate to legitimacy by proclaiming a new and outright global right of pre-emption. If the proclamation is taken literally, it is a call to chaos in or around fifty or more countries. In that environment, the work of the United Nations peacekeeping forces will never be done. Certainly the world's lone superpower should not seek to take on this one.

In effect, the Secretary of State has articulated an essential operating principle for the United Nations, not for the United States or other individual nations. It is time to limit the use of such action by nation states, not to expand it. Pre-emptive and preventive strikes should be employed by the United Nations only under the most demanding of circumstances, and in light of hard information. If nation states take part, they should do so under UN leadership. Except in the face of imminent attack, no version of the option should be available to anyone else. But to avoid injustices, the UN has to be equipped to hear and respond to grievances on a timely basis. That need was recognized by inclusion of a standing UN reaction force in the United Nations Charter, but it was never implemented. Freedom from harassment, attack, or threats of attack has to be confronted as a global issue that concerns everyone on the planet. On this, as on many global issues, the common good is best served by a common strategy carried out by the United Nations.

US POLICY TOWARD ISRAEL—STOP PRETENDING
December 2002

Last week, State Department Spokesman Richard Boucher expressed deep US concern about recent civilian casualties, including the death of UN director of reconstruction, Mr. Ian Hook, resulting from Israeli military actions. That expression of concern, as far as it went, was appropriate and timely, but Boucher went on to say that the United States remains solidly behind Israel's efforts to combat terrorism, and he concluded by saying that Washington's concerns are not a condemnation of the Israeli offensive.

That formula appears designed more to avoid offending Israeli leadership and US Jewish voters than to secure corrective action. The Israelis seem to treat the formula as a continuing carte blanche endorsement of their actions in the West Bank and Gaza. They normally reject rather than respond to any criticism.

In the meantime, under an asserted 'war on terrorism', the Israel Defense Force (IDF) operates without restraint throughout the West Bank and Gaza, keeps three million Palestinians under rigorous curfew and surveillance, has brought the Palestinian economy to a standstill, destroys homes and properties only alleged to be related to militants, protects old and new settlers as the settlements continue to expand, and regularly shoots people who are only suspected of being terrorists. On the other hand, the Palestinians, who have no army, are not supposed to fight back; if they do, they are treated as terrorists.

It is time for the United States to stop pretending that any part of the IDF operation in the West Bank and Gaza is acceptable. Israeli shootings of people who have neither been tried nor found guilty of crime, the IDF occupation, continuing settlement building, and Israeli treatment of the Palestinians as inferior are constant provocations to which the Palestinians respond with suicide bombings or other retaliatory attacks.

Both Israeli and US models of the War on Terrorism involve disturbing erosion of the justice system and of national sovereignty. Israel has the only armed force in Palestine, and we have not objected to the IDF use of accusation and suspicion as justifications for killing Palestinians. The US, therefore, has bought into a corruption of the international justice system by placing the fight against terrorism outside the law. The United States moved into this same shadow land with the assassination of six suspected al Qaida members in Yemen. Israel ignores any sovereign rights the Palestinians may have or aspire to enjoy. The US has indicated that in the War on Terrorism, national boundaries may not deter attacks on suspected terrorists.

US tolerance for Israeli excesses in the West Bank and Gaza is a reflection of our own creeping loss of moral focus. The Israeli treatment of Palestinians is not right, and we know it. We may use the Palestinian suicide bombings, as the Israelis do, as an excuse for the occupation, but those bombings are constantly provoked by IDF actions. As a rule, the United States would be working overtime to terminate the occupation of any other country by a hostile army, but not in the case of Israel. We would be screaming for explanations of such attacks as the killing of Ian Hook, but not from Israel. We would hold any other aid receiving country to legal standards of accountability and performance, but not Israel. And we encourage the Israelis in their attitude toward international criticism or responsibility by ignoring Israel's acquisition (with US, UK, and French help) of weapons of mass destruction. We ignore Israel's failures to comply with more than 30 UN resolutions, while pounding Iraq for far lesser infractions.

The "special relationship" with Israel has been a cornerstone of US policy for more than half a century. However, from the beginning it provided political cover to Israeli excesses, starting with the systematic expulsion of Palestinians from their homes and property in the late 1940s, to which we did not object. In recent years, it has provided for greater economic and military assistance to Israel than to any other country. In fact, US aid to Israel in some years has equaled aid to all other countries combined; if the currently requested package goes through, it will be more than twice US aid to all other countries in 2003.

What have we gotten for those enormous investments of our national prestige and treasure? Rewards are hard to find. The US Congress decided to fund the peace process initiated by the Camp David Accords by giving half of worldwide US assistance to Israel, Egypt, and Jordan, mainly to Israel. But at present and for the indefinite future Israeli excesses in the West Bank and Gaza—sustained by US funding—are likely to remain the chief stumbling blocks to peace in the Middle East. Our largely uncritical support of Israel, despite continuing excesses, has alienated much of the Arab world and many others as well. And now, unless effective ways are found to moderate Israeli behavior toward the Palestinians, our future is at risk due to increasing terrorism by people sympathetic to the Palestinians and/or opposed to Israel.

The solution is not rejection, but a more balanced

relationship. We cannot continue to acquiesce in Israeli military destruction of the Palestinian state. Polite criticism accompanied by unwavering support is a giant hypocrisy. We have to work on getting and keeping the Palestinians on a path to peace, but Israelis have to recognize that the special relationship is a two way street and must also start delivering on their part of the peace process. Israel must accept that much of its current predicament is its own doing, and therefore the only way out is for Israel to behave responsibly toward the region and its neighbors. Israel should begin to repay its enormous debt to us, variously estimated at $85-250 billion, instead of using its clout with the US Congress to get that debt forgiven.

Finally, we cannot allow the War on Terrorism or the special relationship to undermine the values that have made our country great. No relationship with any country is worth that order of sacrifice. It is time to stop pretending that the relationship in its present form is a good thing. It clearly is not, and it is costing us dearly with everyone else.

AID TO ISRAEL—TIME TO SET CONDITIONS
January 2003

In the past few days, both print and electronic media have reported that Ariel Sharon will present a request to the US for $15 billion for 2003. That request will be in addition to $3 billion that Israel has received each year from the United States since the 1967 war. In 2001 dollars—adjusted for inflation—the Christian Science Monitor estimates that Israel has received about $240 billion in assistance—an average of $8 billion per year in grants and loans—in the past 30 years. Among them, Israel ($240 billion), Egypt ($117 billion), and Jordan ($22 billion) have received more US aid in those three decades than all other US aid receiving countries of the world combined. The amazing feature of this situation is that while other aid receiving countries have run up long-term debts to the United States, Israel has not. The reason is the US Congress regularly forgives each new loan to Israel.

Sharon can ask for these incredible amounts of US aid without a care, because the record shows that Israel will never have to repay it. Moreover, Israel enjoys several advantages over any other aid recipient. Aid is provided at the beginning of the year in a lump sum with no strings attached. Israel is not required, as others are, to spend the funds in the United States. Israel also benefits from highly US subsidized joint R&D programs.

It is time we Americans take a hard look at this picture and ask bluntly what is in it for us. The aid to Israel, Egypt, and Jordan was part of the deal for signing the Camp David Accords. The aim of both Camp David, and later Oslo Accords, was peace. Where is it? Today, the region is further from peace than it has been at any point since signature of the Accords. Why? The official Israeli answer, regularly not disputed by US leadership, is Palestinian terrorism. We should weigh against that answer (a) IDF occupation of the West Bank and Gaza, (b) continuing Israeli settlement building in both zones, (c) Israeli assassination of Palestinian activists/militants, (d) systematic IDF destruction of Palestinian homes, businesses and infrastructure, (e) Israeli preemption of the lion's share of water in the region, (f) Israeli treatment of Palestinian Muslims and Christians as second or third class citizens, and widespread discrimination against Sephardic Jews—although the latter situation has improved over the years.

The truly remarkable feature of the foregoing equation is that the only response the Palestinians have made to this pattern is periodic terrorism. For anyone else dealt with in the way the Israelis treat the Palestinians the response would be all out war.

The standard Israeli justification for the foregoing pattern is that Israel has a right to defend itself. Even when they are politely critical, US officials always insert an affirmation of the Israeli right to self-defense. What Sharon is saying with the current aid request is Israel needs $18 billion this year to defend itself against an unarmed population that is under the control of an occupying army. Really? Then what would it cost to defend Israel against an enemy of roughly symmetrical military power? Fortunately for US taxpayers, there is not one in the region, so we are not likely to find out.

Sharon might go on to argue that the Israeli economy is in the pits, and the country needs the requested funds to get the economy back up and running. However, the bulk of the economic cost lies in support of IDF operations. A good deal of the economic downturn in Israel is due to loss of tourism and other side effects of the IDF conduct of operations and the Palestinian response to them. The bottom line for this calculation is that giving Israel the money it wants to defend itself is merely pouring US taxpayer funds down a rat hole. We could better use these funds here at home.

The International Monetary Fund appears to have concluded that the solution to the Israeli recession lies in Israeli decisions on such matters as the occupation of Palestine. Therefore, in its annual report the International Monetary Fund stated that Israel is entirely able to cope with its recession without US help.

The larger issue concerns where real US interest lies. Despite a virtual US and Israeli official mantra on this, Israeli and US interests are not identical. The Israeli assertion that it is the only democracy in the region is only superficially true. Israel has elections, but from the beginning it has been run by an elite of Central European Zionists. By the accounts of Israelis, the Sephardic Jews are still less than equal to the Ashkenazi, while the Muslims and the Christians are a tier below that. Most recently, Sharon's party and other rightist groups have sought to disenfranchise Palestinian Muslims and Christians altogether. Sharon's own party faces charges of vote buying and racketeering. Democratic processes work about that well or badly in neighboring countries.

A second assertion is that Israel is a strong ally of the United States in the Middle East. We are speaking here of the same Israelis who deliberately attacked and tried to sink the USS Liberty with all hands aboard, killing more than 30 American sailors in the process. We are speaking of the same Israelis whose behavior toward everybody else in the region makes Israel, and by association the United States, the enemy of Islam. We are also speaking of the Israel whose leadership, at least its hard right, harbors territorial ambitions that would be destructive not only of the interests of Palestinians but other regional societies, notably Lebanon, Syria, and Jordan, as well. Moreover, any alliance that might exist is constantly undermined by the fact that Israel has a nuclear arsenal that is the spur for the nuclear ambitions of Iraq and Iran. Finally, we are speaking of an ally who not only is a dependant, but who wants us repeatedly to pay for the privilege of the relationship.

Given the IMF view of the Israeli financial situation and the desire of the Bush team to keep Israel out of the way in any Iraqi invasion, the current aid package should be considered a bribe.

The time obviously is past for the United States to extend aid to Israel with no strings attached. Immediate decisive actions are required by Israel: (a), withdraw the IDF from the West Bank and Gaza. (b), stop assassinating Palestinians. (c), stop all further settlement development activity. (d), set up and activate a program to dismantle the existing settlements as soon as possible. (e), stop building the wall. (f), hand the holy places of Jerusalem, all of Jerusalem in fact, over to the UN for administration so that the world's Muslims, Christians, and Jews are guaranteed access.

It is also not sensible to provide assistance where there is no compelling need. Nor is it sound US foreign policy for the United States to go along with indiscriminate and unlawful Israeli use of US supplied military equipment and weapons as the IDF now operates in the West Bank and Gaza. If we write the next check, we should surround it with real expectations for progress on issues that matter to us in the Middle East. Israel should start by carrying out its commitments under the letter and spirit of the Camp David and Oslo Accords.

In exchange for those actions, which are the minimum necessary to demonstrate Israeli worthiness as a member of the family of nations, the Palestinians must stop terrorist attacks.

Suicide bombings of the past few days are a serious setback. Critics of the Sharon regime say that he needs the bombings in order to justify his program to expel the Palestinians. If that is so, the Palestinians tragically play into his hands and prolong their own agony.

What must happen next has little to do with who may be at fault on any given day. The initiative lies with the Israelis because they are the occupying power. Israeli withdrawal is an essential first step. All Israelis and their supporters must understand that the Palestinians have no incentive to stop those attacks so long as Israeli leadership remains on its present course. Conventional military power favors Israel, but economy of force favors the Palestinians. The Israelis are systematically destroying Palestine, but the Palestinians are conducting a successful war of nerves. No one is winning.

Scanning the world media and the Internet, one can see that a growing number of Israelis, American Jews, and Jews in other countries deeply feel the truth of the foregoing paragraphs. As shown in writings by Uri Avnery of Gush Shalom and others, many of them delicately balance a growing concern about the future survival of Israel with an increasing shame about Israeli repression of the people of Palestine.

Some of these Israeli critics see the unreality of the situation and assert that easy access to US financial support is a corrupting influence that they would like to see terminated. A significant minority would accept Israeli adoption of the kinds of austerity and conservative financial management programs the international financial system expects of other aid recipients, at least so long as it would show that the Israelis can stand on their own feet

To make such habits a reality, the US Congress must stop passing laws that routinely forgive Israeli debts to the United States. That means the very powerful Israel support groups in this country, such as AIPAC should back off, stop a corrupt and deeply imbedded practice, be at least moderately fair, and stop pressing the Congress for abnormal, even immoral amounts of aid to Israel. This under the table practice abuses both the trust and the good will of the American people, but it goes unchallenged because, aside from a handful of foreign affairs junkies on university campuses and in the US Government, most Americans pay no attention or, perhaps, do not care.

Peace in the Middle East is plainly in the interest of the people of Israel; it is a travesty for American taxpayers to have to pay Israeli leadership to undertake the effort to achieve peace. In short, it is time to get real, because the conditions of the current relationship are a cruel fantasy for everybody concerned.

ON THE RELEVANCE OF THE UNITED NATIONS
February 2003

In the heat of debate to justify a war on Iraq, top US leaders have attempted to make UN acceptance of the US position a test of the validity of the United Nations system. President Bush did precisely this at his ranch in Crawford, Texas, last Saturday, and asserted again in a speech Wednesday that the United Nations had a last chance to prove its relevance by adopting a resolution which the United States, with British help, will propose in a few days.

This week, members of the Bush team have gone further by asserting that the UN will destroy its legitimacy by failing to back the US war plan. Like many of the throwaway lines Bush is fond of using, such as Ariel Sharon is "a man of peace", these comments (many of which Bush may actually believe) are part of the in your face and personal style Bush and particularly his Secretary of Defense have adopted for putting down people who disagree with them.

Bush team members are unwilling to confront the real issue: whether a war on Iraq is necessary or the best way to disarm Saddam, or whether disarming Saddam is even important at this time. Questioning the relevancy and the legitimacy of the UN is a dangerous challenge to the only organization the world now has to deal with a host of problems. Neither the United States nor any other country can or should want to tackle them alone. At the top of that list are AIDS, world hunger, human rights, failures and deficiencies in the nation state system, and the real war on terrorism.

Those problems cluster around the global issues that gave rise to most, if not all, of the world's terrorists: Hunger, poverty, disease, social, political, and economic injustice, political exclusion, and matters of cultural, ethnic, or religious diversity. If not addressed, those issues will continue to generate new terrorists faster than they can be cut down in any war on terrorism the United States can mount. That is simply because the present War on Terrorism is designed to capture, confine, kill, or counter the existing terrorists, not to deal with the root causes of terrorism.

The US foreign assistance budget is neither large enough nor well-targeted enough to do much work on the global issues. With at least a third of that budget going to Israel and more than half going to Israel, Egypt, and Jordan together, the rest of the developing world receives very little. Meanwhile, as part of the bargaining around support for the war on Iraq, Israel is asking for $18 billion (to stay at home and fight its own battle) and Turkey is asking for and may get $30 billion (to support US war plans). Between them, these two countries are asking for almost 6 times the entire US aid budget to play their non-combatant, virtual bystander parts in the Iraq war.

Those war related expenditures and the de-facto bribes that may be paid to African or other members of the Security Council to get their votes are stark reminders that the US case for war with Iraq is weak. A weak case and signs of US desperation to get a favorable UN vote have perverse effects on the US position: Members of the Security Council and regional countries see plainly that the US can be had in the diplomatic bargaining. On the other hand, US eagerness to obtain a favorable UN decision belies the Bush team charge that the UN lacks relevance.

In fact, the United Nations has the only forum where the United States can legitimate its plans, assuming they should be legitimated. During the Cold War, NATO may have been a legitimizing forum, but that no longer works. If the debate were properly focused by the Bush team, it would be about the legitimacy of the war, not about the standing of the UN. As shown in peace demonstrations in many countries last week, messengers from many parts of the world are saying the war is a poor idea. Killing the messengers or belittling them will not improve the plans. As the debate is being pursued, the UN is not standing in the way. It is serving in loco parentis for dealing with truculent and stubborn US posturing.

Several truths about the situation are obvious: The risks of terrorism cannot be greatly diminished without resolving the global issues. The real war on terrorism is not now being fought by the United States. War on Iraq will not do anything significant to diminish world terrorism. Whoever takes the lead in the real war on terrorism must have global access. Only the UN has the standing needed to tackle the global issues. Only a serious and sustained attack by all nations on the global issues will assure any success in the War on Terrorism. The outcome will never be perfect; the irrational element will always be there; and some protection against terrorism will always be necessary.

The United States on its best day cannot substitute for a detached international organization that is charged and funded to do this work. But the United States with its wealth and technology can fuel the process. The risk is that, on the courses being taken by the Bush team, with only about 4.6% of the world's people, the United States will make itself irrelevant to managing the present conflict environment. Since 9-11, US leadership has done an incredible job of blowing its opportunity to attack world terrorism by too narrowly defining the problem, too exclusively defining the victims who matter, and too assiduously protecting the Israelis whose actions against the Palestinians are the current most potent generators of terrorism.

Over the long haul, the roles and capabilities of the United Nations system must be enhanced and their funding must be markedly increased. Instead of an immature effort to undermine the UN, the United States should take the lead in assuring the UN has every tool it needs to be effective. As a general matter, the United States and governments everywhere rely on the UN specialized agencies in aviation, communications, health, labor, maritime affairs, and other areas. At the same worldwide level of attention, an attack is called for on the global issues. There is no hope of resolving them without a sustained UN-led international effort, because doing anything about them is a slow and patient process, even with adequate funding.

In moving to support the UN, the United States must stand for consistency and clarity on the most frightening aspect of the present and future threat of terrorism: The availability of weapons of mass destruction to nation states and potential leakage to terrorists. Few really quibble with the effort to prevent additional countries from acquiring such weapons. But that outcome is not attainable in a world where the strong may have such weapons and the weak may not. There is no solution but to suppress them all. No one but the weapons owner will ever agree that he or she has any unique right to own such weapons. Their mere presence will generate that horrible fear, envy, or longing of the have nots that has led us to where we are.

In the end, this problem can be managed only by detached leadership, and no nation state is capable of providing that. The four-tiered system that now exists cannot be sustained. That system consists of: (1) The pre-1967 members of the nuclear club who are in the nuclear Non Proliferation Treaty; (2) the Indians and the Pakistanis who are admitted proliferators outside the NPT; (3) the Israelis who have weapons and are not admitted proliferators but are outside the NPT, and protected by the United States; and (4) everybody else who is not allowed to have such weapons. The obvious inconsistency of this system is part of the problem of dealing with Iraq, North Korea, or others such as Iran.

Another part of the problem is the availability of various weapons technologies and precursors from many developed countries for which no effective single export control or monitoring authority exists. The present honor system obviously works quite well to make trouble for us. The unintended troublemaker has been the Eisenhower "Atoms for Peace" program under which technologies that can lead to weapons are permissible for peaceful nuclear power programs. Weaknesses in export control are shown by the case of Iraq where whatever capability exists derived from inputs of the United States, Germany, Russia, and others, while Israel's weapons were made possible with French, US, British, South African, and other support.

Some version of the International Atomic Energy Agency with teeth is likely to be the only long-term solution to proliferation problems. The UN is the only organization with any developed potential for overseeing that role. But the most intractable problem will be to persuade existing nuclear powers to shed their weapons.

The proliferation problems facing the UN, if it is properly given the mission, grow more complex daily. Given modern electronics, electromagnetic pulse weapons, modern explosives, delivery systems, and related technologies, the modern military force is a weapon of mass destruction without benefit of WMDs as such. Viewed realistically, recent civil wars and insurgencies in West Africa have demonstrated that concentrated numbers and reckless uses of small arms amount to weapons of mass destruction.

US and British uses of U-238 or depleted uranium in the first Gulf War as a tank killer charge introduced a low grade nuclear weapon onto the modern battlefield. Tens of thousands of Iraqi and American casualties resulted from exposure to those devices. Those devices remind us that the ultimate weapon of mass destruction is, as it always has been, human intemperance.

In short, for the UN, the future proliferation problem is not just technical weapons of mass destruction, but the sheer mayhem that is possible in modern warfare. The immediate UN challenge is to prevent that mayhem from being visited upon Iraq.

TAX CUTS, FOOD STAMPS, AND COST FREE WAR
March 2003

Wednesday night, President Bush authorized an attempt to assassinate Saddam Hussein and his core leadership. That move violated a long-standing international rule against killing heads of state. White House spokesman Ari Fleischer justified the attack by saying that Saddam and his staff are legitimate targets because they lead Iraq's armed forces. Of course, if leading their armed forces makes legitimate military targets, then these new rules make the US Commander in Chief and his national security team equal candidates.

Last week, USAID announced it had sought and received bids from major US construction and development firms to rebuild Iraq after the war at a cost of $ 900 million. The assumption in this case was that Iraq could be put back together for about $40 per head after so-called "shock and awe" saturation and destruction by America's own panoply of mass destruction weaponry. Those are only the tips of a foreign policy iceberg that is astoundingly simplistic.

On the day that Bush launched the Saddam takeout attempt, Republican members of Congress quietly indicated that work would progress without interruption on the administration's $1.3 trillion tax-cut. In short, the Republican ideology that is so avidly espoused by the Bush team—lessen the tax burden of the rich and starve government down to size—is cruising along through totally untroubled waters.

To any reasonably detached economic thinker, proposing or carrying out tax cuts at this time are signs of incipient insanity. But Democratic leadership, awestruck by the country's warlike posture and the actual onset of war, is unable to engage the simple thought that the Bush tax cut plan must be met head on.

Meanwhile, our armed forces struggle with an ironic twist on making war on Iraq. The Bush team actually offered to pay billions of dollars—in the form of assistance no doubt—to governments that support UN approval of the war, while the families of a sizeable number of American ground troops whose lives are on the line are expected to live on food stamps. Even with pay increases that have been approved by Bush, the lowest ranking soldiers are paid at rates comparable to those of workers in minimum wage jobs. The severe risks of war in Iraq have not moved the administration or members of Congress out of the fantasy world of small government and low taxes long enough to correct this pay gap. The same mentality has caused the Pentagon to fumble the ball on procurement of body armor for troops in Iraq.

The Bush response to questions about the costs of war on Iraq and its aftermath is to tap dance on some days and side step on others. Such dancing around could be based on any of several premises. One is that the war will be over quickly and the cost will not be high. Of course, on the day after, costs move immediately to cleanup, recovery, and promised nation building. Those will not be small, and the $900 million figure for a war recovery program is hardly realistic, even granting that is a nice piece of business for corporate friends of the Bush team.

A second premise is that others will pick up the tab. It is

notable that few of the 30 or so members of the "coalition of the willing" have forces in the endeavor, and it would be even more notable if many of them put any money into the war kitty or the reconstruction. Most members of that group are not financially positioned to do a great deal. In fact, they are in need of assistance that they may be expecting for joining the coalition.

A third basis for Bush not facing costs is that they might well be covered by sales of Iraqi oil, to be sure by American companies. Paul Wolfowitz said so repeatedly in his confirmation hearings for Undersecretary of Defense. Various experts take opposing views. Much of the oil revenue will have to be devoted to feeding and caring for the Iraqi people. After years of neglect, to bring the Iraqi fields up to higher levels of output is expected to take years. In any event, counting on oil revenues to pay the American war costs would be a gross travesty against the Iraqi people. Even so, if American companies do gain a handle on Iraqi oil production and export, do not count on their profits going toward Iraqi reconstruction.

The most obvious reason for not talking about costs is that they would place the Bush tax cut program in a ridiculous light. Many estimates, even including a Russian one, place the costs of the war itself at between $80-100 billion for the first year. That does not include recovery or occupation costs. With the deficit already at an all-time high, and borrowing already occurring rapidly under a new debt ceiling, finding room for tax cuts will take a lot more than devotion to ideology. But paying for this war is only the tip of another iceberg. It does not count the costs of maintaining the American presence around the globe to assert the superpower role of counter-terrorism military policeman that is being acted out in the War on Terrorism. Whichever way he turns, Bush faces harsh realities and a need for candor with the American public about how we will pay the costs of his policies. But to use one of his card playing metaphors, candor is not his long suit.

BUSH AND THE BLACK BOX
June 2003

The idea that we cannot predict the future is among our most stoutly held beliefs. Sayings such as the Spanish "Que sera, sera," (What will be, will be) help get us and keep us comfortable with the thought. But not everybody agrees that when we look forward we should expect to see nothing. One writer, William B. Williams, sketched a way through the mist of the future with a device he called "the black box". In his book, <u>Future Perfect</u>, published in 1995, Williams advised his readers to think of a black box that you put items into from one side (the present) and take them out from the other side (the future).

He makes a strong case that you can look at the box from either side with good result. You can look at what you are putting into the box now and predict what will come out in the future. That is the field of the futurologist. You can look at what has come out of the box and determine what was originally put into it. This is the field of the historian.

Williams argued that with clear-cut, practical inputs to the black box, you could predict outcomes with some certainty. Of course, uncertainty is always present, and our projected straight lines can easily turn into futuristic squiggles. If you look closely, smart business people use something like the black box all the time.

We need to introduce George W. Bush and his core team to the black box, because they have been putting some risky and messy stuff into the box without really focusing on what will surely come out of it tomorrow. Here are some likely examples.

The Kyoto Protocols—One of the first Bush foreign policy decisions was not to sign the Kyoto Protocols. Bush did not argue with the case for the Protocols; he merely said that he saw no point in agreeing to an accord that the Senate would not ratify. That means as our leader he chose not to fight the battle of getting the largest polluter on the planet in line with the global need to control greenhouse gases and to meet a modest national goal of cutting US emissions of such gases to 93% of our 1990 level by 2012.

We are the leading polluter because we are the leading user of fossil fuel. If the leading polluter refuses to lead the way, it is likely that not only less developed countries, but also many signatories of the Protocol can use our posture to drag their feet. This means that Bush is leading the pack in the wrong direction. Unless the US sees the light and helps others do so, future historians can say with conviction that the Bush decision and its waves of effect on others allowed fossil fuel use and generation of greenhouse gases to go out of control. Present futurologists can argue that our planet, in 2050, will be a colossal mess.

Bush almost changed this prospect when he talked glowingly about hydrogen fuel programs, because hydrogen does not pollute, but he did not put any money into it. Go back to "We are the leading polluter…"

Population control—All of the world's great religions venerate human life, and a few venerate life in any and all forms. But the extreme right conservatives of Christianity are the only people who now insist that we must create it. If the Chinese, Indians, and others had followed the American conservative Christian line—no contraception, no abortion—there would probably now be more than 4 billion Chinese and Indians instead of more than 2 billion. And the global population would approach 9 billion or more.

Meanwhile, at most, a few million North American Christians would insist that the world go forth and procreate without restraint. That means do nothing to avoid pregnancy, even if life all around you is at the bottom of the human condition, and the carrying capacity of the system in numerous places is facing exhaustion. Bush has signed off on refusing aid for family planning programs in any of the 75 countries where the US has an AID mission and program.

But look at the American political, economic, and social elite, including the Bush family, and show us that crowd that produces large families, abstains from sex, and doesn't practice birth control. What Bush and his supporters are putting into the black box is a moral hypocrisy. As we have seen for decades, what will come out of the box is growing human misery punctuated by explosive global issues that produce more terrorism and violence than any of us can manage. What comes out of this black box is our own undoing.

Tax cuts—Bush came into office fixated on his plan to cut taxes and give money back to the rich. That was clear because he proposed to cut taxes before he had been in office long enough to find out what it would cost to run the government. He put a 1.3 trillion dollar tax cut into the black box with no thought of the consequences and no visible interest in how that would play out over the decade in which he planned to implement it.

Guessing what will come out of this box is not rocket science. Several thoughtful analysts told Bush that the prospective budget surplus would disappear, that deficit spending would mount, and that any prospect of repaying the national debt would be jeopardized, if not lost altogether. He has now put more cuts into the box, cuts designed to reward, by thoughtful estimates, only the top one percent of Americans.

It is easy to see that several things will come out of this black box. Burgeoning debt, shrinking government services, and a progressive retreat of the United States from the lead role in foreign economic development are only the first echelon of nasty things that will emerge from it. The resultant growing disparity between rich and poor will increase social, political, and economic tensions in the United States, and the risks of domestic terrorism will increase. These are dynamics that can cause the lone world superpower to collapse of its own mismanagement.

The War on Terrorism—The Bush team answer to 9-11 was to declare a War on Terrorism, rush off to Afghanistan where Osama bin Laden and his al Qaida supporters were said to be hiding, and to depose the Taliban government that supported him. Into the box went a concentrated dose of military activity that drove both Taliban and al Qaida forces into the outback, left the warlords in charge across this isolated and difficult country, and established a new government that now controls little more that the immediate area of Kabul. What now is emerging from the box is the same kind of US neglect that led to the Taliban after the retreat of the Russians.

In the meantime, perhaps a serious and comprehensive investigation of the origins of 9-11 has been conducted, but the Bush administration is preventing release of the report. The rationale for keeping it under wraps is that it may shed light on sources and methods of intelligence collection. If that intelligence is no better than what was used to justify the war on Iraq, why should we care? This team is praying that the black box has a delay switch on it and that nothing embarrassing to the administration will come out until it no longer is politically important.

At the same time, ignoring the causes of terrorism, the War consists mainly of pursuing an elusive bandit who has no country, who does the Ayatollah Khomeini one better by appearing only on dubiously authentic cassette recordings, and who yanks us around with some frequency by provoking orange or red alerts. What is going into the black box is an administration fixation. This single-minded focus on al Qaida will emerge as a failure, and world terrorism will emerge largely if not entirely undaunted by this campaign.

The business of government—Our basic problem of national management, as many municipal jurisdictions have discovered, is letting politicians run the business of the nation. Our formula presently is sorely imperfect, because our need for public business management is perennial while we not only allow but vote to limit the tenure of elected officials who are able to learn and tackle governance only for specified short periods of time. When all the fuss is over, we probably both choose them and replace them without any reference to actual needs of governance.

No business would wait for two years to get rid of a defective chief executive. But we do it routinely through adhering to scheduled elections.

What we probably need, to satisfy the political requirements of a democracy, is an elected advisory board of politicians. But to satisfy the requirement for continuity of management for the nation's business, we need a permanent body of system and sector managers. That is what the Civil, Foreign, and Military services are supposed to provide.

Politicians in general put into the box on their first day in office a cynical disdain for professional public servants. More often than they would acknowledge or necessarily deserve they in fact get the world's best professional support.

The Bush version of this was to create a new Homeland Security Department that would not be covered by civil service rules. What he wanted to put into this box was a cascaded array of political cronies. He still needs to pay the piper, but what is likely to come will be a group devoted to keeping their jobs, pleasing their bosses, and getting them reelected. This was once called the Jacksonian spoils system, and around it the black box spewed corruption.

Uses of the United Nations—Prior to the founding of the

League of Nations, transnational alliances tended to be of the sort represented by contending groups in the Cold War, a cluster of powers aligned against common enemies. What the League tried to do was bring together a cluster of powers that were colonial empires. The UN is unique in this sphere because it has succeeded in acquiring the participation of virtually all constituted nations on the planet. With that membership, it is of potential great value to the lone world superpower and to microstates like Fiji. The collapse of the Warsaw Pact and the decline of NATO and other regional groupings present a basically flat earth to the UN system.

With help from its members, the UN can manage a host of global issues in ways that can preserve the integrity of the nation state system. No power should place the United Nations in the situation of contending with a single or small group of nation states for policy control of a global issue. The Bush team has done this with Iraq. The global issue is management of arms proliferation. How the main weapons proliferator in the world can grab the high ground or insist on unique control of this issue is tricky.

What Bush has put into the black box here is a backward walk into the anarchy of unilateralism. If he is not careful what he will get out of the box is a badly damaged international system which the United States desperately needs to provide detached global issue management. That will lead to diminished position and prestige for the United States, and to a future much bleaker and harder than it needs to be.

Iraq—Take a modest sized and populated country and let it be run unopposed by a tyrant for a generation. Ignore him except when he gets in the way, Use him as a foil to befuddle other enemies, do business with him when it is profitable, and then make a diligent effort to kill him when you grow tired. Take his country and let his people mill around for a while. The black box is unforgiving on this. What comes out the far side is chaos.

Belittle, bully, and ignore others—The black box is

peculiar on this subject, because some of the worst leaders never are made to pay for their sins. Perhaps the cynics are right in suggesting that the rest of the world cannot do a lot for us. But moving through the black box are over six billion of them and less than 300 million of us. We can cow this crowd with superior weaponry and the aggressive will to use it, but when we come out of the box headed in inimical or hostile directions, the rest of the world, if it decides to, can do us enormous, perhaps even fatal damage. People who pass through the global black box typically reward cooperation and devour lone wolves.

Ultimately, the black box has dilating and diluting powers over events. It plays on the asymmetry of human decisions, actions, and capabilities. Eighteen fairly ordinary but determined people can transfix a nation of 300 million. That nation with shocking and awesome power can find itself shadow boxing with a chimerical enemy. For anything worthwhile to come out of it, at this point the box needs an input of careful, enlightened self-interest. It is hard to tell whether our present leaders have the vision to see the need or the wisdom to make such an entry.

THE OUTSIDER ROLE IN TRANSFORMING ISLAM
August 2003

From the beginning, the Bush administration has shown that it has at best limited regard for the Constitutional separation of church and state. George Bush's early introduction of so-called "faith-based initiatives" has been followed by a pattern of special favors to religious groups. Non-sectarian groups have been critical of this habit with little effect. Bush and key Republican leaders who work most closely with him have cultivated the Christian right and in turn have forged close links to Zionists, especially leaders of Israel's Likud party. However, to date, no foray into Christianizing American policy has gone so far as National Security Adviser Condoleezza Rice along with close-in neoconservative supporters of the President.

In a recent speech in Dallas, Texas, Rice apparently abandoned all other rationales for the US presence in Iraq and said that bringing democracy and free markets to the Middle East is "the moral mission of our time." She also is reported to have said that this mission could take at least a generation to accomplish. Norman Podhoretz, a leading light of the neo-conservative Bush supporters, called this mission "the reformation and modernization of Islam."

Rice and the neo-conservatives have leaped suddenly from the high precipice of fear for our lives to the high mission of transforming Islam. This leap is quite startling. It puts the President, but more importantly the United States, in the role of beginning a crusade against traditional Islam. The Podhoretz theme particularly sounds like a declaration of war on Islam. At minimum, it will fuel the al Qaida recruitment of new terrorists, while turning Islamic governments generally away from us.

This agenda bespeaks a fundamental misunderstanding, outright ignorance, or both about what is happening in most of Islam. It uses the behavior of extremists, in essence the agendas and actions of, at worst count, less than 100,000 individuals including all of al Qaida and its loose affiliates, to define the spiritual and political desires of more than one billion Muslims. While the Rice/Podhoretz formula is now targeted on the Middle East, it does an enormous disservice to Muslims the world over.

Fundamentalist Muslims, meaning those who seek to observe the practices and follow the teachings of the Koran, have problems of coping with the modern world that are about on a par with the problems of fundamentalist Christians. The problem for both is a pervasive set of influences that challenge their faith and practices. In the modern world of electronic, print, and film media, and the Internet, there is no sheltered place. Such exposure is an intense secularizing pressure that practicing Muslims fear erodes traditions and provides new and frequently corrupting behavioral examples. At the same time, secular groups criticize religious leaders who are too far behind the curve, that curve defined as the leading edge of "modernizing" influence.

The Islamic vectors for the modernizing process are business and professional people and the young, especially urban youth and university students. In countries such as

Saudi Arabia, Egypt, and Iran the younger generations are likely to share a belief in the idea of secular governance. They combine that with a goal of overturning present oligarchic or autarchic governments, and in the case of Iran, a fundamentalist one.

On the religious side, leading clerics and Islamic thinkers of recent times have been Shiites, the Ayatollah Khomeini in Iran, and Sheik Mohammed Hussein Fadlallah, the spiritual leader of Hesballah, in Lebanon. The United States is "the enemy" because it is the bringer of modernizing influences, as well as the ally of the oligarchs supporting the status quo.

In this picture, "reformation" of Islam is a poor choice of words. The task is not reform, but adaptation, and the danger of adaptation, is departure from traditional values. The young in Muslim countries are not only at odds with the fundamentalists, but opposed to existing governments. Those elements comprise a struggle of serious consequence for Islamic societies.

Islam will not be responsive to promptings for change from the outside or by outsiders. What change may come must come from inside, and that has always been a slow process. Moreover, it is important to keep in mind that in Islam God speaks Arabic and Mohammed was only his recording secretary. This forecloses any systematic textual study of the words of the Koran, or any study/analysis of the historical context. Those are two limitations Christian reformers have not had to contend with since Martin Luther and the release of the Bible from its Latin stranglehold. The struggle is how to benefit from new technologies and new ideas without sacrificing belief systems. No one does that well or quickly, but the fundamentalists of all faith systems do it least well.

What must be faced is that this kind of pressure brings out the worst in fundamentalist Christians, Jews, and Muslims. All three systems generally eschew resorting to violence, but the extremist fundamentalists take to it when they see their systems threatened. The young, however, are most often fighting battles that are not about faith but about freedom. That, unfortunately, is where we are, and all of us must understand it or we will destroy ourselves. The solutions of these problems cannot be left by default to the fundamentalists in any society, but at the same time it is not productive to provoke the fundamentalists, the extremists of true believers, to acts that can destroy a society.

In this environment, the Rice/Podhoretz strategy is a dangerous path and should be abandoned. At best, it would be seen in Islamic countries as uninformed meddling. At worst, it would be taken as a provocation to holy war.

A slow process of persuading leadership is most likely to work with Islamic societies. In time new generations will (a) give ground to younger generations who will bring their own mixtures of belief and pragmatism to the task, (b) weed out the hard line extremists among the fundamentalists, but leave room for pacific fundamentalist behavior, and (c) encourage moderates to speak up and publicize their words; this has been working recently in both the US and Egypt.

Suppressing the young produces one kind of revolution. Suppressing the Mullahs produces another. When they end up on the same side, as in Iran, the combination is deadly because the traditionalists and the changelings may share a common enemy: us.

In approaching this challenge, it is worth remembering that Islamic societies have been wrestling with modernization for at least two centuries. Egyptian, Sudanese, Pakistani, Iranian, Lebanese, Tunisian, and other scholars, mostly Sunni Muslims, have written and thought a great deal about it. Moreover, the intensity of the pressures in this struggle has grown with each new generation of technology, especially information systems.

Osama bin Laden and al Qaida represent an anti-modern pressure on Islamic societies. However, except for alliances with extremists, an al Qaida presence is acceptable in few Muslim countries. Thus bin Laden is also an outsider attempting to transform Islam. His dream of an Islamic Caliphate is a pre-medieval scheme. His chance of achieving that is somewhere between dim and none. But he uses every modern device at his disposal to challenge the authority of Muslim governments. His minimum success may be to make the task of dealing with fundamentalist extremists more difficult for each of those governments.

Presently, the pressures in Islamic societies are enormous. However, the number and extremity of violent actions remain small for Islam as a whole. In most Islamic countries, the problems of modernization are complicated by poverty, lack of education, and disease. But inexpensive information and entertainment systems are everywhere promoting change. Those systems challenge even the most repressive of governments, because the systems are carriers of both secularizing and liberalizing thought. They will in time lead to more diverse societies.

Adopting the transformation of Islam as a moral imperative of American policy will not succeed because it puts critical choices in the wrong hands. Recognition of the complexity of the issues for Islamic societies and steady, enlightened promotion of diversity within those societies will accomplish as much as outsiders can achieve. Change will take time. Christians would be deeply offended and angered if an Islamic government adopted an assertive reformation policy toward them. Muslims are likely to find such a Western or Christian interventionist policy equally offensive.

AMERICA'S MARGIN FOR ERROR
December 2003

To justify a pre-emptive strike against Iraq, Secretary of Defense Rumsfeld told the Congress before the invasion that America has entered a new world. In this new world he said, "Our margin of error is notably different." In the context of his remarks, he was most concerned about possible failure to move decisively on the pending military attack of Iraq or on future military actions against al Qaida. "We have entered a new security environment," said Rumsfeld, "one that is dramatically different than the one we grew accustomed to over the past half century."

Our entry into this new world did not just happen. The changes that brought it about occurred over a period of decades with developments such as the slow decay of the communist system, the fall of the Berlin Wall, the collapse of the Soviet Union, large increases in world population, growth in poverty, hunger and disease, and the global emergence of present patterns of terrorism. As discussed in the article on Pre-emptive Regime Change, the "dramatic difference" is the new uncertainty, fear, and policy confusion created by the Bush administration doctrine of pre-emptive war.

Terrorism was already a thorn in our side in the 1970s. It became a bigger one in the 1980s. Even though the number of terrorist attacks declined through the 1990s, our terrorism worries grew because we saw the potential for terrorist acquisition and use of WMDs. However, while we were struggling with the horror of possible WMD events, the 9-11 planners and terrorists showed us that massive shock and destruction can be delivered without them.

Attacks in the past two decades have also shown that the enemy is usually not a country. The enemy can be anywhere, can use the most destructive devices that science or ingenuity might contrive and money can buy, but is more likely to use conventional explosives or so-called IEDs (improvised explosive devices). Moreover, the enemy is likely to be in complete charge of when, where, how, and why such an attack might be delivered. Terrorists are most likely to hit softer, unprotected targets.

Rumsfeld's statement and the whole neo-conservative hawk fixation on attacking Iraq show that the Bush team believes we can beat terrorism globally with unprovoked attacks on specific countries. The track record is not promising so far.

The margin for error—Rumsfeld did us a favor by stating the problem in terms of possibility for error. However, "margin for error", our zone for making mistakes without severe consequences, is a better term. Rumsfeld and those around him are thinking about how we militarily position or pre-position worldwide to deal with the next threat. The tragedy of his statement and the neo-conservative hawk mindset is that they do not come close to appreciating America's true margin for error, either now or in the coming decades.

Our present situation—The United States is a superpower because of its nuclear weapons and other sophisticated weaponry, not because of the numbers or the readiness of its forces. Rather, reliance on National Guard and reserve personnel to eke out force structures in time of need means that both readiness and numbers are constant constraints.

Whether responding to those constraints or just ideologically wedded to the idea, Rumsfeld and his personal following tout a lean, mean fighting machine. This force would go in on the heels of standoff weaponry shock and awe attacks that leave little work for the troops. That indeed was the Gulf War II scenario, but only for the first few days. Iraqi developments since May 1, 2003, have shown major flaws in that design.

On the ground Iraq is a mess. Sources familiar with the situation say there are not enough people, with the right skills, in the right places, with the right mission tasks. As the Coalition chief administrator, L. Paul Bremer, has discovered, those shortcomings cannot be corrected fast enough to stay ahead of creeping chaos. Bremer's main problem may be that he will run out of time. Iraqi guerrilla attacks, Shi'a and Kurdish political maneuvers, and a recently awakened Sunni minority appear to be spreading panic in and around the White House.

The boost in domestic popularity provided by taking Saddam, possibly by bargaining with his Kurdish keepers, appears to have contained that panic for now. However, in Iraq, the main US postures are contradictory; the process of handing over governance to Iraqis is being confounded by a US political need for speedy results, while the military approach is being driven into an ever more harsh posture by constant insurgent attacks. Unless a handover acceptable to Iraqis can be carried out, and unless the killing stops, a pall hangs over a Bush re-election chance in 2004.

The striking demonstration in this situation is that the United States simply does not have enough forces on active duty to meet the obligations set by the combined neo-con agendas of the War on Terrorism and the continuing war in Iraq. That this same group is even now setting its sights on Syria and Iran is truly dim witted. The United States does not have much room for error here. Rather, the Bush team practices of pre-emptive strikes, unilateral action, and the infantile "you are either with us or against us" definitions of major power relationships irritate and frighten others. They isolate the United States, thereby increasing pressure on limited resources and reducing the margin for error.

Our basic situation—How potent is the superpower? The US, the world's third largest country, has only about 4.6 percent of the world population. That means more than 95% of the people and a much higher percentage of the problems with the human condition are outside the United States. Estimates vary, but in terms of energy and other vital production materials, the US is using as much as 25% of key resources, such as oil, to maintain its lifestyle and export parts of it to others. We can live this way for some indefinite time through imports of raw materials and finished goods, supporting technologies, and bright people. We can pay for all of that by exports of advanced technologies and products or services, going into debt abroad, and we can live off the rewards of offshore investments.

In long-range economic terms, our system is vulnerable. It is engaging because it is so productive of innovation and wealth, and on that basis it has prospered and grown even through times of progressively declining domestic resources. Increasingly we have substituted technical achievements for physical resources. We can continue to do that, but the system is vulnerable because its prosperity and growth involve deep and vital interdependencies with the rest of the world.

The US miracle cannot be sustained without these connections. Can we sustain these connections by peaceful and cooperative means? If not, can we enforce them by coercive and military ones? Our margin for error is defined by the challenges we must meet to sustain our status and position.

Unhappy with our vulnerability, the hawks in and around the Bush team appear to have decided that as the lone superpower we can maintain an umbrella over our markets and vital relationships through exports of military power.

Recent steel tariff disputes and the appearance of mad cow disease in the US demonstrate just how out of touch the neocons are with the realities of the US situation.

US military power looks awesome, but we are, as noted, less than 5% of the world's people. Significant projections of military power are personnel rich. The smartest of our weapons demand large capital investments, and human support for upkeep, operations, and protection. Thus, we can be in many places at once with only token forces. Token forces, as we saw in Somalia and are seeing elsewhere, become handy targets to enemies. Even sizeable forces in Iraq are being constantly harassed, and our casualties since the war are now well beyond wartime losses.

That realization ought to force us to be pragmatic. What we must have are astute applications of Occam's razor, the sharp logical tool of an English friar that strips the fat off our usual satisfying answers. The answers that cover all the facts in this case make up several bundles. Military power alone will serve only some of our interests in the global system. To broaden the free-zone within our margin for error we must judge carefully what super powers we have other than military, and work systematically to apply them.

Rumsfeld is probably right in suggesting that our margin for error has changed, but he is mistaken in thinking that unilateral exercises of military power can fix the problem. On some levels, the situation could be changed to our benefit if we properly apply the other "super powers" such as the moral, spiritual, and practical support we had from the rest of the world in the days right after 9-11. What are the critical sets of facts we must address?

The nation state system is in trouble. While there is no official count, an estimated 50 or more nation states are failed or failing. Seventy-five or more states, including the United States, have resident terrorist groups or individual terrorists, or support groups. Groups in 20 or more states want separate states of their own. Such groups include the Kurds and the

Shi'a, quite likely the Sunnis in Iraq. Groups in 35-40 states want to overthrow the government, either for regime change or revolutionary reasons. That includes virtually all of the Islamic fundamentalist groups allied with al Qaida.

The overriding problem of the most troubled states is that too many people are poor and under-represented or not represented at all in their country's decisions. Such shortcomings are often packaged with repression, injustice, and other human rights problems. Those defects make the failed and failing states into primary terrorism generators that threaten everybody.

Weapons proliferation is endemic. As the situations show starkly in the Congo, Liberia, Sierra Leone, and much of the Sub-Sahara region, the proliferation of small arms is a bigger and more imminent threat to many countries than the possible spread of weapons of mass destruction. In Sub-Sahara Africa the unofficial death toll in a half-dozen countries reaches genocidal proportions. Proliferation of small arms, mainly from the United States, Western Europe, Israel, and Russia, is a global, real-time plague. These problems stem largely from the policies of exporting countries, and new victims pay the price every day for gross inattention to a global need for control of such weapons.

Then there are the states that seek or have WMDs. Excluding friendly powers with such capabilities, the threatening ones (numbers somewhat speculative) include a dozen with nuclear weapons programs, 13 with programs for biological weapons, 16 for chemical weapons, and 28 with ballistic missiles programs. This cluster (a frequently changing one) includes many of the failed and failing states. The threats against them are largely internal, but these nations are armed against foreign and domestic enemies. Most seem attracted to taking their war-making capabilities into space. This threat, in turn, drives the US interest in a missile defense system.

The overarching problem is that in an unstable world any

weapon or weapons system becomes an attractive nuisance. For half a century, the United Nations has endeavored to prevent proliferation of nuclear weapons. The UN has failed, in part, because it is totally unrealistic to expect that such powerful bargaining tools can be confined only to the states that already have them. Other factors include (a) the US Atoms for Peace program that may itself be the doom of non-proliferation, and (b) US disregard (at best) or, as asserted by critics, US connivance in Israeli acquisition of nuclear status.

Possession of nuclear weapons by India, Pakistan, and Israel, all outside the Nuclear Non-Proliferation Treaty, has put an elephant in the room for all to see and for anyone who can to copy. North Korea may try to join that group by asserting or proving that it has at least one workable weapon and delivery system that threatens South Korea or Japan. Other WMDs, chemical or biological, are loose on the planet because the technologies are unavoidably allied with legitimate applications, easier to apply than nuclear and, in some degree, can be made in most countries.

At present, US leadership is opening the gates of further proliferation by openly seeking to develop more powerful and smaller battlefield weapons using nuclear technology. Perversely, such smaller weapons are likely to be more attractive than the old city levelers to other governments and terrorists. US action is giving proliferation new scope if not new life. The margin for error of everyone narrows a little each time any country breaches the weapons proliferation boundary.

Terrorism threatens all countries and peoples. During the past two years, terrorist attacks have occurred in at least 60 countries each year. While as many as 20 groups are Islamic, at least half of the Islamic groups are clustered around or have sprung from the Palestine conflict. The majority of terrorist groups are not Muslim, and they tend to remain focused on local agendas. Al Qaida, because it is well funded and has received enormous publicity, is able to recruit new members from countries where no resident terrorist group exists. Individual and unaffiliated dissidents find al Qaida attractive. Countries with Muslim populations have groups with primarily domestic agendas, but al Qaida has appeal to terrorists of all colorations. In part because the United States treats it as the principal terrorist enemy, al Qaida prospers.

The neo-conservative agenda, if played out in this already negative environment, will make us more enemies than we have ever had before. The enemies will not necessarily be in one country prepared to go to war with us. They will be members of groups in various countries, mainly focused on their domestic agendas, but prepared to hook up with effective terrorism delivery systems and support groups such as al Qaida to accomplish their goals. Though the result is not a global network, groups that can be influenced and assisted by international terrorist organizations reduce the US margin for error.

US policies are major terrorism generators. The pockets of terrorism we attack tend to survive and regenerate. By US estimates some 3,000 al Qaida terrorists or affiliates have been killed or captured since 9-11. Other estimates suggest, however, that al Qaida largely has recovered from such losses and remains about as powerful as it was before 9-11. The reason for this is simple: As noted earlier, we go after the terrorists, not the causes of terrorism. In the states where terrorist groups are most active, the effects of the global issues are most depressing. Some analysts consider non-participation to be the leading problem, but desperate human conditions have prompted young and educated elites to enter an armed struggle on behalf of the poor.

Killing the terrorists who are created by and emerge from this environment does no enduring good. Rather, it makes matters worse because the survivors feel injured by the loss of their only advocates. Moreover, the US fosters future terrorism by encouraging the affected states to suppress their out-groups.

Out-groups such as the Kurds in Turkey and Iraq, Indians in Peru and Bolivia, Burmese hill tribals such as the Naga in India and Mianmar, the lesser tribes, ethnic and religious groups in Africa, Latin America, Asia, and the Middle East are not as communities easily provoked to violence. However, activists of or in favor of them are the sources of terrorism. Those activists are now being heard from in many places, either promising terrorism, complaining about US policy, or sniping at US personnel as shown recently in Kuwait, Saudi Arabia, and elsewhere. As the situation in Iraq now shows, those activities against US personnel and facilities will multiply. In this arena, US policies and activities already appear to be at the margin of tolerance and it is not likely that local authorities can prevent attacks.

The Middle East conflict remains toxic. The position of Israel in the troubled Middle East must be put and kept in perspective: It is an area of US policy with major failings and continuing potential for error. While the official position of the Israelis is that they are the perennial victims of terrorism and are only defending themselves, Israeli policies and actions in Palestine are the most active sources of new terrorism in the whole region.

The Road Map for Peace in the Middle East, launched by the US, the UN, the European Union, and Russia, appears unlikely to prosper. A heavy performance burden rests on the Palestinians, but the Map will lead nowhere until the role of the Israelis in creating and sustaining this conflict by taking their property and displacing the Palestinians is squarely admitted and dealt with.

US policies, including economic and military assistance on an exaggerated scale make Israeli excesses possible. While cited in earlier articles, it should be stated again here that US ignoring of Israeli use of US supplied weapons to repress an unarmed population is a major problem. For these and other reasons, the Map, the Geneva accord, or any plan, if it prospers, will require fundamental change in the US-Israeli relationship because it is a zone in which the US constantly errs.

The limits of military power—Military power can deal with only a few of the challenges the US faces abroad. Unfortunately, the military solutions applied abroad typically do the people most in need little, if any, good. That may be due in part to the fact that the interests being served are ours, not theirs. Up to now, when we have gone in somewhere militarily our goal has been crisis management, abatement or termination of actual or potential threats to US interests, the end of active conflict, followed by an early exit. Our goal has not been nation building, regime change, or even regime improvement, but settlement of immediate military issues, e.g., restoring the peace. Recent vacillation over a peacekeeping role in Liberia was a good/bad example.

Our troops in Iraq see every day that the occupation is serving as a wakeup call for dissidents. It is easy to assume that all of the disgruntled people in Iraq are former Baathists and Saddam adherents. However, Saddam suppressed a good deal of inter-tribal and ethnic/religious strife that has now resurfaced and will have to work itself off. Our effort to maintain peace puts our people in the middle of those conflicts; in addition, our people have to face the risks associated with small-scale insurgency and lawlessness. Our forces cannot fix the future because the Iraqis must learn to live peacefully together, something that for a century or more they have done only under pressure. Our best shot will be some limited steps in that direction.

The major problem in the weakest countries is that neither our efforts nor those of the whole international community have ever been enough. The problem is not merely quantity of assistance, but quality of involvement. Peacekeeping efforts, if they succeed at all, buy time for troubled communities by reducing or shutting off conflict. That is insufficient if communities suffer from lack of resources. Impatience and frustration grow. Scarcity conditions tend to rekindle conflicts. A comprehensive restorative and/or developmental effort is called for in the majority of cases, and that seldom happens. Iraq is lucky because it has intrinsic wealth, but the people must learn to work together.

Global poverty is growing. At the present time, More than a billion people subsist on less than a dollar a day. After a long decline, extreme poverty is increasing in the United States, but poverty conditions in the rest of the world are much worse than they are here. In poorer countries, conditions are not improving rapidly. Poverty is outpacing development.

The need in roughly half the world is for developmental assistance, and financial support, both public and private, on a greatly augmented and sustained scale. Failure to respond to this need has been our most common international policy error for decades. In 2002, the UN recorded $59 billion in Official Development Assistance, with the United States and Japan between them accounting for one third of the total. France, Germany, Britain, other European Countries, and Canada accounted for much of the rest. But only five countries met or exceeded the UN specified goal of contributing .07% of gross domestic product in 2002. The US regularly achieves about one seventh of its .07% goal.

Copycats are not easily contained. Several writers and commentators have pointed out that an exclusive writ does not exist for the United States to abandon foreign policy rules that have worked for at least half a century. The United States and other advanced countries have worked diligently to wean countries away from such foreign policy aberrations as pre-emptive strikes, assassination, hot pursuit or other border-crossing tactics, peremptory detentions, and abuses of prisoners.

Driven by the neo-conservative hawks, the United States is becoming a role model for the bad actors. The restraint on others that was achieved by efforts to promote the US/European example was always spotty, but the abandonment of such restraints by the United States itself is a major setback to good governance. The United States will pay for this, not only through less considered treatment of Americans abroad, but also through loss of respect for American positions on key global issues and emulation of policy aberrations against both US interests and the interests of other countries. Unless corrected, this will greatly reduce the US margin for error in the coming decades.

The bottom line—Several analysts, beginning immediately after the first Gulf War, have argued that the United States makes a great mistake trying to go it alone. It uses our blood and treasure to be a world policeman. It does not pay our dues to the UN—the only global organization that can help.

The hawks are trying to carry the world policeman role to a militarist extreme, to be the world's sole military power. To assert that role, our leaders are bending and breaking the basic rules of international behavior we learned at great cost during the past century.

In addition, as noted in earlier articles, US policy is to keep the WMD genii in the bottle worldwide. However, we are openly experimenting with both bigger (bunker busters) and smaller (tactical) nuclear, chemical, explosive, and electronic weapons.

Our biggest and perhaps even fatal error may be failure to contain the spread of our best bad ideas. The very information systems that make us powerful also broadcast our most advanced ideas, military and otherwise, and further reduce our margin for error.

Our problem is that as wealthy as we are, we are not big enough or rich enough to rule the world. With the US and other developed nations at the top, the global system is not an orderly pyramid. It resembles a needle standing in a mud pie. It is an awkward system to administer even with enormous resources and worldwide support. If our budget and fiscal policies remain the way they are under the present administration, those policies will squander the rest of our dwindling national net worth, and we may be too poor to rule the world anyway. In any case, we will need all the help we can get to keep our place in it.

Living within a narrow margin for error that has been created by our bad habits and our misguided leadership is our assignment. Unless we get this right, the New American Century of the neo-cons, which was always a pipe dream, is already a lost cause. Even more important, the United States will have blown the chance to lead that was offered to it by most countries after the evil deeds of 9-11.

WE HAVE BECOME THE MAIN PROBLEM
April 2004

With his book, <u>Against All Enemies</u>, and his interviews, including his March 21, 2004 Sixty Minutes session with Leslie Stahl, Richard Clarke has put the Bush administration in a state of high confusion. The costs of that state of mind for US interests and for prospects of world peace are mounting daily. The situation brings into sharp focus two key areas of long term Bush team confusion: Before 9-11, the great bulk of terrorism in the world was not directed against the United States. After 9-11, the Bush team has done an incredible job of increasing the risks to Americans everywhere.

In her statement and responses to questions before the 9-11 Commission on April 8, National Security Adviser Condoleezza Rice tried to contradict all of Clarke statements about Bush administration performance, but it was not a convincing rebuttal. How can the Clarke recounting of events and the Bush/Rice statements of administration actions and intentions occupy the same space? The problem facing the administration is they cannot.

On the immediate struggle against possible terrorist

attacks, Clarke is largely right and the administration is largely wrong, but neither is looking at the global struggle against terrorism. Rather both are bogged down in the "who struck John" Washington politics of the War on Terrorism. That will burn mega volumes of media space and professional time to no purpose because, the global challenge of terrorism notwithstanding, we have become the main problem.

The evolution of our situation is compelling. Before we invaded Iraq a year ago, the most turbulent terrorism generators on the planet were churning away in Palestine, and we were doing little about them. The Palestinians get most of the blame, but every Israeli action respecting the West Bank and Gaza has been provocative. Heavy handed military operations, targeted assassination of the elderly Hamas leader Yassin last month, and more recently his successor, Rantissi, aggressive bulldozing of homes and businesses, and the travesty of the "wall" have assured that terrorism generators run full blast. And the Israelis are using money and equipment supplied by the American taxpayer to do it.

Prime Minister Sharon's recent threat to throw out all so-called illegal Palestinians in Israel once the wall is finished is just another hot coal on this fire. Israeli hardliners can be assured that enough suicide bombings and other attacks will occur to keep the Israeli public properly cowed and agreeable to present extremist policies.

The Israelis contend that any actions the Palestinians take to fight back against the Israeli occupation and its excesses are terrorism. That view fits a Middle Eastern conflict model in which national armies can terrorize whole populations, but individuals who fight back are terrorists. By signing on to the Israeli side of this conflict, the US says the Palestinian people have no rights, no dignity, no claims they can assert against an occupying force, and no actions they can take to defend themselves. The Palestinians are dehumanized in this process.

The ultimate put down of the Palestinian people, and sad

proof that there is no administration understanding of the causes of terrorism, occurred in the Bush meeting Wednesday, April, 14, with Ariel Sharon. So far as the Palestinians are concerned, Bush gave away the store. He gave Sharon carte blanche to choose which settlements—the so-called "facts on the ground"—the Israelis will keep or even add in the West Bank. He personally withdrew any right of the Palestinians to return to their ancestral homes. In short, Bush pulled the plug on Palestinian hopes for the future.

Alongside Palestine, Iraq has an increasingly familiar look. The view from the Coalition Green Zone in Baghdad is that people who fight back against occupying forces are either malcontents or terrorists, probably allied with al Qaida. The promise, or threat, is that the bad actors, the militants, will be punished. In light of sharply increased attacks over the past few days, US civil administrator in Iraq, L. Paul Bremer, and US military spokesmen, have stated categorically that the Iraqis who fight back are terrorists, and the US will not negotiate with them. In short, the US is now using the same dehumanizing strategy against the Iraqis that Israel uses against the Palestinians.

Moreover, the US has used this strategy from the beginning of the post 9-11 war in Afghanistan. It asserts that suspected terrorists, whether or not members of al Qaida, have no rights and may be confined indefinitely without recourse.

This strategy has perverse effects in both situations. To be sure, a number of Iraqis and Palestinians cease to openly resist, but their sympathies are clearly with the people who actually do fight back. They provide the fighters with shelter, money, food, weapons, transportation, and assistance, and they do not appear to press their tribal or religious leaders to find a political solution. Meanwhile, the fighters are told they have no choice but to give up, but because they appear to believe that they will only be trading their compliance for submission, they fight back more vigorously.

This all or nothing approach, which appears very satisfying

to hardliners, accomplishes nothing except to make more people angry and ready to resist. The trend of conflict in Iraq brutally bears this out.

A de-humanize-the-enemy strategy is paired with another commonplace failing of the Bush administration that was mentioned in earlier articles: Nothing is being done about the causes of terrorism. In her statement to the 9-11 Commission on Thursday, Condoleezza Rice delivered her entire justification of Bush policies around terrorism without once mentioning the causes. Only on questioning did she admit that conditions in Afghanistan had been allowed to deteriorate badly before any real effort was begun to improve conditions of life in that country. After the US defeated Taliban rulers who had controlled pretty much the whole country, warlords who were enlisted by the US to achieve that defeat were allowed to reassert their control of major areas of the country.

As seen by some observers, Hamid Karzai, the chosen national leader installed shortly after defeat of the Taliban, actually has become little more than Mayor of Kabul. Meanwhile, the country is back in the heroin business.

Rice committed another major error in her response to questioning when she said that the way to respond to human needs in the area is to introduce democracy to defeat Islamic fundamentalism. What if the great majority of Muslims want an Islamic society? The notion that Muslims can overcome the impact of modernization and the effects of severe scarcities in their societies by revising the way they select their leaders is incredibly naïve. But the tragedy of it all is that her assessment totally ignores the powerful terrorism generators that have existed for half a century in Palestine and that are daily more intensively turned on in Iraq.

From the perspective of service to US national interests, the Washington debate is almost totally sterile. There can be no winner. If the Bush team succeeds in asserting that it actually knew what it was doing before 9-11 and was taking the necessary steps to protect the country, its critics will say "But the towers were knocked down." If the critics succeed in convincing the public that the Bush team screwed up, he will likely lose the 2004 election. However, the country's protection against a future terrorist attack may not be made better by his loss. US actions since 9-11 have created new sources of terrorism and aggravated existing stresses in many societies.

The administration view implants a sense of hopelessness in American minds. It gives an impression that the United States has a set of implacable and unreasonable enemies whose anger is not our fault. It promotes the view that nothing can be done about such dangers but fight back.

This assumption is not only false; it is most dangerous because it raises feelings of victim-hood and fear in our country that are quite enervating. Much of the Israeli public has been enslaved by these feelings for half a century.

Such feelings appear to be growing in the United States. The frustrations that are generated by them in turn sustain an unhealthy tolerance for violent remedies that only feed the problems.

Dislike of US policies and actions has grown since the Iraq invasion, but as discussed in the article Why the War on Terrorism Will Fail, the primary targets of terrorism in other countries, including Islamic ones, are not the United States or its citizens. However, we can bring ourselves into the "enemy" camp by one-sided support for Israel and insensitivity to the real injuries being inflicted on the Palestinian people, by supporting repressive leaders, or simply by supporting constituted governments in countries where there is significant popular dissent. We can be the enemy, as we are in Iraq, by carrying out an unprovoked and illegal attack on another country. We can be the enemy by trying to suppress the nuclear ambitions of other countries while seeking to expand and improve our own enormous stockpiles.

In short, our own actions have triggered quite a bit of

the risk of terrorism against us. Therefore, by changing our behavior, we can do something to reduce that risk.

There is an odd twist under the title of Richard Clarke's book <u>Against All Enemies</u>. The complete phrase is "Against All Enemies Foreign and Domestic" and that is an apt phrase, because under Bush and neo-conservative leadership, the United States has become its own worst enemy. Bush has cemented that position by the concessions he made Wednesday to Sharon, giving away Palestinian rights the United States does not own. Kerry will be tarred with the same brush if he does not immediately disavow the Bush concessions. But both Bush and Kerry have indicated strong support for Israel and neither is likely to risk loss of Jewish support in the coming election. For the same reason, neither appears likely to favor retreat from the hard line now being taken in Iraq. We therefore may be locked into stoking the flames of terrorism worldwide.

Instead of just allowing that to happen, we should put terrorism into proper perspective. Terrorism is an asymmetrical struggle in which small, even weak, adversaries can do large and powerful states a great deal of harm. There is no convincing evidence that terrorism can be defeated by military means, even though special operations make good adventure TV programs. There is convincing evidence that economic and social improvements in a society reduce tendencies to violence.

In trying to defeat terrorism militarily, the Bush team has made terror attacks a more critical risk for the United States by making new enemies in much of the Middle East and by offending friends virtually everywhere else. The war on terrorism is globally provocative in the same manner as Israeli attacks in Palestine.

There is hope in this situation. Many of the challenges are problems of our own making, and many of the possible solutions are in our own hands. We can abandon the hard line attack strategy in Iraq as a first step toward reducing the number of enemies our country is making. We can hand the Iraq recovery over to the United Nations—assuming they will take it, and that will get us out of a nation-building role we have bungled from the beginning. We surely can recognize that a one-sided and thoughtless approach to Palestine is an enormous terrorism generator and must be corrected. We can recognize that terrorism is a product of multiple weaknesses in many societies; we can put the energies we are wasting on war into combating those weaknesses.

All of those steps would take us a long way toward reducing the risks of terrorism. We must first admit—at least to ourselves—that we are a big part of the problem. Getting our country back on its historic course will do the rest.

WHERE DID YOU SAY THE BUCK STOPPED?
May 2004

Harry Truman minted the model of presidential responsibility when he posted this sign on his desk: "The buck stops here". Truman's political history was hardly as pure as the driven snow, having emerged from a Midwest political machine through flaky compromises that identify Vice Presidents. He was almost a terrorism victim himself when Puerto Rican nationalists tried to assassinate him in front of Blair House—he was walking across the street from the White House. Truman made some tough decisions, including A-bomb attacks on Hiroshima and Nagasaki, and he took his share of flak, e.g., for war in Korea, but he never wavered from the principle of his sign.

The White House is a complicated place. Popular TV versions of it depict high-level power users and abusers constantly doing crisis or priority or personal things, some of them in the national interest. But the White House staff version of Truman's sign is: We cannot afford to be uninformed about anything that matters to the presidency. That statement is not a mantra; it is the main driver of every White House staffer's job description from clerk to chief of staff. Their task is to serve the President at all times on anything that may require a decision or just presidential awareness. It is exhausting, mostly thankless work, but staffers do it.

Now about Abu Ghraib.-The only way to determine exactly what and when the President knew about what went on in that American run prison is to be inside his head. Ample evidence exists that there was an almost constant flow of information to the White House on prisoner abuses in Iraq. It began as early as mid-2003 when the International Committee of the Red Cross began to file reports with US government officials. That flow heightened in late 2003/early 2004 when senior officers began to submit a series of investigative reports.

Defense Secretary Rumsfeld has said he informed the President of the abuse reports in February 2004. Moreover, recent articles, notably Seymour Hersh in the New Yorker, call attention to a special access program led by Rumsfeld that calls for means that rely on torture for extracting information from prisoners. There was fire where the Red Cross said there was smoke, and an ICRC report of multiple abuses was hardly the low level complaint of a non-entity, especially when the ICRC report said the abuses were systemic and "tantamount to torture".

Despite all the complaints about the lack of information sharing across agency lines, even the agency stovepipes—their protected lines of communication upward—reach the White House. Therefore, the ICRC complaint would have been reported back through the chain of command to Washington, and it would have appeared without fail in the baskets of the national security and/or public affairs staffs in the White House. At this point, the well-honed reflexes of the staff would have assured that a summary report of the problem would be provided to the President. His Chief of Staff could have withheld it, but why?

President Bush is saying, however, that he knew nothing about the problem until he saw the report on Sixty Minutes.

Basically he is saying "The buck did not even get here." There are several ways to view that assertion: (1) It is true because nobody told him; (2) staff submitted a report, but he did not read it; (3) he read the report, but did not remember it or think the subject was serious; or (4) his actions and statements were considered easier to defend if he were ignorant than if he were informed.

Maybe we can be kind and assume Rumsfeld's report to Bush was not actually a "buck". However, based on the evidence, knowledgeable people in Washington conclude that Bush knew about Abu Ghraib, and knew that what went on there was part of a special access program for gathering intelligence, but he thinks he can defend himself better by appearing ignorant. In short, he and his campaign handlers think it would hurt his chances less if he denied it, even if he had to lie to do it.

But what about the national interest? Right now, more than at any point in the Bush presidency, we need a leader with good judgment and integrity. The whole Abu Ghraib performance says both are lacking. Ever since Bush's aircraft carrier declaration that major combat was over in Iraq, the situation has gotten worse for two reasons: (a) We have been trying to beat the Iraqis into submission; and (b) they make increasingly clear they won't have it. In simple terms, the Coalition war strategy went from "shock and awe" in the air to brutalize or kill on the ground. Things have gone downhill at each step on this path.

Experienced analysts are saying this is a make or break moment for the United States, not only in the Middle East. It is certainly not a golden moment for the Greater Middle East Initiative the United States is promoting as a means to modernize Islamic countries. If we can come forward with good explanations of what happened at Abu Ghraib and other prisons, if we clean up our act—including ditching the neo-con architects of this policy, if we voluntarily compensate those individuals and their families who bore the brunt of this misbegotten approach to war, if we honestly turn Iraq back to its own people, and if we leave as gracefully as possible, the situation can be retrieved.

Our leaders must start restoring our country's pre-Iraq standing in the world community. However, the task of bringing the United States back to its place of leadership in the family of nations will take new leadership, even a new brand of leadership in Washington. We need someone who is prepared to admit and act on the facts. We need someone who is prepared, not to set our values aside, but to show that our system works to protect us. The buck truly does stop at the Oval Office.

BUSH HAD A DREAM DURING THE CONVENTION
September 2004

In accepting the Republican nomination for President on September 2, George W. Bush plunged into a strange reverie. Ignoring the mess that actually exists, Bush said: "As the citizens of Afghanistan and Iraq seize the moment, their example will send a message of hope throughout a vital region. Palestinians will hear the message that democracy and reform are within their reach, and so is peace with our good friend Israel. Young women across the Middle East will hear the message that their day of equality and justice is coming. Young men will hear the message that national progress and dignity are found in liberty, not tyranny and terror. Reformers and political prisoners and exiles will hear the message that their dream of freedom cannot be denied forever. And as freedom advances, heart by heart and nation by nation, America will be more secure and the world more peaceful."

While we must all pray for and work to achieve such outcomes, the Bush speech is a dream that totally ignores the real situation and the actual prospects for the Middle East.

The real situation is that the United States invaded a country that was not threatening the United States in any way. In the process, the United States killed more than 10,000 Iraqis, wounded at least ten times that number, many of them women and children, destroyed much of the Iraqi infrastructure, imprisoned thousands of Iraqis, tortured many hundreds of them, and put our young men and women in harm's way for no vital national purpose. In August 2004, US losses ran to more than 66 killed and 1,100 wounded.

The real situation is that the Bush team is talking about invading Iran when the US does not have adequate forces to occupy Iraq. The real situation is that Iraqi control and ownership of its enterprises, including oil, have been covertly compromised by sales to foreign businesses, including Israelis. The real situation is that with bases springing up at every convenient location in Iraq, the US is signaling that its intent is not to leave. The real situation is that the Iraqis face more years of occupation by foreigners, meaning also years of outside interference in their internal affairs.

In Afghanistan, the real situation is that there are not enough foreign, US, British, or other forces in the country to assuredly pacify even the remnants of the Taliban. The War on Terrorism began here, but it is bogged down for want of forces, and some say for want of Bush team interest.

Somewhere in the outback between Pakistan and Afghanistan, Osama bin Laden and his core al Qaida team may be operating in comparative safety to plot horrendous attacks on the American economic and financial infrastructure. Potential attacks on such "icon targets" in the United States are said to be high on the al Qaida list. However, if those leading institutions at this stage do not have sufficient built-in redundancy to survive such an attack without disruption, we have three emergency preparedness problems instead of one: (a) We have leadership that is inattentive to our system needs. (b) We have spent billions on homeland security without meeting preparedness needs. (c) We have produced sitting ducks.

With respect to Palestine, in the past several weeks the prospect that the Palestinian people will ever "hear the message that democracy and reform are within their reach" has grown dim. Bush has signed on to the complete Likud agenda for expelling the Palestinian people from their homeland. Sharon is taking advantage of the inattention to foreign policy details that typically is bred of a presidential election year, and he is moving briskly forward to annex the West Bank. Since the beginning of March 2004, far from responding to US diplomatic urgings to stop new settlement activity, Israeli authorities have approved almost 5,000 new construction requests in at least fourteen settlement areas. The real situation is that Sharon and his Zionist supporters are moving as rapidly as they can to render the idea of a Palestinian state entirely moot, regardless of what happens to the Palestinian people.

Nothing the United States is doing or talking about doing in the rest of the Middle East is capable of delivering the opportunities for young people that Bush dreams about. Right now, Israeli leadership is contemplating raids into Syria to deal with Shiites—a group called Hizballah (Party of God)—who sympathize with the Palestinians and fight on their behalf. Right now Israelis are working with Kurds in Iraq to mount operations against Iran. The Israelis assuredly are not doing this against US will. All of this is street news, not intelligence. Pressure appears to be mounting among leading neo-cons in the Bush team—and encouraged by Israel—to attack Iran to prevent that country from achieving home grown nuclear weapons. The overt Bush team agenda, therefore, is riddled with actual and potential conflict situations, none of which contribute to a climate for peaceful change.

In the real Middle East situation, there is no moment to seize. Such dream-like promises as Bush reflected in his speech Thursday night are destructive because they offer a hope that is unreal. They breed disappointment, because in the most tragic sense, the Bush dream is a lie. Not because the things he muses about are undesirable. Far from it; they are devoutly to be wished. They are lies, because the real US intent is being wreaked on the landscape for all to see.

The Bush team vision collides with the needs and expectations of Middle Eastern peoples. It has an unreal perspective on what and how long it might take to achieve changes many Muslims want in their societies. It displays little understanding of what writer William Pfaff calls the interactions of terrorism with Islamic religion and nationalist goals. The Bush vision demands that no Middle East country have nuclear weapons except Israel. The key ingredients are oil and Israeli security. That vision is a hard sell to anyone but Bush team members, Israeli extremists and supporters. Unfortunately, John Kerry has embraced virtually all of it.

While George Washington did not necessarily envisage the financial, business, and political complexity of our present operating system, he certainly foresaw the corrupting patterns of influence that now drive our political processes. In his Farewell Address, he expressed concern that the way our emerging political system would work "opens the door to foreign influence and corruption...thus the policy and the will of one country are subjected to the policy and will of another."

The present Middle East reflects a situation Washington could have had in mind. Both Republican and Democratic Party leaders have pledged the same allegiance to Israel to gain or avoid losing swing votes in November. As a result, Israel has become the very type of foreign entanglement that President Washington warned us about. And if both candidates live up to their commitments to Israel, no balanced, reasonable, or potentially successful policy that serves American interests is likely to emerge in the next four years. Instead, the region is in for very hard times indeed.

Both George W. Bush, or, if elected, John F. Kerry, should take Washington's caution seriously, because the immediate danger is a growing separation between vital American interests and American foreign policy. That spread is more serious than the immense distance between the Bush dream speech and the realities of the Middle East.

IN DENIAL ON NUCLEAR PROLIFERATION
February 2005

With growing stridence, the United States is making a high profile effort to persuade Iran to abandon its alleged nuclear weapons program. Both State Undersecretary John Bolton and Vice President Dick Cheney give the highest priority to halting Iranian nuclear activities; US threats of what happens to Iran if it does not cease and desist are hardly veiled. Just how does a layman know what is going on here, and why? The combination of deception to protect military options, deceit to keep the public from knowing what is happening, and a Bush/neo-con habit of telling anything but the way it is, means the picture we get is frightening, but also badly distorted.

There is great confusion on exactly what Iran is doing. Iran is unlikely to tell what it knows. But the main distortion in the picture is the behavior of the United States. While publicly devoted to curbing the nuclear ambitions of Iran, Syria, and North Korea, the US is totally silent on Israel's large nuclear arsenal and soft-spoken on likely programs of countries such as Taiwan. Meanwhile, advocates in the United States

Government openly call for research, design, and production of new generations of nuclear weapons.

Redefining the battlefield—Scarier than weapons design and manufacture, the United States appears engaged in a creeping redefinition of conventional warfare. Since the beginning of Gulf War I, the US has deposited several thousand tons of nuclear trash through the use of depleted uranium weapons on both Iraqi and Kosovo landscapes. Long before, both the United States and former Soviet Union had developed battlefield nuclear weapons, e.g., artillery shells, and small, tactical nukes for air drop. Where the Russians are going on their activities is not clear, but the United States is setting the worst possible example of nuclear proliferation while aggressively attempting to prevent the birth of any new nuclear states.

What is the goal? The true subject of US behavior does not appear to be nuclear non-proliferation. If it were, the US would be pounding tables everywhere to eliminate nuclear weapons no matter who has or may have them. However, all the while pushing to rid Iraq of non-existent nuclear weapons and pressing North Korea and Iran to cease and desist from uranium refining programs that can lead to weapons, the US is seen, especially in the Middle East, as merely trying to keep for itself and Israel a regional nuclear monopoly. As Middle Easterners and many others see it, the name of the game is not non-proliferation, but retention of nuclear advantage.

The troublesome facts—To a layman, there are several facets of this problem that are worrisome. (a) The United States and other nuclear club members (Britain, France, China, and Russia) are not showing any real signs of getting rid of their weapons. (b) The United States, while reducing stockpiles, seems launched on a major modernization program. (c) Doubtless other nuclear club members are not standing still, although budgets and other resources are a major constraint. (d) North Korea and Iran are currently targeted want-to-be nuclear powers. (e) They are almost certainly not the only other countries trying for this brass ring.

The US program, and other likely reactions to it, obviously will broaden the range of nuclear weapons uses, and it presents an undeniable picture of proliferation, not control. The result is that any real non-proliferation leadership of the United States is lacking, a genuine non-proliferation spirit is simply missing, and in that atmosphere the persistence of nuclear weapons on the planet appears assured. The have-not countries see powerful demonstrators of the enduring desirability of nuclear weapons as attributes of national power.

To make matters worse, any approach to non proliferation is highly selective. No real effort is being made to either curb or eliminate Israeli weapons, or for that matter the weapons of India and Pakistan. Maybe it would be foolish, even perilous to try, but the approach looks to the rest of the world like an aggressive, even arrogant, attempt to maintain nuclear exclusiveness, to preserve and limit nuclear power because it provides the ultimate weapon for dominating other societies. Another troublesome fact: As one of its few budget cuts in the national security area, the Bush team severely slashed the budget of the Nunn-Lugar program that is aimed at reducing the risks posed by possibly loose nuclear weapons and unemployed nuclear technicians in Russia.

All non-nuclear powers have to struggle with a fundamental national security decision: Can they trust the nuclear powers not to use the bargaining weight of nuclear weapons against them? The Middle East answer to that question is "No!" Depleted uranium has been widely used in Iraq; other equally, if not more noxious devices, reportedly were used in the destruction of Fallujah. Meanwhile, mainstream media report that the United States and Israel are both looking for bunker busters powerful enough to disrupt Iranian and any other deeply buried and would-be nuclear program. Weapons of that power are likely to be tactical nukes that would create their own mushroom clouds.

What is the truth? Current US leaders may be driven by a realistic appraisal that it is no longer possible to put the genii back in the bottle; the only real option is to control the size, shape, motives, and applications of the genii. That appraisal would commit the world to a lasting condition of nuclear haves and have nots, while decisions about who is who would be maintained by nuclear blackmail. For better or worse, that is almost certainly the inevitable outcome.

That appraisal is a sad commentary on our ability to control a major global evil. It is also the doorway to a frightful, self-fulfilling prophecy in which the world will either destroy itself or become bound in an iron-fisted matrix of a few nuclear powers dominating a world of vassal states.

The role of "dirty bombs"—Creeping nuclearization of conventional warfare is America's future. The gateway weapons are "dirty bombs". We hear much about them as so-called radiological weapons that may be the first nuclear entry of terrorists. But the United States has introduced a defacto dirty bomb because it has used depleted uranium weapons widely on the battlefields of Iraq and Kosovo. Depleted uranium is incorporated into armor piercing ammunition and other projectiles because it provides greater mass, meaning a more penetrating or destructive edge. It is also the core of steel encased armor on tanks, because the enhanced mass provides a protective edge that potential enemy armorers have not yet overcome. The unavoidable side effect, however, is radiation contamination of both friend and foe. Such radiation effects account for much of the 30% US casualty rate the Veterans Administration has recorded for Gulf War I.

In the competition between arms and armor that has gone on for millennia, the current battle is being fought with the earth. Governments seeking to protect their programs, devices, plans, and key people, now bury them ever deeper beneath the ground. The challenge is how to penetrate those bunkers; Iran reportedly has dug in deeply in many different locations.

So the outlook is not ideal. An ideal perspective for non-nuclear powers would be that of a nuclear club and outriders all diligently seeking to reduce and eliminate their weapons. That would represent a benign environment free of threat. But the present environment is aggressively threatening. Whether or not they intended the world to know it, the United States and Israel are now actively thinking about destroying large parts of Iran to prevent that country from going nuclear. They are looking for weapons powerful enough to penetrate far enough to eliminate deeply buried operating sites. Thus, as implied in Cheney and Bolton statements, Iran is a defacto victim of nuclear blackmail. North Korea will also be if it persists in its nuclear ambitions; the only real deterrent may be likely Chinese reactions to any attack on North Korea.

These equations are globally destabilizing. They help proliferation and terrorism flourish. Because they contribute to uncertainties that unbalance the outlooks of many societies, they add to the incentives of dissidents, opposition groups, and active terrorist organizations to take advantage of the situations. Lacking nuclear tools, the groups motivated by such situations will use conventional devices. The 9-11 attacks should have shown us how effective conventional devices can be.

The perverse nature of the present nuclear policies is that they preserve a nuclear standoff among club members while stimulating the rest of the family of nations to use every device and subterfuge available to become a club member. Unfortunately, the materials are both available and profitable to sell. The atmosphere for real non-proliferation is totally contaminated.

At the same time, nuclear weapons appear to deter only nuclear weapons. Conventional devices are available to the least significant of users. Thanks to the proliferation of Semtex and C4, virtually anybody anywhere can, albeit illegally, get powerful explosives, and the Iraq landscape is increasingly destroyed by them. If those explosives are not to be found, fertilizer and fuel are available. Equally worrisome, biological and chemical weapons are easily available to any country that has medical, chemical or pharmaceutical production facilities. The principal deterrent to any such weapons is not other weapons, but some way to keep people from becoming angry enough to use them. The Iraqi spectacle says we are not even close to that discovery.

Facing us is the slippery slope. Having crossed the boundary between nuclear/chemical/biological and conventional war, there seems no turning back. Rather, the prospect is that governments who might have felt "We really don't want to do this" will shift to "We can't afford not to do this." In that frame of mind, the conventions of war will slowly drift toward unbounded use of nuclear devices. The struggle to keep new nuclear powers from emerging will become more acute. Non-proliferation as now pursued will only encourage proliferation.

The global evil we now face cannot be turned away without a concerted effort by people who know this landscape well and are dedicated to putting the genii back into the bottle. America had that potential once, and America must regain it, first by curbing its own ambition. The notion that the leaders of non-proliferation can also be the leading proliferators is a denial that will destroy us all.

DEAL WITH AMERICAN TYRANNY FIRST
February 2005

In his State of the Union address February 2, 2005, President Bush used the last six-hundred words or so to outline a new war on tyranny. "America will always stand firm," he said, "for the non-negotiable demands of human dignity: the rule of law...limits on the power of the state...respect for women...private property...free speech...equal justice...and religious tolerance." He then summarized future behavior by saying: "America will take the side of brave men and women who advocate these values around the world—including the Islamic world—because we have a greater objective than eliminating threats and containing resentment. We seek a just and peaceful world beyond the war on terror."

All of these sound right for the world's most powerful democracy. With them, and other supportive lines in his speech, Bush transformed the war on terrorism into a war against tyranny. And that, again as words, sounds OK.

Why, then, are more people around the world now expressing alarm or disbelief and not satisfaction with the President's announcements? The simplest answer that covers all the facts is that the present American behavioral model is wildly at odds with the language of the President's speech. Much in present American behavior would need to be fixed to get our country's own model on track.

Deal with insults to human dignity in Palestine. Today, more than three million Palestinians are waiting for the promise of a Palestinian state to become real. They have suffered expulsion from their ancestral homes, witnessed the destruction of their homes and farms and businesses, endured willful expropriation of limited water supplies, watched their children gunned down by he Israel Defense Force, experienced the assassination or imprisonment and torture of militants, confronted the spectacle of separate roads for Israelis, found the land of their would-be state turned into Bantustans by a meandering Israeli 24 foot concrete wall, and suffered the confiscation of their property in Jerusalem. The final indignity is they still carry the blame for everything that prevents peace in Palestine on their backs. If the President wants to prove his assertion that the demands of human dignity are non-negotiable, he can start with Palestine.

Stop the US assault on equal justice. Prisoner torture and abuse at Abu Ghraib, Guantanamo and other prison facilities under US or "friendly" government control have engraved a cruel pattern of unequal justice in the public mind. To get to that point, US military, CIA, and supporting contractors have ignored or set aside well-established rules of war, the Geneva Conventions on treatment of prisoners, the US Constitution on individual rights, and, in the President's own words, "the limits on the power of the state." To get our country beyond this complete collapse of civility in our society, President Bush can start by instructing his newly-confirmed Attorney General to withdraw the torture memos written during the last four years and substitute rules that are consistent with US law, with the international obligations of the United States, with the Uniform Code of Military Justice, and with commonly held concepts of human rights. President Bush can also see that at least a handful of the senior civilians and uniformed military officers responsible are disciplined for their roles in these excesses.

Strike a blow for private property. Most of what is modern Israel exists on private properties that had belonged to Palestinian families for generations. That land was mostly taken, sometimes in bloody massacres, by destruction and expulsion of people from hundreds of villages and farms. The Israelis have used a de facto eminent domain to achieve these results. They have either taken over or destroyed the Palestinian homes and businesses that were on these properties and have consistently resisted the idea of return or any compensation.

Israelis can enjoy the property they have taken without paying the Palestinian owners, while the former Palestinian occupants live in refugee camps or struggle with abject poverty in towns and villages scattered across the West Bank and Gaza and throughout the Middle East. Either of two choices would honor the rights of Palestinians in private property: Compensate them or their descendents for their losses at fair market value, or allow them to return and resume enjoyment of their ancestral homes. In his stance on Israeli-Palestinian peace efforts, President Bush should stand for either or both of those choices depending on cases. All other choices amount to Israeli confiscation and theft, aided by the United States.

Restore the rule of law. The rule of law has been badly mangled since 9-11. The first and most striking example was that the Congress, with little evident debate, once again ceded its constitutional war-declaration powers to the President. The second was that, with hardly any examination, the Congress passed the Patriot Act, which opened the gates to systematic reduction and averting of constitutional protections for individual liberties. A third was the unprovoked invasion of Iraq in violation of established rules of national sovereignty. Another was a decision of Defense Secretary Rumsfeld to initiate military intelligence covert operations without any legislative consultation or authorization. A fifth was the virtual castration of the CIA in an effort to make intelligence collection and analysis an acolyte of Presidential policy, in short, a propaganda machine. When added to the illegal invasion and occupation of Iraq, the continuing abuse of prisoners in US custody, and the rendition of prisoners to governments that practice torture of prisoners, US actions since 9-11 have done much to discredit the United States. Unless the President cleans up this landscape, he has no product of value to sell to the rest of humanity.

Get the global picture straight. The promise: "America will take the side of brave men and women who advocate these values around the world," fully implemented, is an invitation to chaos. The situations vary widely by countries. In some cases, the advocates of democratic or representative systems are either governments or loyal oppositions actively engaged in politics. In many cases, the seekers after representation or advocates of human rights are in out-groups; some of these groups are the spawning grounds for terrorist groups or terrorist attacks. The State Department typically reports on more than sixty terrorist organizations, only about a third of them Islamic, and a goodly portion of the so-called Islamic ones are involved in the Palestine issues.

About half of the groups worldwide appear to seek regime change principally to achieve full participation in national life. The problems at root are often extracts of cross-cultural, ethnic, religious, territorial, and historic frictions.

The President can help by assuring that the understanding of these situations is widespread in government and the public, and that appropriate efforts are being made to support solutions. The war on terrorism has effectively contradicted such efforts by encouraging and financially or technically assisting various governments to suppress their indigenous "terrorists", quite a number of them "brave men and women who advocate these values."

Fix the conflict between words and deeds. At present

there is an enormous gap between the President's words and America's deeds. His words are particularly out of phase with (a) an unprovoked invasion of Iraq, (b) a threatened assault on Iran, (c) reported covert operations against Iran or Syria, (d) repeated intimations of intent to use force against North Korea, (e) US support for free-wheeling Israeli operations in Palestine, (f) US association with the recent attempt to overthrow the democratically elected President of Venezuela, (g) continued support for autocratic and/or repressive regimes such as in Egypt, Saudi Arabia, and Pakistan, (h) US treatment of enemy combatants, (h) reported US plans to keep Guantanamo and other prisoners confined virtually forever without any legal basis for doing so, (i) extension of the Patriot Act to further undercut human liberties in the United States and make those changes permanent, or (j) continuing US work on nuclear weapons with implied plans to use one or more, e.g., to take out deep bunkers in Iran or North Korea. In its current edition, The Economist described the basic US approach as "Democracy at gunpoint".

President Bush could profitably use the remainder of his years in the Oval Office to tidy up this mess. If he were to do so, our country and the rest of the world could write off the experiences of the past three years as excessive outbursts due to the shocks of 9-11. It could be widely agreed that the United States needed some time to right itself. If the President wishes a genuine and well-earned legacy, this is the way to go.

VINDICATING AMERICAN DEMOCRACY
April 2005

Over the past several weeks, mainstream American media have practically swooned over the elections of sorts that have occurred in countries of the Middle East and elsewhere. Reflecting comments from official Washington, they have been full of praise for balloting in Iraq, in Palestine, and retrospectively for Ukraine. The prospect of an election in Lebanon has been imbued with virtually millennial significance. Their overarching judgment is that political spring is flowering in the Middle East. Their bottom line is the assertion that all of this is the first product of President Bush's promotion of democracy. On a more cautious note, The Economist, a London voice, sums it up with such terms as the idea of "Democracy for Arabs" is no longer "the stuff of foolish dreams" while the idea that the Israelis and Palestinians would negotiate a settlement "is no longer ridiculous."

The primary reason for these rhetorical flights is a desperate Washington leadership search for good news from the Middle East. One reason is an effort to validate the President's State of the Union declaration of a war on tyranny. Another reflects way-paving for future pre-emptive US/Israeli moves, for example against Iran. A fourth reason is the desire of many people in the Middle East and elsewhere to achieve representative forms of government and greater participation in decisions affecting them. But that dream is at least several generations old, and it has been suppressed by the weight of American and European colonial policies.

A "flowering" of the desire for participatory government in countries where self-selected/externally supported elites have ruled for decades could prove, like Aladdin's genii, difficult to put back in the bottle. The acid test will be a demonstration that the United States not only means what President Bush has been saying, but also knows what those statements mean when translated into national forms of governance.

An even harder test may be US willingness to accept whatever "summer" of governance that "spring" leads to. There is virtually no public evidence of such openness in recent American policies and decisions. So, what is driving the liberal sounding promotion of democracy everywhere by a US leadership that up to now has pursued a basically military and unilateral interventionist agenda?

There may be no single response to this question, but answers to several related questions are a good place to start: What is the much touted Project for a New American Century really about? What were the policy effects of the 9-11 attacks? Exactly why did the United States invade Iraq? What is the War on Tyranny really about?

The Project for the New American Century (PNAC)—A report called "Rebuilding America's Defenses", prepared by a Washington think tank called PNAC became the guiding light of the first George W. Bush administration. It still is. The main focus of the report was on defense and military strategy matters. The drafters were looking at an America that was preeminent, but which faced growing difficulties with sustaining that position. Such a perspective could reasonably have been taken as a sign that the United States, with, as the report says, "no global rival," certainly no comparable military rival, had time to cool it for a while and watch developments. The PNAC drafters thought otherwise.

A fundamental situation that confronted the United States at the start of the George W. Bush administration was the prospect that most big, global political discussions would be about economic and environmental issues. In that context, the most heated debate would likely arise around competition for increasingly scarce materials and, as one of the more than 1,300 scientists involved in the just published Millennium Ecosystem Assessment commented, a need to "manage the global economy to produce a fairer distribution of the earth's resources."

A new handwriting had appeared on the wall: **To maintain peace and prosperity for the many, world leaders must find mutually agreeable ways of allocating the impact of scarcity.** (writer words and emphasis) With increasing world population and a growing number of successful competitors, the United States faced no real choice but to work with others to find some way to address the resource allocation issues.

However, the PNAC crafters saw the future dominated by variously competitive military challenges, a game in which, in their view, the United States must position itself to maintain total dominance. If the PNAC crafters saw the finite and demanding dependence of military power on assured economic success, that vision is not evident in the report. Aware of the coming economic complications they may have been, but focused on the elements of cooperative economic problem solving they clearly were not. Rather, their "four core missions" were: (1) how to defend the American homeland, (2) how to fight and win multiple and simultaneous, major theater wars, (3) how to perform the "constabulary", that is, world policeman role, and (4) how to transform US forces to exploit the "revolution in military affairs."

Those missions required the US, as the PNAC report

found to: (1) maintain nuclear superiority, (2) reform military personnel strength, (3) reposition forces to respond to strategic needs, (4) modernize forces, ```(5) stop spending on non-PNAC defense projects, (6) develop and deploy missile defenses, (7) control space and cyberspace, (8) insure US force superiority, and (9) increase defense spending.

That agenda is both bellicose and strident. As noted in an earlier article in this collection, it translates, as <u>The Economist</u> recently headlined, into promotion of "democracy at gunpoint."

The 9-11 attacks—Numerous critics have suggested that in its early days the new Bush administration was deflected by the PNAC report and its authors and supporters within the cabinet from any real consideration of America's needs or the needs of any other country. Growing scarcities of critical materials may have been noted by them, but did not surface in public discussions. Instead, the administration acquired an imperial agenda, but even PNAC did not keep the President from moving ahead with his tax cut for wealthy supporters. The path to realization of PNAC plans involved wiping out the budget surplus handed on by the Clinton administration, then building a mountain of debt to finance defense expenditures. Those tendencies were reinforced by the 9-11 attacks that presented a glittering new opportunity.

Whether or not the 9-11 attacks qualified as a new Pearl Harbor, the attacks were used to justify launching the War on Terrorism, first by invading Afghanistan. As PNAC enthusiasts saw it, this was the beginning of World War IV (they say that the Cold War was III) or the Long War, an enduring struggle for world domination. The most vital effect of 9-11 was that it provided the rationale for abandoning defense budget conservatism and for increasing defense spending. The American public was too shocked and troubled by the events and too uninformed about neo-conservative intentions as spelled out by PNAC to pose any objections.

The neo-cons were off and running. Against no specific national enemy, without a global rival, America would arm to the teeth to deal with a non-state actor, Osama bin Laden, whose forces numbered a few thousand. 9-11 was not only a unique American tragedy, it has proved to be an enduring attack on the American system because of the distortions in behavior, law, domestic, and foreign policy that have been adopted by the Bush administration in its name.

Why did the United States invade Iraq? The Bush team is responsible for much of the debate about why the United States invaded Iraq. Oil, either access to supplies or control over distribution, was always an obvious rationale. But openly going into Iraq for oil was a universal no, no. Since every country has some interest in the subject, being too obviously predatory and greedy gets attention. Iraq was not and never had been a threat to the United States, so that excuse would not and did not fly. Weapons of mass destruction, guilt for alleged past crimes committed during the war with Iran—when the US supported Iraq—or simply disposing of a despot whose human rights abuses were numerous, would have to do, and they did until the Iraqi arsenal proved to be empty.

Oil aside, the assault on Iraq was a PNAC-inspired, neo-conservative driven "shock and awe" demonstration of American military power. The apparent PNAC theory was that if you have all that weaponry but never use it, nobody thinks you mean it. In PNAC terms, the world policeman utility of US military power needed to be demonstrated. Besides, Saddam was never loveable, and with the media and official Washington vilification of him that accompanied the run-up to the war, he became a natural for the part.

Not able—or willing—to tell us why we invaded Iraq, the Bush team chose democratizing Iraq as its political mantra. The people of Iraq, who had been variously bombed, humiliated, and starved for more than a decade by the United States and sometimes Britain, obviously deserved better than that. How about turning the place into a democracy? L. Paul

(Jerry) Bremer, who had been the American administrator of Coalition operations since early in the war, made an incredible move in that direction in the hours before his departure and the handover to an Iraqi interim government.

Bremer decreed a model system: Everybody would be subject to a flat tax of 15%. All economic activities would be fully open to foreign participation and ownership and repatriation of profits. His rules—or those dictated to him by Washington—declared by fiat, would not be subject to modification by the Iraqis once they took over. In six months, the Iraqis would hold a democratic election. That was to be Iraqi democracy to an American neo-con heart's desire, pre-wired from floor to ceiling.

What Bremer dictated, complete with a draft constitution, was the formation of an Iraq friendly to foreign business and finance. It would have a democratically elected leadership that would accept his scheme without question, and be a friend to Israel to boot. That was a PNAC agenda, but to get there, Iraq was to be an instant democracy of sorts, just as its first election was to be sort of democratic. Many candidates did not identify themselves to the electorate for fear of being killed, polling places were not designated for fear they would be destroyed, and parties did not announce their programs or candidates for fear of being targeted. The whole election scheme was pursued while the country was under military occupation and sporadic attack. Those actions are extreme departures from normal election procedure. About half of the Iraqis came out to vote and that was the only democratic decision on the landscape.

US officials talked in a desultory manner about pulling US forces out of Iraq, but in the meantime, the US was building at least fourteen very permanent looking bases in Iraq. One view of those bases is that they are a colossal waste. The other view is that permanent bases mean the US has no intention of leaving Iraq, period. The current and next rounds of Iraqi insurgency are stimulated by Iraqi objections to that plan.

They want their country back, and some would even take it back with Saddam in power.

What is the War on Tyranny? Facing a growing body of Americans who want our troops back home, along with growing negativism to the neo-con agenda, Bush devoted part of his second State of the Union message to the new war on tyranny. As much as anything, that appeared to be razzle-dazzle to take the public eye off failing strategies in Iraq. He talked about bringing democracy to the Middle East. He talked about ridding countries of tyrannical regimes and about hearing the appeals of believers in democracy whose aspirations have been frustrated in many countries. In that whole discussion, he never mentioned a military threat or an economic problem. He floated the war on tyranny as an idealized leadership plan for countries that did not have—and therefore needed, allegedly wanted—a western style democracy.

Vindicating American democracy—American democracy has been badly used and mauled in the Iraqi experiment. Iraqis know that they had an election in January, but the run up to the election was anything but peaceful; the validity of the outcome, partly due to the non-participation of the Sunnis, was questionable. Moreover, the election process was dampened by the belief of many that the outcome had to be a government that both accepts and tolerates an enduring American presence. Bremer had sealed that impression with his last minute decrees.

That question—whether the US forces will stay or leave—is hanging in mid-air despite the fact that US forces are stretched to the limit to sustain the presence in Iraq, and there are mixed signals from political and military figures on drawdowns and pullouts. As the Shi'a and Kurd dominated national assembly tries to form a government, already weeks overdue, it is under obvious, constant pressure to avoid asking the US and other Coalition forces to leave.

The problem is that conventional results of a democratic

election would yield an Iraqi government ruled by the Shi'a in cooperation with a strong Kurd minority, possibly leaving out the former ruling Sunni. Just below the surface lies the prospect that this government could easily be Islamic, if not necessarily fundamentalist. Thanks to the Baath and in great measure to Saddam Hussein, Iraq has the largest secular population in a Middle Eastern state, even though it is politically untried. Though a secular government appears unlikely, the secular elements appear to have enough influence among both Shi'a and Kurds to moderate the Islamic influences on governance. That kind of outcome could be reached without US involvement. Whether it would emerge with the US on the scene remains to be seen. In fact, concerns about or real objections to a US presence may well drive the outcome toward Islamic extremes because Shi'a firebrands, such as Moqtada al-Sadr, could capture a lead from the respected Shi'a clerics.

However this turns out, it appears unlikely to be a victory for American style democracy. It is more likely to present an amalgam of influences including the newly elected representatives (candidates selected by tribal, clerical, and communal procedures), the tribal chieftains, and the clerics, basically a transitional Middle Eastern system of governance.

Vindicating American democracy and demonstrating that ridding the world of tyranny is a genuine US goal can result from the Iraqi experiment if Americans in the Green Zone and in Washington give the Iraqis enough room to work this out. However, that depends on whether any new Iraqi government will be receptive to and cooperative with American plans. If those plans include retention of control over Iraqi oil, US bases, and selection of an Iraqi leadership that will go along with such an outcome, American democracy, in Iraqi and other Middle Eastern eyes, will stand as a farce, not different from other colonial gambits to get and keep control.

The real trial in Iraq centers on whether the Bush team and its neo-con/Zionist supporters will risk losing control of both Iraqi oil and a dominant military position in the region. It is obvious they believe they could lose both by letting the Iraqis themselves decide what they want and what form of government they want to obtain it. Viewed in this light, it is not American democracy that is on trial in Iraq, but American leadership intentions and the integrity of the Bush team.

There are two possible outcomes on the table: If the American players in Iraq insist on one that curtails Iraqi control of their country, democracy will lose in the Middle East and elsewhere by default, no matter how the situation is explained. However, if American players are prepared to support creation of a genuinely independent Iraqi government and to work out ways of doing business with it, democracy will be vindicated in many minds everywhere. On the other hand, domestic opposition to the war could mount, as it now appears, and the Bush team could find continued occupation of Iraq unsustainable.

The global challenges—On a global scale, the vindication of American democracy depends on how US leaders decide to deal with the growing scarcities of key resources. That means not only how they deal with the major resource supplier countries such as Iraq; it also means how US leaders, both business and government, will agree to deal with the allocation of scarce resources among potential users. The PNAC approach is pre-emptive in its intent, and in the anticipated organization of the United States, to deal with this future.

The formula is pure, old fashioned "beggar thy neighbor" economics, enforced by superpower military dominance and implemented with superior buying power, granted with borrowed money. Acceptance of this formula by the world financial community is probably the key item on the Paul Wolfowitz agenda as the new head of the World Bank. Its key elements are high materials prices, low wages, and burgeoning American debt. That formula attracts resources and wealth to the rich, while delegating low income and poverty to the poor, and scaring the daylights out of people who carry the debt. It avoids any concept of equity; it will place the United States increasingly at odds with the rest of the world, and increasingly at risk of economic failure.

The situation calls for Bush team realization of the need for processes of adjustment that are not now clearly on the Washington agenda. However, there is totally sufficient knowledge of the actual and pending world resource situation to make sound judgments about future distribution and use of all key resources. If the outcomes are pre-emptive or even aggressively assertive through buying power, then both American leadership and American democracy will be impugned. If it is reckoned that all potential users are equal, and some equitable system is developed, then American leadership will be vindicated and with it American democracy.

At issue are how the world's only superpower should adjust its lifestyle, and how it should adjust the trappings and uses of its power to accommodate the needs and interests of others. Democracy indeed could flower if the answers are any good. But the answers have to conform to the dictates of America's founding fathers: "We hold these truths to be self-evident, that all men are created equal..." Honest and even-handed carrying out of that principle would surely vindicate American democracy, proving that it is not only a way to run elections but also the way to conduct fair dealings among equals.

FEMA WAS A VICTIM OF TERRORISM
September 2005

When Hurricane Katrina blew ashore last weekend and started to disassemble much of the Gulf coast, several things started to unravel. First was the demonstration that response teams were not equipped to deal with such a severe emergency. Communications largely did not work—an incredible situation in the day of cell phones and satellites. Coordination of federal, state and local response capabilities was absent, in part because they could not talk to each other, but, equally if not more important, because they had not drilled intensively to develop well-honed responses. These failings, along with the emergent horrors of destruction of Gulf coast cities such as Biloxi and the flooding of New Orleans, created a firestorm of criticism that, sadly, was well deserved. That need not have been, and it should not have been if the Bush Administration had moved ahead with well developed plans FEMA had, at least from the early 1990s, for building and improving the national disaster response system.

During the early 1990s, Bill Clinton's first term in the White House, the Federal Emergency Management Agency

(FEMA) was well focused on building a credible national system for managing emergencies. Several critics said that under FEMA Director, James Lee Witt, the organization was finally on the right track. With support from consultants, FEMA staff developed a program called Survivable Crisis Management.

Before moving into a critique of the present situation, it is very revealing to look at the work FEMA had in progress. To promote and develop its Survivable Crisis Management (SCM) program, FEMA published two guides: An <u>Introduction to Survivable Crisis Management</u>, and the <u>Survivable Crisis Management Development Guide</u>. Key paragraphs of the Introduction explain the situation and the requirement very clearly.

"During the last decade, our Presidents declared 250 disasters across the United States and territories. Those events cost almost $7 billion in Federal disaster assistance and affected millions of people. Such numbers indicate that a costly disaster can strike any community at any time...

"If you are the Governor, the Mayor, the chairman of a county board of supervisors, or the leader of any emergency response organization, you have the legal responsibility to manage the consequences of any emergency that affects your jurisdiction, regardless of its cause."

"**To assure that you can respond effectively to protect and assist people your emergency response capabilities must survive the emergency itself.** (emphasis added) No matter what causes the emergency, you must be able to direct and control emergency operations within your State or local jurisdiction and coordinate with other jurisdictions and the Federal Government. The ability to survive and continue to direct and control emergency operations and continue to govern is called Survivable Crisis Management (SCM)."

"FEMA's goal is a nationwide network of statewide SCM capabilities, all compatible with each other and with those of the Federal Government."

Under SCM, FEMA set out to create and coordinate national capabilities to deal with virtually any foreseeable emergency. The spectrum cited in the guide is a three-tiered set of risks.

Lowest risk events are: Nuclear War, Major Conventional War, and Insurrection.

Intermediate Risk events are: Terrorist Incidents, Theater War, Major System Failures, Low Intensity Conflict, Nuclear Incidents, and Small Scale Attacks.

Highest Risk events are: Hurricanes, Earthquakes, Tornados, Major Fires, and System Failures.

As Katrina and a season of heavy Atlantic storms have emphasized, natural disasters are the hard end of this spectrum. Their consequences may be made more severe by system or human failures.

Two fundamental premises of the FEMA approach to SCM were **(a) a basic emergency response capability is needed to deal with any disaster, and (b) key preparedness elements are common to all emergencies** (emphasis added). Several home truths were well understood. The plan could not be accomplished without a lot of coordinated effort across the whole emergency preparedness system, from state and local to federal. The plan required exceptional attention to communications, meaning that the emergency systems had to be sturdy enough to survive even extreme emergencies. Effective coordination in any given emergency would depend on well developed and well rehearsed operating practices and protocols. To assure creation of a coordinated nationwide system at all state and local and federal levels of emergency management, probably several billion dollars would be needed. To lead that effort, FEMA had to be a Federal Government organization of well-funded and influential status in the Federal system.

We may never know how well the SCM system would have developed or how well it would have worked in an emergency such as Katrina. The basic concepts are still reflected in FEMA's strategic plan, relevant courses are regularly offered at FEMA'S Emergency Management Institute, and SCM itself is offered as a course by the International Disaster/Fire and Training Institute. But the promise of SCM has not been reflected in the response to Katrina. Why?

Because FEMA was downgraded in the creation of the new Department of Homeland Security. FEMA lost its cabinet level status and access. Funds that could have gone to building the SCM or any comparable system were used to create the new Department. The central focus of national emergency preparedness, especially after 9-11, was shifted to terrorism and warfare. The Clinton era name, SCM, was probably a no-no in the new Homeland Security Department, but the concepts were sound; all the new administration needed to do was pick its own pet name.

In this instance, FEMA was a victim of two kinds of terrorism. The first was a Bush administration focus on global terrorism that stole the money as well as the management priority. The second was a power struggle in the new Department that stole the power and influence of FEMA and sent it into decline. Perhaps crudely stated, FEMA was a victim of the Bush Administration fixation on Osama bin Laden. More simply, perhaps, FEMA was a victim of the Bush/neo-con fixation on terrorism, fortress America, and projecting military power abroad.

Many people have had severe misgivings about the War on Terrorism, the focus on warfare that has dominated US governance for the past five years. Given the performance of the system in the early stages of this hurricane, we can only shudder at what might have happened in a major terrorist incident. For the Bush team and for all of us Katrina is a wakeup call.

SCM might not have been the last word in emergency

management for the country, because every emergency management jurisdiction knows the problem is a moving target and it takes money, dedication, and skill to stay on top of it. But if SCM had been in place and functional, the response to Katrina would have been a lot better organized, lives and property would have been saved, and the life of our country would have been much less disrupted. At this moment, it is already clear that Katrina will cost us a great deal more in lives lost or disrupted, property damaged or destroyed and money for recovery than 9-11. The biggest enemy was not Katrina, but our own lack of national level readiness to deal with it.

PART TWO
THE WAR ON TERRORISM

CAN WE WIN THE WAR ON TERRORISM?
November 2002

On November 5, 2002, voters made it clear that they favored the War on Terrorism by electing Republicans. They did not vote on any version of the War or on any means to conduct it. Rather, they had to assume that the President and his advisers would conduct the war in accordance with American law and practice and with due regard for the rights and interests of other countries, and that we would win. We should examine those assumptions very carefully.

As declarations go, the War on Terrorism doesn't fit. We usually declare war on a country or a bloc of countries. After 9-11, we went after the Taliban and al Qaida without declaring war on Afghanistan. After ousting the Taliban, we helped install a nominal new government, nominal because the major tribal chiefs of the country have not sworn allegiance to it. With local help, US and British forces began searching for al Qaida members, but experience shows this campaign may never be finished.

This war cannot be contained—the enemy is able to flee into other Muslim countries, or elsewhere. Before 9-11, al

Qaida had alliances in Egypt, Sudan, Saudi Arabia, Yemen, Ethiopia, Somalia, Pakistan, and Afghanistan. Potential safehavens also exist in Malaysia, Indonesia, and the Philippines.

Widely scattered cells make it hard to attack al Qaida. Even with host country agreement, we cannot station US forces everywhere needed. That problem is not easily resolved, but the assassination of alleged terrorists in Yemen last week with a remotely controlled device presents a controversial option.

Based on administration statements and actions, the rules for this war now appear as follows: (a) The war itself will remain undeclared. (b) The enemy has a name but no country. (c) Efforts to get at the enemy could render national boundaries irrelevant. (d) Assassination will be used as a weapon. (e) Once targets are identified, we will attack them remotely if need be. (f) Countries where al Qaida hideouts exist may not be consulted before we attack. (g) We may not wait until we know that our targets are the right people. (h) Pre-emptive strikes will be made to deal with threats.

The implications are clear: The Bush administration is adopting the terrorist's own rules of war. One must ask whether this war is important enough to warrant abandoning established principles of statehood and foreign policy. However, a critical question is: Can we win the war?

The answer to both questions is no! Abandoning the rules invites everybody to play without rules. Ignoring national boundaries gives others equal rights to do the same. Killing people without trial or proof of guilt invites anarchy. Using assassination is an invitation to political chaos.

Military power does not stop terrorism. In the past two years, Israel invested more than ten billion dollars in IDF operations in Palestine. But the IDF killed or captured only about 1,500 Palestinians, most not proven terrorists. Worse still, IDF, the top military force in the Middle East, could not stop suicide bombers. Our forces spent a year in Afghanistan without corralling al Qaida. In the meantime, al Qaida may have carried out several terrorist operations, at least one against US forces. Moreover, as the IDF shows repeatedly in Palestine, the human costs are simply appalling. In Palestine, the lives of thousands of innocent people were disturbed, permanently changed, or destroyed for only a handful of terrorists.

Military sprawl across this problem is costly and inefficient. Perhaps because it recognizes that fact, the Bush administration seeks less bulky tools such as assassination and other covert operations. Unfortunately, such devices revive the messy practices of the Cold War without offering any reward; the war just goes on.

The War on Terrorism goes on because it does not address the primary causes. If we define winning as stopping terrorism for all time, not a prayer can help the present strategy. US strategy focuses on eliminating the present generation of terrorists. Under that strategy, nations are invited to work with the US on controlling terrorists in their own countries. If those nations cooperate, they do so by repressing the out-groups in their countries whose most angry or discontented members are the terrorists. Angered and frustrated by further repression, those out-groups grow the next generation of terrorists. As a result, the War on Terrorism is self-feeding and it can never be won.

The same rules apply to War on Terrorism as to all other wars. No real progress can be made until the fighting stops. Only then can we focus on the problems outlined in the next article—"Fighting the Real War on Terrorism"—that are the global breeding grounds for terrorism. Those problems exist in at least a third of all nations. If we do not recognize this situation soon and move with other nations and the United Nations system to deal with it, we are all doomed to perpetual conflict. Our best chances lie with dedicating many more aid resources to solving those problems and shifting the fight against terrorism back to law, diplomacy, and the justice system.

FIGHTING THE REAL WAR ON TERRORISM
December 2002

After 9-11, the United States launched a War on Terrorism to rid our country and the world of this menace. That War got off to a brisk start, ousting the Taliban rulers of Afghanistan and attacking the hideouts of al Qaida and Osama bin Laden. The war bogged down in Afghanistan because there are many places to hide and al Qaida has allies in several potential safehaven countries. Critics say the War bogged down because the US botched the capture of Osama bin Laden. That error certainly was compounded by employing the established warlords whose self interests probably led them to let Osama escape. But Afghanistan is only the beginning because terrorist groups exist in 75 or more countries. Ultimately, that War cannot succeed because terrorism grows out of deeply embedded, complex global issues that the War on Terrorism does not address.

Where real effort should be—USAID statements present the problem clearly. As AID Administrator Andrew Natsios observed in a statement in May 2001, USAID has missions in 75 countries. In 50 of those countries major conflicts occurred during the past five years. Most of those countries have terrorist groups that existed before we ever heard of al Qaida. Those countries are among the least developed economically and the least modern politically.

The real enemies in the war on terrorism exist because the out-groups in those societies face exclusion or non-participation, social, political and economic injustice, poverty, ignorance, differences of ethnicity, culture or religion. Many of them live outside the mainstream of society, and in areas where they see the environment that sustains their often primitive lifestyles being systematically destroyed. Official US, UN, and other government statements cite the critical roles of these global issues in world terrorism. But the attack by all governments and the UN is weak and misdirected.

Where Do We Go Wrong? The global effort falls far short of need. The US economic and humanitarian assistance effort is larger than the programs of all other aid-giving countries combined, but it will be about $8.5 billion in 2003. That looks like a lot of money, but if it were distributed evenly among the weakest third of the world's people, it would amount to only about $4.00 per person. However, it is odd that polls regularly show Americans generally believe our assistance effort is much greater, even several multiples of the actual amounts. It is both interesting and disturbing that politicians generally do not work to dispel that illusion.

The money does not go where it is needed, and it is far from evenly spread among recipients. Half of US AID funds go to Israel, Egypt and Jordan, with the lion's share going to Israel. In effect, Congress decided to pay for the Middle East peace process with the existing aid budget, forcing sharp cuts in assistance to all other countries. Congress cut assistance more when the Cold War ended. Thus, aid to the 70 or so needy countries amounts to less that $2 per person per year. Annual aid to Israel amounts to $600-800 or more per person.

The largest human needs for assistance exist in Asia, Africa, and Latin America, where the money is spent on programs to grow more food, improve health, cope with the AIDS/HIV pandemic, and to democratize countries and reduce conflicts. Little to none of the money is spent on economic growth.

What became of dedication to growth? In the 1950s and 1960s, development economists argued that rapid economic growth was the key to escape from under-development because growth advanced the critical indicators: income, employment, education, health, and political and economic modernization. However, in the 1970s Congress put the brakes on US funding for growth, because politicians see no domestic political pizzazz and little foreign policy reward for it. At the same time, growth strategies fell out of favor with development economists.

Moreover, there were some bad examples of the focus on growth in the 1950s and later that soured political thinking about economic growth among diplomatic professionals. One case in point concerned the Iraq Development Board which, political officers say, operated with such disregard for political realities that it precipitated the coup against the English-installed monarchy in 1958, the first of several events that preceded the takeover by Saddam. The average Iraqi saw no improvement in his daily life, could not see or did not understand the possible value to him of big projects, became convinced that foreigners were stealing his country's oil revenues, and was happy to see the foreigners thrown out. That perception probably strengthened Iraqi interest in promoting creation of OPEC to protect Iraqi oil earnings, and Adnan Pachachi, one of the most respected members of the recent Iraq Provisional Authority, was a key architect.

The World Bank now suggests that early development economists had it right by making economic growth the first priority for the poorer countries. The key ingredient in underdeveloped societies is scarcity. Growth in income and the alleviation of scarcity produce improvements in the quality of life across a broad set of indicators. In sum, we may have wasted several decades by placing growth at the bottom of our priorities.

The Terrorism Generators—Even with a quick turnaround, scarcity can drive the terrorism generators for years to come. The numbers of people left out, angered, frustrated, and rendered militant by problems of overcrowding and poverty are likely to grow at frightening speed because most of the 3-5 billion people to be born between now and 2050 will be born in the poorer countries.

This is the wind in al Qaida's sails. If advanced countries do nothing to reduce the economic and social distances between "North" (wealthy) and "South" (impoverished) countries, Osama bin Laden and the leaders of other terrorist groups will exploit the growing gap to generate new outbreaks of terrorism.

What needs to be done? Along with increasing the aid budget, Congress should require that assistance go to the people who need it most. US diplomatic efforts should encourage sharp increases in assistance from other governments. The wealthy of the planet need to put in the resources required for serious developmental work, and to keep working the problem until results are assured.

How do we get to the future? Assuming that we do not destroy ourselves en route, we can get to the future in two ways. One is to continue present trends that assure we will face endless conflict and constant threats of terrorism. The other is to lift the bottom of the human condition by dedication and sacrifice to improve the quality of life for everybody. President Bush and a number of others may not accept either of these choices, but we need to start down this road now and make our destination clear to everyone. If we help the weak, they will help us contain terrorism. If we do nothing, we must learn to live in fear.

THE COST OF BECOMING PREDATOR
January 2003

A few weeks ago US operatives used a Predator drone to launch a deadly missile attack on six alleged members of al Qaida in Yemen. Reports in non-US media indicate that this attack was set up by the US Ambassador and CIA agents as a covert operation on Yemeni territory and without full knowledge of Yemeni authorities. It raised profound misgivings in many places about apparent US adoption of a policy of assassination as part of the War on Terrorism; it offended Yemeni officials. The real shocker was the suggestion by unnamed US officials and experts that this kind of attack could be mounted anywhere and the US was likely to do so without prior announcement to the country whose territory may be so invaded.

In a not surprising follow-up to the US action, according to UPI, the Israeli intelligence agency, Mossad, now plans to attack so-called terrorist targets in the United States as part of a hardening Israeli approach to attacks on Israel and on Israelis in places such as Kenya. Since Sharon and his war cabinet, including Mossad director, Meir Dagan, define as terrorism any aggressive response or reaction to Israel Defense Force or Mossad attacks on the Palestinians, the floodgate is open to attacks on Israeli-defined enemies anywhere in the world. This decision could be merely taking a page from the US book, but former Israeli intelligence officers suggest the matter has been under discussion for some time.

The United States and Israel appear bent on following a policy that is fundamentally destructive of the integrity and stability of the nation state system. Sharon may think that the Israeli lobbies in the United States are powerful enough to defend him and his government against any adverse reactions from American leadership if Mossad carries out an attack in the United States, and the Bush team seems to think that the United States can do likewise in unannounced foreign countries without generating a firestorm of protest. The US carried out pre-emptive attacks in Afghanistan and Sudan, allegedly for their roles in harboring the perpetrators of al Qaida bombings in Kenya and Tanzania. They were hardly screaming successes operationally, but they have become benchmarks in the declining credibility and respect for the United States in much of the world.

Potential impact of any serious pursuit of assassination policies by the US and Israel will be neither subtle nor confined. There is a certain arrogance and stupidity in the notion that these two countries can pursue such a policy without encouraging any government with a grievance against another to copy it. The notion that a government can send its agents abroad to wipe out aggravating dissidents in their safe havens in the United States and in Europe has already been tried by Libyan dictator Qadhafi.

Washington has witnessed one such attack in the infamous Chilean Letelier case. Pulling out the stops on this type of aggression will have consequences that no one with any sense would want to see.

Ironically, the United States will be the main loser. Our international reputation is already being systematically destroyed by the Bush administration. Pre-emptive strikes, remote controlled assassinations, un-supported war in Iraq, and unquestioning support of Israeli actions against the Palestinians are undermining decades of good standing that America has enjoyed in most of the world. But that is only the beginning.

The Statue of Liberty is an enduring symbol of American openness to the poor and the oppressed of the world. Ancestors of millions of Americans owed their presence here to the reality of that invitation. In recent years, hardly any of the 190 or so countries of the world have not been represented in the business, tourist, spiritual, educational, or migratory traffic to our shores.

In those numbers are many dissidents and protesters of the world. They include Sikh militants, Cuban exiles, members of the Lebanese group Hizballah, Palestinian refugees, and countless others. Up to now their safe-haven in the US has been a protected place. Many of them can be the natural targets of governments they or their friends and followers have offended, or to whom they may be threatening. Unless the United States vigorously fends off Israeli or any other invaders seeking to murder their enemies here, that safe-haven will evaporate and the resulting violence will harm Americans.

Our system, with all its problems, is still the best there is. We should not trade its integrity, or permit others to erode its security, for the illusory victory that assassination might bring. We should not fool ourselves that this weapon can be controlled. It can just as easily be used against us.

WHY THE WAR ON TERRORISM WILL FAIL
June 2003

The Bush administration now has more than eighteen months experience with the War on Terrorism. The principal events of that war have been (a) deposing the Taliban in Afghanistan, (b) scattering the leadership and membership of Taliban and al Qaida to unknown locations, (c) capture and confinement of several hundred grunt level "combatants" now confined in Guantanamo, (d) highly publicized capture of several middle to senior grade al Qaida leaders, and (e) a growing body of complaints that the Bush administration is conducting a systematic assault on civil liberties of both Americans and aliens.

The hawks pursue the War on Terrorism as if it rivals World War II. But putting the rhetoric aside, just how serious is the global terrorism problem? How amenable is the problem to warlike solutions? Recent data and analysis suggest the War is too big, too harsh, too military, and likely to fail.

Every year, by Congressional mandate, the Department of State publishes Patterns of Global Terrorism. Thematically, the report for 2001 was dominated by 9-11; the newly released report for 2002 focuses on al Qaida. However, these reports—part of a continuing series going back to 1982—provide the best and most comprehensive global picture available in unclassified form. Taken together with the previous report for the year 2000, it is timely to take a worldwide look at what has happened in international terrorism in a three-year period that brackets 9-11, and during the past decade, to judge how well this war faces the problem.

Global data do not actually tell the story. Before the 2001 attacks, the smallest number of international terrorist attacks in the past two decades was 274 attacks in 1998. In 2000, there were 426 attacks. In 2001, there were 348 attacks. Data for 2002 recorded only 199 attacks. Taken as given, these numbers seem to say the War on Terrorism is going like a house afire. But a decade-long look at State's data before and after 9-11 shows that terrorism is much less a global problem than it was in previous decades. In the 1980s terrorist attacks averaged 550 per year. In the decade ending in 2002, attacks averaged about 360 per year. Several questions about these data need to be considered.

Where and how are most acts of terrorism carried out? Colombia and India accounted for more than half of all international terrorist incidents during 2000-2002. In that period worldwide attacks averaged 323 per year. Colombia had 134 attacks each year, while 50 occurred each year in India. In 2001, more than half of the recorded attacks (194) were in Latin America. Except for the four 9-11 attacks, the other attacks occurred in Asia (68), the Middle East (29), Africa (23), and Europe (17).

How serious an international threat does that pattern reveal? To get an answer to that question, State developed a data series for Significant Terrorist Incidents, meaning those that involve deaths, injuries, serious property damage, kidnappings, or hostage takings.

The Colombia pipeline bombings are typically excluded from this category. The goal of Colombian groups is to disrupt the pipelines to get government attention to their followers' political, economic, and social justice demands; they do local damage to pipelines but seldom are there any casualties. Over the past decade, these bombings have averaged 90 per year.

Attacks in India typically are considered significant because there are usually casualties and property damage. However, they are a unique category, because most of these attacks occur around the dispute with Pakistan over Kashmir or the desire of many Kashmiri to be free of either country. During our three-year period, attacks in India averaged about 50 per year, with the highest number being 67 in 2002.

With the Colombia pipeline bombings and other non-significant incidents removed, the State data list about 400 significant attacks—an average of 133 per year—during 2000-2002. But 40% or more of those attacks occurred in India alone.

How much of that threat can be met by US action? While the United States works diplomatically and through the United Nations with both Indian and Pakistani governments to relieve tensions and move the two powers toward resolution of the problem, the US-led War on Terrorism has little or nothing to contribute toward resolving the Kashmir dispute. Moreover, our operations with national police and military forces in Colombia are conducted in connection with the so-called War on Drugs. In either case, these activities would go on without reference to the War on Terrorism.

In effect, the global pattern of significant terrorist incidents, excluding India, is less than 100 attacks per year; the frequency of attacks was declining before 9-11. Stopping those attacks, and/or dealing with the groups that cause them, is the worst-case current mission of the War on Terrorism.

Most terrorists operate in home territory. The picture becomes even clearer when the groups that operate and stay entirely at home in their own countries are taken off the stage. That can be done, since such groups represent no threat to US homeland security. Strictly speaking, the United States is not threatened everywhere by terrorists, even though US businesses and Americans in many countries face some risk. Most groups represent varying orders of threat to the stability of governments in their countries, but that is not America's war.

How well does the pattern fit a concept of war? State designates 36 so-called Foreign Terrorist Organizations, several of which operate outside their own home states or regions. State reported on 38 other terrorist groups in 2002 for a total of 74 groups. At least seven groups are focused on Kashmir; eight are focused on Palestine; six are focused on Northern Ireland. Six are al Qaida and suspected affiliates. Upward of a third of the groups operate internationally. Except for the attacks of 9-11 and the earlier (1993) attack on the World Trade Center, direct attacks by any group on the United States are rare.

International attacks in North America present another clarifying picture of where terrorist harm is done. Over the period 1992-2002, State records 30,825 casualties—all nationalities worldwide—of which 5,105 were in North America. Over 99% of the casualties in North America were associated with the 1993 attack on the World Trade Center and the events of 9-11. That means about one casualty out of every six resulted from international terrorism in North America, but in the other nine years of this period, only eight deaths due to international terrorism occurred in North America. In the average year, virtually all casualties occur in other parts of the world. The highest number of casualties (11,872) in this 11-year period was in Asia. Next were Africa with 6,032 and the Middle East with 4,160.

The Anti-US Threat—The State data through the 1990s to the present make it clear that the War on Terrorism was launched in response to a single day's events. Before 9-11 there was no new or broad based threat of terrorism against the United States, nor do the data for 2002, or the recorded pattern of events since 9-11 suggest that there is such an exceptional threat now. Rather, most terrorists are national groups who attack targets in their own countries. As a rule, Americans who become casualties are living, touring, or working in other countries when attacked or caught up in attacks on others.

Why the War is too big -A review of attacks on US citizens or property does not indicate an exceptional threat against the United States. In the period 1992 through 2002, State records a total of 1,333 incidents involving US targets. But 1,014 of these incidents were Colombia pipeline bombings, so the real number of terrorist incidents that involved US citizens or facilities was 321, including all known or suspected anti-US attacks by al Qaida. That is about 30 incidents per year scattered across most regions of the world in as many as 30 countries. Leaving out the 1993 and 2001 attacks on the World Trade Center, the annual worldwide incidents averaged about 11-12 American deaths and 80 wounded each year. In 9-11 attacks, 1,440 Americans died and 90 were wounded. There were 6 deaths and 1,000 injuries in the 1993 WTC attack, mostly due to smoke inhalation.

These data do not provide a basis for any worldwide War on Terrorism. However, frustration with these facts and the continuing affront of international terrorism probably led Bush advisers in the wake of 9-11 to suggest global unilateral and invasive counterterrorism strategies. Their conclusions, conveyed by actions and words, were that (1) the United States would take pre-emptive action worldwide to destroy the terrorists in their home bases, and (2) the United States could win the War on Terrorism through military engagement.

The immediate body count appears to favor such military action, until the US War on Terrorism casualty lists are published. The President has said that more than 3,000 al Qaida terrorists have been accounted for "one way or another." Those numbers crudely match the number of casualties suffered in North America on 9-11. But look at the asymmetry of the process. The terrorists did their deeds with 18 people equipped with hijacked airplanes.

The US evened the body count score by fielding tens of thousands of troops, engaging the forces of several allies, spending many millions of dollars to support long logistical tails, and putting our entire national law enforcement and intelligence system into the fray. Satisfying? Perhaps. Effective? Not demonstrated. The body count frankly shows an awkwardly high price for each kill or capture in the War on Terrorism. That count shows a depressing economy of effort on the other side.

The War is too harsh. The Bush administration, especially the Justice Department, has decided that the only way to deal with terrorists is to deny them due process. This appears to be based on a judgment that a politically motivated crime is worse than an ordinary crime; that judgment makes it ok to ignore the Geneva Conventions. That judgment also casts aside the Law of Land Warfare that is taught rigorously in all US military colleges.

The comparison with normal justice processes is a national embarrassment. Every year the perpetrators of 12,000-15,000 proven homicides receive the most careful due process before being confined or put to death. Meanwhile, 600 or so US labeled "enemy combatants" are held at Guantanamo without rights to counsel and under conditions that include (a) torture of prisoners in US confinement, and (b) export of other prisoners, with US knowledge and consent, to even more abusive prison environments. In its most celebrated terrorism trial involving a US citizen, the United States convicted Timothy McVeigh of killing over 260 Americans, in his own terms for political reasons, after a long and properly conducted trial.

There is no clear or present danger—There could be only one reason for going to the extremes now being demonstrated by the US military and justice systems in dealing with suspected al Qaida members or supporters: That these individuals themselves represent a clear and present danger to the survival of the United States. That has not and probably cannot be proven for any of them. However, the pattern of attacks has been used to justify assassinations of suspected terrorists.

Both strategies indeed may represent frustration and the urge to kill, but we lose three or four times as many people each year to homicides than we lost in the past decade to terrorism, including the casualties of 9-11. To preserve our own system and to convince the rest of the world that we have not lost it, we should get back to normal.

The value of military force is not proven. The doctrine that seems most appealing to the hawks around President Bush is that direct military action is the most effective available response to terrorism. A quick glance at military experience against terrorists anywhere in the world would show little success. Constant Israel Defense Force occupation in the West Bank and Gaza with thousands of troops, tanks, gunships, and bulldozers—and assassination of suspected terrorists—have not stopped suicide bombings in Israel. Indonesian use of military force against Jemaah Islamiyah did not prevent the deadly Bali bombings of October 2002. Some battles may have been won, because, since 9-11 and start of the War on Terrorism, al Qaida has lost significant numbers of adherents and some key leaders, but it has been able to reconstitute and remains a viable threat.

On balance, use of military force against terrorists and brutal uses of police power appear only to aggravate tensions that the War does not seek to address. US and coalition operations in Afghanistan are a sad case in point. They may have been successful as military operations go, but they left the terrorism problem largely unsolved, because they did not put in motion any political, economic, or social institution building measures to address the enormous weaknesses in Afghan society. As a terrorism generator, Afghanistan was left as fertile as a Petri dish loaded with bacteria and nutrients, and Iraq clearly has been turned into another one.

It is time to regroup. The bottom line is that raw success with killing individual terrorists does not demonstrate the utility of military intervention. Creation of new terrorists from communities and support groups that often are brutalized in military operations typically undoes any gains from military attacks.

What would be the framework for scaling back this enterprise to something more consistent with the logic of the problem? We could start with a critical look at the actual anti-US terrorism record. America suffered more than 2,500 dead and wounded in the events of 9-11 and the 1993 attack on the World Trade Center, but the United States had averaged only 80-90 casualties per year throughout the decade. Moreover, more than half of the Americans killed in terrorist incidents during 2002, e.g., during attacks in Bali, the Moscow theater and at Hebrew University in Israel just happened to be in the target zone when the attacks occurred. There was nothing obviously anti-US about these attacks, and that accidental quality is often the case where Americans get caught in terrorist attacks.

In that light, the national preoccupation with terrorism rests awkwardly among the causes of death of US citizens each year. Over the past decade, the United States lost roughly 400,000 people to highway accidents, about 150,000-200,000 of those deaths due to drunken driving. The country lost upward of 300,000 people due to suicide and over 200,000 by homicide. More than 150,000 of the suicides were teenagers. In that period 1,562 Americans died in terrorist attacks and 1,790 were wounded in such attacks.

9-11 was a shocking and unexpected attack that appears to have taken us more by surprise than it should have, given the world terrorism environment. It would be a major national victory if we were able to avoid another such attack. The question is what would it take to assure that outcome? That question cannot be answered with certainty. We could erect a perfect barrier against the outside world only to discover that, as demonstrated in Oklahoma City, we may have a badly wired, homegrown fanatic who wants to destroy our society.

The practical reality is that the task of dealing with the current generation of terrorists is a relatively small part of any serious campaign against political violence in society. Iraq was well on its way to becoming three states the moment Saddam Hussein fell, and nothing that has happened so far in the US occupation has changed the prospect that Iraq will come apart. Ultimately the individual parts may be regrouped with other similar single group identity areas into new or already existing nation states, e.g. Kurdistan uniting populations now scattered Iran, Armenia, Turkey, and Syria. Indonesia is attempting to manage a range of ethnic, cultural, and religious stresses that may well force it to disintegrate to find peace. Sub-Sahara Africa is seething with tribal discontents that offer ready prospects of violence on a genocidal scale. Perhaps a third of all nation states face internal pressures that from time to time boil over.

Those are the terrorism generators in our present. They will dominate our future unless we begin to address them now through development and reform of the global political economy and the nation state system.

So, we come to an irreducible three part future strategy for dealing with terrorism: First, always up front will be the need to deal with people who hold hostages, carry bombs, or threaten other depredations. As State and most federal agencies recognize and practice, this task consists of political, diplomatic, law enforcement, health, and social services challenge, with some but quite limited military inputs. However, the Bush administration emphasis on a "War on Terrorism" has taken the focus off this campaign in favor of a military charge.

Second, attack the global issues to assure that the present generations have hope and future generations have a better life. Many key US, UN and other officials recognize this need, but they do not have the resources, or in present leadership, the political support to deal with it.

Third, rearrange national boundaries and systems of

governance so that the frictions of the present system are abated and the class struggles within failed and failing states are reduced or eliminated. This task addresses a genuine historic can of worms, but there can be no solution to terrorism in many parts of the world unless these problems are resolved state by state in some amicable way.

There is no shortcut through these problems. The present War on Terrorism is a political, partly revenge motivated shortcut. That is why it will fail.

DANGEROUS IMAGININGS IN THE WAR ON TERRORISM
September 2003

Last Sunday night President Bush gave us two startling new reasons for being in Iraq: Iraq, he said, has become the "central front" in the War on Terrorism, and by fighting in Iraq, our troops are attracting terrorists from all over the world. If we kill them in Iraq, they will not attack us at home. Deputy Defense Secretary Paul Wolfowitz appears to have originated this argument on his return from Baghdad a few weeks ago. US civil administrator, L. Paul Bremer, echoed the thought on his return to Baghdad from a recent visit to Washington. The concept is akin to hanging fly-paper from the ceiling and waiting for flies to gather. The suggestion that global terrorism can be fought successfully in this manner is absurd.

How has the analysis of the Iraq challenge gone astray? The first error was to call any Iraqi who objects to the US/Coalition presence a terrorist. That makes it convenient, if analytically weird to call the effort to pacify the Iraqi people—who did not attack us or even threaten to attack us—the central front in the War on Terrorism. The second error is to heat up conflict in Iraq at a time when the need is to calm the situation. The third is to use the War on Terrorism as an excuse to prolong the occupation: Since terrorists are alleged to be "streaming into the country," even as a minor part of the insurgent activity, the occupation must be continued—the argument goes—even augmented to assure public safety.

Focusing the War on Terrorism in Iraq does not fit the facts. At the beginning of the Iraq war there were about 75 terrorist groups, 60 of them active enough to merit mention in the State Department annual report. None of these groups was operating in Iraq at that time. One reason for their absence is that most of the world's terrorists are not Muslims. Most terrorist organizations grew out of long-standing complaints against governments in their countries of origin, and they fight their battles at home. In Iraq, the groups with terrorist connections or histories, mainly Shi'a or Kurdish, had and still have axes to grind other than with Saddam Hussein or the United States. But the US presence provides an opportunity to pursue the causes that Saddam Hussein ruthlessly suppressed.

Assuming that the current Bush team rationale does embody some reality, the potential impact on our forces in Iraq is deadly. We are staking them out in all the Iraqi trouble spots with no choice but to wait for the insurgents and/or the terrorists to find them and attack. We are letting those who oppose us decide the strategy; in the "Bring 'em on" scenario our antagonists, whether insurgents or terrorists, will determine when and where each battle will be fought. The high level US sources of these statements are telling incoming terrorists that they can have a killing field in Iraq for taking their best shots at the Americans or British troops. No doubt our troops have been put deliberately in harm's way before because that is in the nature of warfare, but the blatant suggestion that our troops are bait for the enemy is a warped new wrinkle.

Terrorist numbers will not be diminished by the Iraqi

campaign. Al Qaida's latest tape, played on Al-Jazeera TV in the past few days, says that far from being decimated, bin Laden's creation is alive and well. Reported al Qaida recruitment and training are increasing. Meanwhile, Iraq has become the latest training ground for terrorists. For years, Libya has catered to terrorist machismo by training them in a desert camp where no one is at risk, but it is a much more he-man experience to train in live combat situations. Both sides produce trained and hardened killers on the battlefield. And it is worth recalling that bin Laden and al Qaida are graduates of the Mujahideen experience in Afghanistan, many of them the products of US training.

Centering the War on Terrorism in Iraq is a mistake. No determined terrorist is likely to be deterred from striking elsewhere, including the United States. The most recent al Qaida tape makes this threat. Bush team spokesmen are doing the Iraqi people no favors by deliberately advertising a fly-paper-for-terrorists situation that has rained down more terror on the Iraqis than anyone else. US leadership does our troops a great disservice by deliberately placing them in harm's way under the threat of imported terrorists and distracting them from their prime mission of pacifying Iraq. Finally, suggesting to the American public that they will be safer as a result is a promise that cannot be fulfilled.

It is doubtful that military successes against insurgents and terrorists in Iraq will diminish the number or the determination of terrorists elsewhere in the world. It is certain that mauling any large number of Iraqis and foreigners in this enterprise will generate more terrorists. As the Israelis discover relentlessly in Palestine, killing another militant is more likely to generate the next terrorist bombing than it is to prevent it; repeated brutal IDF operations have proved ineffective against single suicide bombers.

Blame for the present mess no doubt can be shared with Iraqi and other Islamic militants or can be attributed solely to mistakes by our forces. But Bush team decisions and statements of recent weeks have helped turn Iraq into a terrorism generator that did not need to be. The sobering truth is that our forces are stuck with a war without a battlefield and with an enemy that is small, elusive, deadly, and becoming bolder. This situation is not a good thing; other governments have good sense to shun it because the facile notion that a war on terrorism can be fought successfully on this ground is not true. The saddest feature of all is that US personnel are distracted by a war that does not help them carry out their primary mission: Get the Iraqi people back in charge of their affairs and get out of there.

The keys to the situation are political, not military. We must work as closely as possible with all Islamic governments to prevent Islamic extremists from calling the tune. The conflict situation in Iraq must be calmed down, starting with shifting from an aggressive military effort to quell an insurgency that exists mainly because US forces are there. Every effort should be made with all surrounding governments to reduce or eliminate the flow of outside terrorists. Right now, the Iraqi people think they are our enemy. That breeds resistance and support for those who resist. Whether the neo-conservative hawks like it or not, we must involve the UN up front and quickly, preferably in charge, because we have no credibility.

There is no glory in leading a losing strategy. We should modify the strategy, recompose the team to make it genuinely international, and get the US go-it-alone crowd out of the way. We should stop pretending that Iraq is a good place to fight the War on Terrorism. While the Iraqi people are under attack and occupation by us, Iraq is the worst possible place on the planet to fight the battle at this time.

OSAMA BIN LADEN'S CUNNING TAPE TERRORISM
October 2003

Saturday, October 18, another bin Laden tape aired on Arabic al Jazeera television. According to the Associated Press, CIA analysts who have evaluated the tape report that references in the tape to recent events suggest that bin Laden is still alive. He remains holed up somewhere along the Afghanistan/Pakistan frontier. Bin Laden used this tape to condemn the government of Palestinian Prime Minister Mahmoud Abbas as a "collaborator government" with the United States. He also taunted President Bush for running the largest Federal deficit in history and for being reduced to scrounging for help and "begging for mercenary soldiers from everywhere."

This tape is the most recent of at least three that have appeared since 9-11. It is said to be proof that Osama retains command of Al Qaida. However, other reports suggest command may have passed to younger lieutenants. The tape follows a video of a few weeks ago that showed bin Laden climbing a steep hill. Conventional wisdom is that those images were an effort to show that he is still active and capable of command.

In the terrorism universe, the tapes represent a unique al Qaida device. They were perhaps matched in impact only by the cassette tape campaign mounted by the Ayatollah Khomeini to overthrow the Shah of Iran. US official analysts use the appearance of each tape to demonstrate that Osama is still alive and that al Qaida continues to represent a global threat. Why is bin Laden using them?

Bin Laden serves numerous objectives with the tapes. He uses them to cajole, sometimes threaten Muslims. He ridiculed Mahmoud Abbas for apparent alliances with the United States. The tapes also serve to unify and expand support for his campaign across Islam, and to undermine secular governments in Islamic countries. Those efforts are not received with enthusiasm by the leadership of any Muslim country. But they have particular appeal to fundamentalists, especially among Sunni Muslims. Sunnis comprise more than one billion of the estimated 1.3 billion Muslims in the world. While there are no statistics, fundamentalists appear to make up only a small portion of Sunni Islam. Bin Laden's ambition is to make that number grow.

The more important question for American policy makers should be: What is bin Laden's goal in targeting the tapes on the United States? For the answer, one only has to look at results. Each tape is a media event. It receives worldwide coverage in mainstream media, despite the fact that initial releases occur through al Jazeera television. At the end of each tape cycle of publication and analysis, the global focus on al Qaida as the prime world terrorism threat has been renewed.

That publicity has been virtually cost free to bin Laden. The continuing focus on al Qaida appears to enhance recruitment. The number of al Qaida affiliates tends to grow despite reported losses even of some key players. But the bottom line of the tapes is that the world superpower and its allies have failed to capture or contain al Qaida. Bin Laden is not untouchable, but he has yet to be touched.

What has bin Laden's publicity achieved for the United States? Principally, it has served to underpin the War on Terrorism. Given the long term downtrend of international terrorism, without periodic refurbishing the global terrorism threat will not sustain the rationale for the War. If the threat is not a constant or growing feature of the American outlook, the War cannot be justified. The tapes receive public attention from officials because they serve to renew that justification. Transferring the War on Terrorism to Iraq has not served this function; rather it has raised questions about the seriousness of the administration in pursuing al Qaida and searching for bin Laden. But it appears that so long as bin Laden and al Qaida are out there somewhere safe, the War on Terrorism is safe.

Bin Laden plays a calculated game with American policymakers. He has the resources to follow our doings more closely than we can follow his. He knows that the Bush Administration has put most of its chestnuts into the War on Terrorism and politically could back away from it only with difficulty. He knows that the neo-conservative hawks around the President have focused American policy narrowly to the violent end of the response to terrorism. Those same hawks have led the United States into a needless war in Iraq that is a powerful incentive to Muslims to be at odds with the United States. And these hawks have led the White House to give up more than half a century of defending human rights. All bin Laden has to do is exploit the weaknesses exposed by these warps in American policy.

Bin Laden tapes are a carefully metered version of the 25 cent telephone terrorist attack of the 1980s. All that was required was the threat. Bin Laden tapes are threat sustaining because our officials deal with them that way. Continued viability of bin Laden and al Qaida provide a continuing basis for American belligerence. That state of mind coupled with an ideological bent toward reducing taxes, spending money on military power, and running large spending deficits to carry out those aims already pushes the United States toward financial bankruptcy.

By keeping the United States embroiled in a pointless War on Terrorism, bin Laden hopes to reinforce the negatives of present American foreign policies and to drive the United States into international political bankruptcy as well. In his tape campaign bin Laden is using the asymmetry of terrorism warfare to remarkable effect, applying the media skills of a wealthy non-state actor to beat a superpower. His tapes have made effective non-violent warfare ever since the 9-11 attacks.

Some argue that US leadership has no option but to treat the tapes the way they do. However, the response should be a more carefully considered one. It is obvious that the tapes cannot be ignored. Global media would not allow silence, and al Qaida/bin Laden count on that.

Along with the tape, the public needs a solid assessment of any evidence that exists to either support or contradict the taped message. If there is no independent evidence, the public should be informed that the tapes are unsubstantiated threat statements. The tapes should not be given undue weight, because that makes US officials serve bin Laden's purposes.

TERRORISM AND THE FEAR MARKET
February 2004

Since 9-11, our country has been on conditional alert against a possible terrorist attack. Before 9-11, we were vaguely conscious of the possibility of terrorist attacks and we fitted that risk into a spectrum of perils that ranged from slipping on a bar of soap in the bathtub to being on a plane when it was blown out of the sky; a broad, random, dour, but not readily personalized set of risks. We took it that way and learned to live with it. Carefully assessed, the reality still looks much the same, but we are behaving differently. What is going on?

Life on earth is fraught with natural and manmade disasters. Natural disasters can be devastating as we saw recently in Bam, Iran with the number of earthquake deaths approaching 40,000 people. Preparedness between events has steadily improved over the years, but the response is considered, compassionate, and generally focused on recover and rebuild. War is a manmade disaster, but it too ends with recover and rebuild.

What is so unique about terrorism that we respond to it so differently? Why are we prepared to allow our leadership to corrupt our democratic system to deal with it? Why have we allowed ourselves to become enslaved by it in the backlash from 9-11?

We have entered the fear market, where ignorance and perception drive our thoughts, emotions, and responses. This place demands our close attention because we are seldom given enough information to make specific defensive moves credible or useful. Terrorists seldom announce their moves in advance; the attack often is the announcement. They cynically scare us and move on.

Governments are compelled politically to say they are well informed about the matter and are on top of it, but in reality they are seldom either. The next real attack is likely to catch everyone by surprise; no amount of warlike preparation significantly alters that prospect.

How does terrorism compare with other risks? Our reactions to the possibility of terrorism are out of proportion to the facts. In order to understand the problem, it is useful to look at several common risk situations.

To revisit some casualty numbers alluded to earlier, in the period 1996-2002, more than 320,000 Americans died in homicides or suicides. That amounts to about 45,000 people per year. The chance that an American might die this way was roughly one in 6,500. American deaths from terrorism during that period amounted to 1,538, including over 1,400 Americans who died in the 9-11 attacks. In this period, inclusive of 9-11, the chance of an American dying by terrorist hands was roughly one in 1.3 million.

The odds are one in less than 100 that any of us could be involved in an auto accident in the United States. In 2003 the worldwide chance of someone dying by terrorist hands was about one in 2.7 million.

How do we put terrorism in perspective? The uncommon denominator of the events just described is intent. Uncertainty is common to all of it. Homicides are usually an intentional violent act, but most of the other hazards do not involve people actively setting out to do harm to other people. Terrorism involves intentional harm, and the scariest facet of it is not the size of any given attack but the randomness of the prospect.

There is genuine concern in many parts of our society about losses of life through accidents and murder or suicide, but there is no great political furor about any of it. Nor do we seem prepared to deal effectively—assuming that we could—with the mayhem annually perpetrated by use of firearms. Most people respond to the situation on our highways by being more careful, wearing their seat belts, avoiding alcohol abuse, and getting on with their lives. We mostly shrug off the fact that the National Rifle Association and its membership have a political hammerlock on gun controls, no matter what the arguments are on both sides of this question. Why is it that our leadership has been driven to a state of near paranoia by terrorism? Just what is this fear market? How do we put the threat terrorism poses for our lives, property, and lifestyles into some sensible perspective?

Before 9-11, fear was not our organizing principle, but the Bush administration has made it so in the 28 months since 9-11. Terrorism and the shadows of fear around it were centerpieces of this year's Bush State of the Union address. Yet since 9-11 we have not been attacked at home and Americans have experienced only limited attacks abroad. We have instead become the attacker while talking ourselves into a frenzy. Our leadership, our media, and a burgeoning array of firms and organizations that market their goods and services through playing on fear have built and sustain the overblown images we now confront. In effect, fear has become a major marketing tool for government budgets, leadership acceptance, political campaigns, government programs, publishing and media programming, insurance, and other private business activities.

Who are the targets of fear marketing? Americans are the targets. Politicians argue that not telling us about threats is a bad policy. The net effect of current terrorism information policy, notably the national alert system, keeps us apprehensive, and gives the terrorists one of their best tools: fear.

This fear campaign can be effective with us only if we do not do our homework. Start with who we are. Since the end of the Vietnam War and collapse of the Soviet Union, the risk of any attack on the US has been virtually nil. In the past two generations we have had three significant terrorist attacks on our home territory: A domestic attack in Oklahoma City, an attack on the World Trade Center in 1993 and the attacks of 9-11. Meanwhile, there were hundreds of terrorist attacks every year in the rest of the world. The attacks of 9-11 mainly brought it forcefully home that it could happen here.

Since 9-11, the impact of government policy and publicity has been to keep us focused on the vulnerability suggested by the 9-11 attacks. That single day's events have been turned from a single disastrous day into a continuum. Tomorrow, we are counseled, can be like another 9-11. Terrorism alerts stay in the yellow to orange zones. Therefore, we must organize our lives around that prospect. This is a pretty hairy outlook; but we should remember Franklin D. Roosevelt's caution: "We have nothing to fear but fear itself." Then, let us look critically at the available data about terrorism.

What are the terrorism data? For the past three decades our country has coped with a worldwide pattern of terrorist attacks, some of which were deliberately aimed at us, but most that involved Americans only incidentally; we were often in the wrong places at the wrong times. The attacks would have occurred had we not been there because we were not the targets. US terrorism statistics do not make that distinction, counting any attack that involves death or injuries to Americans or American property as anti-US attacks.

The data are distorted in another way, as discussed in "Why the War on Terrorism Will Fail", in that as many as 3 out of 4 so-called anti-US attacks are oil pipeline bombings in Colombia. As indicated above, terrorist attacks are a far smaller source of risk to us than highway accidents, homicides or drunken driving. Moreover, more than a third of all significant terrorist attacks in the years 2000-2002 occurred in India around the dispute between India and Pakistan over Kashmir. To get the problem of international terrorism clear in our minds, it is essential to look at such patterns.

How are we misled? Nothing about the terrorism pattern warrants launching a worldwide "War on Terrorism." Without the fear factor, the threat is not credible. How is the fear factor sustained?

There are several aspects of fear mongering we must assess. One is implicitly to lump together all the small insurgent groups in the world as a more or less monolithic enemy of the United States. This is fallacious, because the majority of insurgencies are directed against the governments or the elites of their own countries.

Such insurgencies exist in many of the 50 or so failed or failing nation states. Some fairly large groups, such as the Revolutionary Armed Forces of Colombia (Fuerca Armada Revolutionaria Colombiana) or FARC, which numbers 15,000 or more, seldom venture out of their own countries. The Philippine group, Abu Sayaff, that operates in the fringes, such as the China Sea island of Palawan, fights in Philippine territory. These groups represent some threat to Americans who get in their way, but they pose virtually no threat to the United States.

Another fallacy is the loose play around the threat of Islamic fundamentalism. Although many Muslims may be closer to their core beliefs than many Christians, Muslim fundamentalists—those who try to adhere closely to the values expressed in the Koran—by no means comprise a majority, and the extremists who commit terrorist attacks comprise only a small fraction of the Islamic adherents of the world who number upward of 1.3 billion people. In fact, mainstream Muslims and believers in secular government who want to depose their elite, corrupt, or oligarchic leaders are far more numerous than fundamentalists. Here again, the primary targets of their energies are their own governments. We become the enemy because we visibly ally with their hated governments, but that threat is largely centered on the national territories of those countries.

What about al Qaida? As his use of tapes shows, Osama bin Laden understands the situations outlined above quite well. Through al Qaida, he aids and abets dissidents in those situations to undercut secular governments or, as in the Saudi Arabian case, leaders who oppose and suppress his brand of Islamism. Such individuals and groups pose a threat to Americans and American interests in those countries, but they are not generally a threat to the United States. Much of the terrorism al Qaida recently has been blamed for has occurred in Islamic countries against indigenous targets. However, to get the attention of their home country governments as well as foreign governments, some Islamic attacks (tourist resorts in Kenya and Egypt and a night club in Indonesia) have been targeted deliberately on places where foreign tourists and business people are likely to be present.

If bin Laden is serious about his scheme to recreate an Islamic caliphate, then much of his terrorist activity and terrorist attack sponsorship will be to destabilize and unseat secular or nominal Islamic governments in Islamic countries. He will try to disrupt the pattern of support that the US and other developed countries long have extended to those governments. This is not an easy challenge for US leadership because disengaging and/or reducing support without losing influence on those governments is unlikely.

Al Qaida and bin Laden are poised to take advantage of any flaws in American conduct or activities, especially in Islamic countries. Iraq is the immediate case in point. There are enough indigenous sources of dissension among Iraqis to sustain more than one insurgency until the Americans, British, and Coalition partners give up and leave.

Bin Laden can leverage investments of resources and people in this conflict to make it worse, but the main sources of trouble in Iraq are indigenous, and they are feeding on the occupation. The argument that what goes on in Iraq is part of the War on Terrorism is window dressing, because outside terrorists would have nothing to do if the battle were not already joined between the Coalition forces and Iraqi insurgents. The Iraq conflict must be faced as a struggle between an occupying force and indigenous sources of resistance, mainly but not exclusively Sunni. Sources and causes of terrorism in the rest of the world are largely irrelevant to it.

How is fear generated? The generators of fear are largely controlled by government attitudes and actions. Their success depends on public fear of the unknown or the unfamiliar. What scares serious thinkers most is the fact that the United States Government is prepared to go to a condition of all out global war preparedness against small groups of non-state actors in sixty or more countries. Even if all the world's terrorists were on the same team, they would still number fewer than the population of Delaware.

In effect, the United States has a wartime President who has declared all out and global war on the equivalent at worst of a micro-state, or as one retired senior American diplomat put it, he has declared war on a tactic, the use of terrorism. Even more pointedly, he has declared war on groups that many of the countries that contain them may find irritating but not sufficiently to go to war.

High level US rhetoric about these groups makes it appear that they are mainly enemies of the United States, but that is hardly the case. The majority of these groups lack the resources or the inclination to go truly international. In many instances they get an international label in State Department reporting because they attack foreigners inside their own countries.

The alert system is harmful. The most pervasive fear maintenance system is the national terrorism alert program run by the Department of Homeland Security. An Orange Alert status was maintained throughout the Christmas and New Years holidays. That was based on rumors and speculations about how effective a major attack would be somewhere like Times Square at midnight on New Year's Eve. A similar alert was maintained during the period around the anniversary of 9-11.

The second most pervasive fear mechanism is media reporting, often inspired by government leaks or press conferences about possible terrorism threat situations, or "expert" speculation about possible terrorism scenarios. Few media appear interested in talking about the chronic problems that generate terrorism in many countries. These reminders do not make good headlines. People who blow things up are more likely to make attention getting headlines than are millions of people who suffer in silence, even if their suffering is among the main roots of terrorism.

The third pervasive threat mechanism is Osama bin Laden's practice of periodically sending the world a tape that Washington officials use to refurbish the threat. The interplay between Osama and US officialdom works to broadcast that Osama is still alive and al Qaida is a real threat. The fear machine works.

A deeply insidious part of the fear mechanism is the unwillingness of honest skeptics and opponents of the war in both parties to speak out against it. Because critics are afraid that the public or their political opponents will punish them for opposing a useless war, they do not speak out against the war. The Bush team cynically uses that fear of criticism to silence opposition to the War on Terrorism.

Where does this leave us? The cumulative effect of all these fear-generating mechanisms is a human condition closely akin to clinical paranoia. Rumor and supposition substitute for facts and information. In that ambiguous state of knowledge we are victims of a bogeyman theory of world terrorism.

We were struggling with world terrorism well before the CIA began training Osama bin Laden and other fighters against the Russians in Afghanistan. What bin Laden has done since graduation is assess and capitalize on the patterns of grievances many groups around the world have against their governments, the dominant elites or religious and secular groups that compete for power.

Bin Laden uses that assessment for recruitment and action against enemies who actually or potentially interfere with his goal of recreating a Muslim caliphate to rule Islam. He did not invent the bogeyman. We did that for him. An elusive, amorphous enemy that was world terrorism before bin Laden is not nearly as satisfying a target as a specific, humanized enemy. He satisfies the need for an enemy. We satisfy his need for identity and influence.

How can we break out of this situation? Data and analysis are available in the public domain to deal with this problem. The State Department annual report, required under Title 22 of the United State Code, and which this writer helped to create in the early 1980s, provides an increasingly clear and comprehensive picture of world terrorism. The report, <u>Patterns of Global Terrorism</u>, provides a sound basis for judgment about terrorist groups and situations in countries where terrorism occurs each year.

Unfortunately, this report apparently is not read by senior officials of the government. If read, its logic is certainly not driving US policy, because using a worst case estimate al Qaida membership accounts for less than ten percent of known world terrorist group membership.

The report itself has fallen prey since 9-11 to an exaggerated focus on Muslim terrorists and al Qaida, but the obvious conclusion to draw from the annual reports is that if Osama bin Laden were to die from natural causes or be killed and al Qaida shrivel to naught, most of the world's terrorist groups and problems would remain with us.

We need a new policy. We need a policy based on knowledge and understanding of those facts, not one that relies on fear and uncertainty. Today the country is being victimized by its own leadership. Ideologues, extremists, and true believers in the utility of military power and direct action drive a national policy that favors pre-emptive war and global domination as the only tools to meet a largely local problem that exists in many nations including the United States itself.

Only the United States now argues that this problem can be met by military means. Fear (of an exaggerated enemy) and uncertainty (about when, where and how a terrorist attack may occur) are the only arguments made to sustain this policy

Is there no good news? On the other side of this situation, we could and should marvel at how calm most people remain under conditions of deep privation, repression, servitude, and injustice. If there ever were a generalized human reaction to these conditions, we could have at least a third of the world's people up in arms. One of the most remarkable results of the Israeli treatment of the Palestinian people is not that it produces suicide bombers, but that it produces so few of them. The Palestinians give us the reassuring fact that even when subjected to extremes of repression, the great majority of people are not prone to violence. The world terrorism threat is as modest as it is because comparatively few of the world's 6.3 billion people are violent.

What can be done about the situation? The War on Terrorism ignores most of the foregoing facts. The President launched a small-scale special operation in Afghanistan. He then kept the country on a war footing to launch a war against Iraq that the facts do not support. He and his neo-con advisers have loosely labeled the conflict in Iraq as "the central front" in the War on Terrorism, but that ignores the obvious truth: a people whose country is invaded will fight back, may have help from outside, and have the right to resist by whatever means available. Moreover, it ignores the fact that if the Pentagon had planned carefully for the post major combat phase of the Iraq war, our forces could have prevented the looting, imposed civil order, denied potential insurgent access to weapons and explosives, and quickly restored electricity, water and sanitation to their pre-attack levels. In sum, such prompt actions could have stopped or certainly diminished the armed resistance that developed.

The War has thwarted attention to the essential struggle. Little to no effort is being mounted to deal with the causes of terrorism. The causes—as cited in earlier articles—are well known to many workers in international organizations and in the United States Government. In the competition for resources, war fighting gets priority. Mitigating or eliminating the causes of terrorism does not.

Trying to reduce or eliminate terrorist attacks without doing anything about the causes of terrorism is like trying to eliminate drunk driving without doing anything about alcohol abuse. That logic would appeal to someone who wants to strike a coin that has a head but no tail. The same logic works for someone who insists on increasing government spending while reducing government revenue. But worse still, this logic works for present policy advocates who appear to believe that terrorists can be hounded or beaten into giving up their grievances.

We actually are not the enemy. The majority of the world's terrorists and their grievances are not in the United States. Most remain within their own countries and pursue battles against their own country's leaders and elites. The United States is often treated as an enemy because it allies with those leaders and elites. Those alliances are prime recruiting arguments for al Qaida. But the only way a global war on terrorism can be justified is to make a convincing case that world terrorism is principally aimed against the United States and therefore justifies a warlike response worldwide.

No such case factually exists. The only case that can be made is that terrorists can attack us at home at any time. In the abstract that is true, but it always has been true. The only other argument that can be persuasive is that such attacks are imminent. That assertion depends on the willing cooperation of the bogeyman. Our leadership now responds to Osama bin Laden tapes with all the certainty of Pavlov's dog (Ivan Pavlov was a late 19th century Russian born psychologist who used dogs in conditioned response experiments.). Terrorism alerts go up a notch. Fear refurbishes public support for the War on Terrorism.

Our government ends up being a victim of the way it handles this problem. Having declared that the problem is serious enough to go to war, and having averred that the "enemy" is dangerous, pervasive, and capable, there is nothing for it but to act accordingly. So long as the War goes on, the media and the public will insist on being informed. It will take considerable honesty, boldness, and integrity to break out of this trap.

Is there a way out? What a mess. But we can break out of it. The critical path is clear: Demand straight talk and question what our leadership tells us. Demand better intelligence and closer attention to analysis. We should never have a repeat of the mismatch between truth and action that is Iraq. Recognize and apply the knowledge our government already has about the worldwide causes of terrorism. Devote needed human and material resources to mitigating these real problems. Promote actual delivery of those human and material resources by all governments that have any to spare. Assure that the world's wealthiest nations stay with it for the long haul.

Shut down the War on Terrorism. Put the task of combating terrorist crimes back where it belongs, in the law enforcement and intelligence communities of all countries concerned.

Our best prospects for making a severe terrorist attack on the United States less likely are contained in those steps. We must accept that perfection is impossible and that uncertainties of the types that commonly beset our lives every day are unavoidable. Terrorism at worst is one of those, but it is less likely than many others. This is the antidote to fear.

TERRORISM HAS HIJACKED OUR NATIONAL PRIORITIES
June 2004

Over a period of many months our country has drifted into a sea of troubles. There are landmark events and dates that mark our progress toward these waters. There are no indications that we see where we are, have identified the reefs, or have started to change course. Just what are the problems? How did we get here?

There is probably no clear defining moment on our path, but the process began, it appears, before George W. Bush was sworn in as President. Bush is said to have had a hangup (Saddam tried to kill my dad.) respecting Iraq that he acquired much earlier, perhaps from his father. As presidential candidate and neophyte President, Bush the younger had been schooled by Cheney and others in the PNAC agenda on which an urgent item was removal of Saddam Hussein. Bush was also briefed by Ariel Sharon who, sources indicate, urged removal of Saddam on behalf of Israel, and helped paint the picture of Iraqi nuclear ambitions and achievements that later was proven false.

The fixation on Iraq was cemented by the events of 9-

11. Iraqi—that is Saddam Hussein—responsibility for those attacks and Saddam's alleged affiliation with al Qaida became a Bush mantra. He repeated those accusations long after it was clear that the facts did not support the charges. At the time, however, the 9-11 attacks provided the reason for a war on terrorism, for the invasion of Afghanistan, and for attacking Iraq.

In the wake of 9-11, US leadership expounded to the public an exaggerated terrorism threat. Perhaps the peak was the argument of Condoleezza Rice that it was vital to act against Saddam before we confronted a "mushroom cloud", i.e., a nuclear attack. At least as indicated by public statements, concern progressed from there toward a state of mind approaching official paranoia.

That frame of mind and the underlying PNAC/neo-con agenda has caused our leadership to consider and apply extreme measures. It has caused them to abandon well-established principles of national behavior. It has led our leaders into us/them depictions of the world around us. It has alienated our friends, confounded our relationships with many countries, put us at odds with one of the world's main population groups, caused us to descend into a racist view of the human condition, warped us toward excessive reliance on military power, beset us with fear, and now leads us to prolix waste of our national resources.

Let's examine how we got into this. Start with a tolerant disdain we developed over the years for violence in other societies. There was a joke making the rounds about bomb throwers that grew out of repeated explosions in the Balkans, now the troubled zone of the fragmented Yugoslavia: "Momma's aim is bad; the copskys all know dad; its little Ivan's turn to throw the bomb." In that way, we dismissed the repetitive evidence of untreated social illness in that region until it exploded into World War I. In our transit to the start of the third millennium we endured many wars, all of them somewhere else. Hundreds of thousands of people died in primitive conflict in places such as Central Africa.

We were not unmoved by this. Our own society remained physically if not emotionally untouched; overall we felt free to go on about our business while people in far away places died in large numbers or were brutalized by repressive leaders. We were hit by terrorist attacks in places such as Lebanon, Kenya, Saudi Arabia, and Tanzania, but since World War II we had not been attacked at home by an external enemy.

9-11 was a crowning moment in a growing perverse romance with terrorism. The strange progression of that day is ground deeply into our psyche. We had been offended by kidnappings in the Middle East and Latin America, shocked by the bombing of our Embassy and Marine barracks in Lebanon, disturbed by damages to embassies in East Africa, and deeply unsettled by a homegrown attack in Oklahoma City. But due to television and radio images and sounds of that morning, 9-11 became part of a common, virtually global experience with how quickly and efficiently our system can be attacked and wounded. No other property of the world terrorism environment had changed. Simply, we had been attacked at home on live television.

In politics, every crisis is an opportunity, and 9-11 made us vulnerable to exploitation by a leadership cluster—the so-called neo-cons—around President Bush. They wanted to move US policy and practice toward the extreme right. They saw 9-11 as the moment—while the people were in shock and fearful of repeated attacks—to move America toward an aggressive and warlike national stance. Specifically they saw movement toward establishment of the New American Century and toward achievement of an Israeli geo-political goal—the total neutralization of opposition in the Middle East, beginning with Saddam Hussein. The transit is, has been, and will be costly.

There is a constant, subliminal debate in American life about what is a proper subject for our leadership to tackle. Are we the world policeman? Most appear to think not. Should we intervene to keep hundreds of thousands of people from dying in genocide in Central Africa? Not enough said yes, soon enough. Do we really care whether several world leaders are dictators or are people elected in dubious processes? Mostly no. Are we shocked by terrorist attacks in other parts of the world? Some are, but most appear not. Do we care how many Iraqis have died at the hands of Saddam or of Coalition forces? Mostly those details are kept from us and we do not protest the censorship. Do we care how many Palestinians are brutalized, imprisoned, killed, or rendered homeless by the Israel Defense Force and Mossad? Mostly suicide bombings that kill or wound Israelis get our attention. Does the assault on civil liberties of prisoners in Iraq, Afghanistan, and Guantanamo really offend us? Maybe, but we have taken too long to recognize that rules that permit those officially sanctioned crimes place our own liberties in jeopardy.

Observing such patterns, the Bush team, especially the neo-con cadre, knew or guessed the limits of the vision of the American public and decided we could be had. Their first deception was the War on Terrorism. Taking our outrage and feelings of being victimized as cover, this group decided to launch a global response that had no chance of succeeding. But it looked good on television and the rhetoric had a satisfying tone: Let's go to war and get these bastards. We fell for it.

We fell for it again with the war in Iraq. Much of the world was opposed to it, but that carried little weight with the Bush team or with the public. We were actually fed a badly concocted cock and bull story to justify that war, but hardly enough people seemed, even later, to mind the incredible deceptions the Bush team used to launch it. There seemed hardly a tremor caused by the unfolding fact that Bush had taken us into a war we did not need to fight in a region that did not threaten us, and where there was no imminent danger.

The bottom line was our future had changed. How our money would be spent, how the lives of young Americans would be invested in conflicts, how our reputation would fare in world opinion, how many threats we would face, and where those threats would originate would all be wrenched into a new pattern. By failing adequately to object, we had drifted into years, if not decades, of pointless war. Our national priorities had not only been scrambled, they had been hijacked.

TERRORISM WAR IS MAIN TERRORISM GENERATOR
July 2005

Last week's bombings in London stoked a fire storm of commentary about the state of the War on Terrorism, about US and Coalition military engagements in Iraq and Afghanistan, and even about the definition of terrorism. The pit was reached with Tony Blair's assertion that they—the terrorists—"will never destroy what we hold dear," because the bombers are not really interested in what the British or the Americans hold dear. They want the Americans and the British out of Iraq and Afghanistan, and an end to the Israeli persecution of the Palestinian people. The high point of this furor was reached, again by Tony Blair, who mused that something must be done about the causes of terrorism.

If it takes a bombing to focus the minds of leadership on the correct path out of this situation, then maybe the London bombers did the world a favor, while actually getting across what they wanted: They want the West to do something about their grievances, starting with an end to the War on Terrorism, because that war is seen by at least a billion people as a war against Islam.

The bombings coincided with a rumbling in Washington about what is terrorism. It seems awfully late in a shooting war to need to define what the war is about, but better late than never. In fact it is a war of definitions: What is terrorism? The definition seems to be moving toward accepting that, outside of legitimate warfare and justified law enforcement, a politically motivated violent attack by anyone, against anyone, anywhere, on any scale is terrorism. That formulation comes close to a universal definition, and it probably will not survive. In won't survive, because it leaves open the prospect that the terrifying acts of military forces, including those of the United States, could be counted as terrorism.

Meanwhile, what will terrorism data include? The emergent new Washington definition bundles into the global problem all of the internal disturbances of the fifty or so failed and failing states by combining so called "domestic" terrorism (incidents that involve only the actors, victims and property of one country) and "international" terrorism (incidents that involve actors, victims and property of more than one country). The new definition, as expected, excludes the actions of military forces. The number of international incidents does not appear to have changed, although the definition of what is a "significant" attack may be under review.

On the eve of the publication of its annual <u>Patterns of Global Terrorism</u> in April 2005, the State Department Office of Counterterrorism indicated the report would not be published for 2004 or for future years. Instead, the legal requirement to report to the Congress would be met only by sending the information to the Hill; it would not be released to the public. That announcement stirred a flurry of accusatives, e.g., the numbers have gone up as high as they were in the 1980s, the US is losing the War on Terrorism. The White House does not want the public to know. Those accusations demonstrated widespread mistrust of Bush team reporting and wariness of its devious information management habits. However, on April 27, the newly established National Counterterrorism

Center published its first statistical report: A chronology of Significant International Terrorism for 2004.

The Counterterrorism Center report deals with the most important categories of terrorism that were covered in the State annual, but the Center report applies a somewhat broader set of reporting criteria, and it reports only on significant incidents—meaning that they result in hostage takings or in "loss of life or serious injury to persons, major property damage, and/or an act or attempted act" that could result in those outcomes. The numbers speak for themselves, and their implications are a problem for the Bush administration because they call the whole idea of the War on Terrorism into question.

The report's main finding is that there were 651 significant international terrorist incidents in 2004. The last time there were that many incidents of any kind reported was in the late 1980s. But the numbers are really not comparable because the database for the 80s included a sizeable number of incidents that were not defined as "significant": Of the 208 incidents reported in 2003, 161, or 77% of all reported incidents were classed as significant. They occurred in 40 countries, roughly 60% of them in five countries: India, Afghanistan, Colombia, Iraq, and Israel, in that order, with India alone accounting for 48, or about 30%.

On its new Internet site, the Terrorism Knowledge Base (a joint venture with the Department of Homeland Security), the Counterterrorism Center has included international and domestic terrorism in a data series that begins in 1998. Thus, compared with earlier State Department reports, the 2004 numbers show radically increased global numbers: Some 2,575 incidents, about a quarter of them "international", occurred in 2004. Over half of the newly tabulated incidents (1,309) occurred in Iraq, Palestine, Afghanistan, and Israel. In the first half of 2005, the concentration of incidents increased: Worldwide incidents numbered 1,650, of which 1,120 occurred in Iraq, Palestine, Afghanistan, and Israel.

The increase in incidents in Iraq is dramatic. In 2002 there were 14 incidents in Iraq. In 2004, the first full year of occupation, there were 790 incidents. In the first half of 2005, incidents in Iraq numbered 883. Iraq appeared to be on a path to more than double the 2004 incident rate. In effect, the invasion of Iraq has become the world's principal terrorism generator.

There has been a brutal rise in incidents associated with the War on Terrorism. In 2002, somewhat more than 20% of worldwide incidents occurred in Iraq (14), Palestine (432), Israel (109), and Afghanistan (65). In the first half of 2005, roughly 70% of the 1,650 worldwide incidents occurred in those four areas, with Iraq (883) accounting for more than half of worldwide incidents.

As the Center report indicates, it is difficult in the Iraqi case to distinguish between terrorist attacks and acts of insurgency. Moreover, the status of victims (foreign, private, civilian, official, and military) is an uncertain cut line between the two. If the outsiders are westerners, they are, as seen by insurgents, more than likely involved in the occupation, therefore, they are a perceivable part of the enemy. Even a cautious judgment indicates that the root cause of the incidents in Iraq is the occupation, together with the uncertainties of governance and the instability associated with it. Therefore, it is probably unwise to class them as terrorism, and the same applies to incidents in Afghanistan. An occupation/war related/ insurgent violence pattern applies better.

Data on incidents in and around the Indian subcontinent make up a big part of the remaining global terrorism statistics. In 2002, incidents in India, Pakistan, Bangladesh, Nepal, and Kashmir numbered 743. That was a quarter of worldwide incidents. In 2004, things quieted down somewhat, mainly in and around Kashmir, but the region still accounted for 8-9% of worldwide incidents. Moreover, use of the "Significant incident" category by the State Department may have been dropped, but it should not be forgotten. Incidents in India and nearby areas typically counted for the largest single block of such incidents before the data base changeover, and the incidents themselves probably continue to be as violent as ever.

The other significant groups of attacks listed in the Center report were in the West Bank and Gaza Strip. In 2004, there were 373 attacks, mainly in Palestine. In the first half of 2005, there were 191, again mainly in Palestine. The attacks in Palestine (the West Bank and Gaza) and Israel are evidence of the continuing Israeli repression of the Palestinian people. There were 12 attacks in Saudi Arabia during 2004, said variously to be associated/promoted by al Qaida, but they were more likely evidence of growing local discontent with the Saudi royals' monopoly of power.

The majority of countries included in the Center report experienced only one or two attacks during the year. Those attacks can be attributed largely to long standing quarrels between out-groups and elites.

Where does this leave the War on Terrorism? In Iraq and Afghanistan the United States leads an occupying force battling people who have every right to object to it. In Colombia and the Philippines the United States has been helping local authorities deal with long-standing insurgencies, so there is a limited connection. Terrorism in the majority of countries covered by the Center report is indigenous, centered on disputes between governments and out-groups that existed long before al Qaida. It is unlikely, that, if the War on Terrorism ended tomorrow, its passing would alter either the status or the outlook for those long-standing disputes.

This poses a draconian set of choices. The United States is the primary culprit in volatile situations in Iraq and Afghanistan. The United States relationship to Israel is a significant driver of Middle East attacks that may harm Americans and others. Thus, the United States, along with Britain and other Coalition members, is the visible proximate cause or at the very least is closely associated with the causes of over 1,300 of the 2,575 terrorist incidents reported by the National Counterterrorism Center for 2004. The situation is worse so far in 2005 because the US is associated in the same manner with more than 1,100 (close to 70%) of the 1,650 worldwide attacks recorded for the year as of June 30.

There is an ironic twist to this situation. President Bush has said repeatedly that it is important to fight the terrorists offshore so they will not attack us in the United States. The London, Madrid, and Bali bombers, and of course the 9-11 hijackers clearly have gotten the same idea: It is quieter at home if you take the struggle to the other side. But that philosophy encourages the export of political violence by anyone who thinks exporting violence will serve his cause.

The President has declared Iraq to be the "central front" in the War on Terrorism. If that is true, it is more provocative than productive. The Counterterrorism Center data show that the War on Terrorism is irrelevant to patterns of terrorism in most societies. However, the War on Terrorism looks like the heart of the problem in Iraq and Afghanistan. Withdrawal of US and Coalition forces from Iraq and Afghanistan, plus a Middle East peace that is fair to the Palestinian people and the Israelis, plus, as Blair said, addressing the causes of terrorism are the key elements of the solution.

PART THREE
THE MIDDLE EAST CONFLICT

PALESTINE—THE PROBLEM AND THE PROSPECT
April 2002

"His Majesty's Government view with favor the establishment in Palestine of a National Home for the Jewish people, and will use their best endeavors to facilitate the achievement of this object, it being clearly understood that nothing shall be done which may prejudice the civil and religious rights of existing non-Jewish communities in Palestine, or the rights and political status enjoyed by Jews in any other country." The Balfour Declaration –November 2, 1917

Introduction—The sheer brutality of Palestinian and Israeli actions in the present Palestine conflict has focused world attention on stopping the death and destruction while trying to find a path to peace. It is important to have a clear fix on how this situation came about, because, as is often the case, the remedies are tied irrevocably to recognition and management of the causes. Lord Balfour started the process, but instead of recognizing Palestine as the home of the people who had lived there for centuries, the League of Nations turned the Balfour Declaration into a mandate that gave the Jewish people—a small minority in Palestine at the time—a national home, if they could achieve a majority. The triumph of the Israelis and the tragedy of the Palestinians began here.

To meet the requirement of the League of Nations mandate, the Zionists encouraged mass migrations of Jews to Palestine, while forcefully and sometimes violently displacing the Palestinians to achieve and retain a majority. Well before the Arab-Israeli wars that began soon after the state of Israel was declared in 1948, the Zionists sought permanent displacement of Palestinians from all areas of Palestine west of the Jordan River.

At the end of World War I, there were about 50,000 Jews in Palestine. By mid 1955, there were 1,200,000 Jews in the new state of Israel, the major infusion being migrants from Central Europe. However, by UN estimates, about 750,000 Palestinians had been displaced, mainly into refugee camps in the West Bank and Gaza. In those two areas and the immediately surrounding states of Lebanon, Jordan, and Egypt, the United Nations reported 3,800,000 registered Palestinian refugees in 2001.

Who Is Responsible? The United Nations, the United States, and other major world governments, the Arab governments, the Palestinians, and the Israelis all share responsibility for failure to deal with the stateless existence of 3,000,000 Palestinians presently in the West Bank and Gaza, many of whom live in impoverished condition. The majority are young people with limited education, limited skills, limited opportunities, and great vulnerability to recruitment, indoctrination, and training by extremists.

While the West Bank and Gaza are nominally under the Palestine National Authority, Israel has in fact exercised critical control over both territories and the conditions prevailing there. Twice in the past decade, for stated security reasons, the Israelis sharply curtailed traffic between Palestinian and Israeli areas, causing abrupt and severe damage to the

Palestinian economy. Recent curfews and curtailments of border crossings for workers in Israel have compounded Palestinian problems of unemployment, malnutrition of the young, and frustration. Palestinian leadership, principally Arafat, is blamed for failing to accept the last Israeli offer to move toward peace. Much of the last Israeli offer was more show than substance, and in any case pressure from other Arab leaders gave Arafat little leeway in the discussion of that central problem.

The tasks ahead—It is futile to expect any way out of this situation without a balanced approach and without restraint on the part of both sides. While the urgent need is to address an accumulation of irritants, not merely the provocations of the present conflict, the immediate task is to recognize what has occurred in Palestine. The most troublesome aspect of this situation is that Jews, whose presence in Palestine was humanely dictated by the need to extricate them from persecution and bondage in Central Europe, are now as Israelis literally the masters of a subject population of 3,000,000 million Palestinians.

As the Palestinians now see it, their safety and survival depend on the decisions, even the whims of a hostile government. To shut down the terrorism generators and to stop the body bombers, the highest single priority today is to change the conditions that sustain that perception. To that end, the tasks for now and the next several months are clear.

Stop Israeli Incursions. In their own interest, the Israelis should cease incursions designed to drive the Palestinians out of the West Bank and Gaza and actively seek a settlement with the Palestinians. However, that is not the goal.

Present Israeli leadership says it is conducting a war against terrorism, but the obvious effect of harsh Israeli military actions is a war of attrition and social disintegration against the Palestinian people. Israeli military moves in the West Bank and Gaza generate the suicide bombings that are then used to justify the next round of harsh military responses, and those simply engender more Palestinian attacks. So far, Israeli forces have been unable to stop these attacks, because in this apparently lopsided conflict, the advantage of the economy of force is on the side of the Palestinians.

The clincher here is that after four generations of refugee status, it should be obvious to the Israelis that the Palestinians will neither leave voluntarily nor desist from fighting back. It should also be clear to everyone by now that the pattern of repressive actions against the Palestinians is both self-feeding and self-defeating. A graceful backing off under a framework such as the one proposed by Crown Prince Abdullah of Saudi Arabia would buy the Israelis peace more quickly and surely than any campaign in the West Bank.

Shut down Palestinian attacks. Until they are recognized as a state, the Palestinian activists are insurgents—a militant resistance to Israeli rule of their territory. But by Israeli and US definitions, the Palestinians have no rights to engage in proto-military activities, meaning forceful acts to defend themselves or to fight back against Israeli attacks. Thus, the Israelis assert that all Palestinian actions during the recent Israeli invasion are terrorism, and that all of Palestine's defenders are terrorists. Whatever the definition, Arafat faces the major task of shutting down Hamas and other resistance groups while Palestinians are under attack. They are not likely to cooperate under present conditions of acute Israeli hostility. To make it possible for Arafat or the Palestine National Authority to succeed, the Israelis must shut down military incursions, assassinations, and settlement activity.

Get on with the transition. Delay in this situation is destructive. The longer it takes to resolve the Palestine question, the more likely it is that further terrorist attacks, in the region and farther afield, will occur. Moreover, the further down the road Palestinian statehood appears the more excuses and opportunities Israelis and Jews from outside Israel, including the United States, have for trying to expand and add settlements. Thus, the map of the West

Bank and Gaza changes by an amoeba-like colonization from Palestinian to Jewish, the frustration of the Palestinians grows, the exposure of Jews in the West Bank and Gaza to hostile acts increases, and the volatility of this already unhealthy situation goes increasingly out of control.

Define national territories. The boundaries of Israel and Palestine must be defined, recognized, and respected by both sides. So-called buffer zones that go beyond the recognized demarcation lines cannot be permitted. "Fences"—a euphemism for the 24 foot high wall the Israelis are building to "contain" the Palestinians—further complicate the situation. For the Israelis to build and maintain a fence around the West Bank and Gaza is in the same class with creating a stockade or prison to house either a subject population or slaves. It would say the Palestinians have no rights, they can be confined without any processes of law, and they can be kept that way at the whim of their neighbors.

Settle the boundary questions. Much if not all of the present conflict could be dealt with if those defacto boundaries were formalized and accepted. Above all, Palestinian leadership would have strong arguments to use with extremists to calm the situation.

Stabilize the situation. Palestine is the special case of a state about to be born. The candidate has both actual and potential leadership. It has some control of a defined national territory, at least of the pieces not covered by Israeli settlements. It has a sort of government, although most of the infrastructure of governance has been destroyed in recent actions by the Israel Defense Force IDF). It is not headless, but the effectiveness and the integrity of its aging leadership have been called into question, even by Palestinians. In every respect, the Palestinian state is transitional. The next stages toward complete independence can be accomplished only under conditions of some stability. Without stability both the organized insurgent groups and rank and file Palestinians who are simply angry will continue to operate out of control.

Get rid of the "refugee" label. The label "refugee" is a barrier to stabilizing the situation. Thinking of one's self as a displaced person creates a sense of uncertainty and insecurity that interferes with living and planning because nothing is seen to be permanent. The Palestinians, the Israelis and the international community must either address the issue of return, which is still on the United Nations agenda, or move on to compensation for confiscated property, which is a long standing subject of UN General Assembly Resolution 194. While compensation is hardly the same as the right of return, it may pave the way for permanent resolution, both physical and psychological, provided it is accompanied by the symbolic return of a few. That was the special genius of the Geneva Accords that proposed Israeli ceding of territory in the north equal to the area of settlements around Jerusalem, which Sharon and others insist must be retained by Israel.

Restore the Palestinian infrastructure. Among the effects of the Israeli attacks in Palestine was the destruction of places of business, government offices, and other infrastructure, including medical services, but above all the security services since both police personnel and facilities have been destroyed. Beginning immediately, the UN should take the lead in marshalling the resources and expanding or initiating the programs necessary to rebuild infrastructure and stabilize and improve the living conditions of the Palestinian people.

Moderate the extremists. Both sides in this conflict must moderate their extremists. From the very beginning in the 1940s, the Israelis used terrorism; they can hardly be surprised that it would be used against them. Efforts to convince the Palestinians to leave, such as the attacks on the villages of Deir Yassin in 1948 and of Qibya in 1953, were deliberate terrorism, as were the 1982 attacks on Sabra and Shatila in Lebanon. The assassination of Palestinian militants has been a matter of official policy, and if carried out by any other government would be considered state terrorism. For the state of Israel to survive and prosper, future Israeli leadership must reject such actions.

Recent furor about Arafat's effort to bring Hamas into the government of Palestine shows a real lack of understanding of the situation. In fact, if Israel had not supported Hamas as a counterweight to Fatah in the 1960s and 1970s, Hamas might not be the potent political, social, and military force it has become. Long ago, the Israelis brought their terrorist extremists into the government, and some of them, such as Sharon, have had major roles, to be sure not always positive. With Hamas or other extremist elements, Arafat or any other Palestinian leader has two choices: He has to deal with them as opponents and cope with the consequences of their actions, or he has to bring them in and deal with the task of keeping them in line. He should be encouraged to do as the Israelis did, and bring the extremists into the process in the hope of moderating their behavior.

Each party needs room and each needs to allow space for mistakes or miscalculations on both sides. It is doubtful that either the Palestinian or the Israeli leadership can guarantee that no attempt will be made to disrupt any peace effort.

Remove the settlements. In order for the Palestinians to establish and run a state of their own, they must have free and unencumbered entry and exit to and from their own territory, and practice and enjoy the usual protocols for treatment by and conduct of relations with other states. This requires that they be free of interference in their internal affairs and be treated as equals, not as a subject people of the Israelis. Those goals cannot become reality unless the Palestinians can take effective control of the West Bank and Gaza territories where they now live. Those goals are not attainable so long as the Israeli settlements remain.

Resolve long-term economic issues. Many of the borders Israel wishes to keep relate to access to and control over water. The present water balance is heavily weighted toward the Israelis, not only in absolute terms, but also in per-capita water use terms. Any long-term resolution of the present conflict has to focus on redistributing access to water in this parched region on a basis that is equitable for all of the people.

Palestine faces a future basically of a landlocked state, except for the Gaza Strip. Like the landlocked states of Europe, it must have and earn rights of free passage. It was incredible that Israel refused to allow the Palestinian head of state to travel, even on a mission that could have contributed to peace. Arafat's ability to control extremists in Palestine was probably reduced by this action.

Settle the status of Jerusalem. The 1948 United Nations partition of Palestine set out three components: The State of Israel, Palestine, and the Holy Places. None of the three religions that have an historic interest in the Holy Places can claim a unique right to them. All have an interest in achieving the goal that the original partition decision was designed to accomplish. The UN should take on the task of administering these sites for all humankind.

Deal with human trauma. One of the principal consequences of Israeli raids and Palestinian suicide bombings has been an accumulation of potentially destructive trauma in both populations. If not effectively detected and treated, the extremes of these conditions can lead not only to terrorism and other lawlessness on either side, but to the disabling of significant numbers of people in both countries. An urgent task for Israeli and Palestinian leaders, and the UN and interested national governments, is to identify the victims of trauma in the conflict region and to undertake counseling and treatment.

The US interest—The most immediate US interest is how to shut down a conflict that has become a serious and escalating generator of hatred against Americans and the United States. Next, the boundaries of the Palestinian state and Israel need to be defined and stabilized. Then Israel must be taken out of the position of maintaining a subject population. The US needs to convince others that it is seeking a fair and even handed solution. Finally, the US has a vital interest in seeing that the terrorism generators on both sides of this conflict are shut down.

Israeli interests—Israeli interests place large obstacles in the path of resolving this conflict. They want a Jewish state, at a time when much of the world moves toward diversity. They want to be free of threats and attacks, and to be treated as an equal among Middle Eastern states. Those two aims are hard to argue with. They want stable and unchallenged boundaries around as much land as possible.

They want to avoid either a return or compensation for the displaced Palestinians, even though critics argue that the Israelis have no objection to compensation, so long as Uncle Sam pays it. They want Jerusalem as their exclusive capital. They want as much control of water resources as they can get. They want the West Bank and Gaza as part of Israel. In this form, the Israeli dream is not attainable without trampling the rights of the Palestinians and engendering unremitting bloodshed. But the Israelis, at least the hard liners, seem not to recognize this reality.

Final thoughts—Lord Balfour stated the correct principles for building the new state, but he possibly did not anticipate that the Jewish exclusivists of the Zionist movement would violate the requirement he set to protect Palestinian rights, and drive the Palestinians out. The current situation has grown from the Balfour, League of Nations, and Zionist decisions, and having matured, or perhaps better, fermented for almost 90 years, there is no going back. A peaceful future requires accommodation by everyone involved. Fairness, equity, realism, and mutual respect have been the missing ingredients. If those qualities are not supplied, the situation will fester. If not abated, the hate, frustration and resentment that now exist will sooner or later unleash a weapon of mass destruction.

THE DELUSION OF TOTAL SUPPORT
April 2002

As the Israel Defense Force incursions into the West Bank and Gaza have advanced, reports have grown that the United States Congress is hardening around unconditional support for Israel in the conflict. Congressional hardening on the side of Israel is driven in part by anger about the Palestinian suicide bombings. But the main drivers are active lobbies for Israel including Jewish organizations in the United States and the Christian Right. The aim obviously is to put Congressional pressure on the Executive Branch to pursue a totally pro-Israeli policy.

So far that pressure has not worked. There are real questions about why Secretary of State Colin Powell spent so much time on his way to meetings with Sharon and Arafat. Was he, albeit unsuccessfully, twisting the diplomatic screws on the Israelis to withdraw from their brutally harsh invasion of Palestinian lands?

One can ask whether the God of Abraham, who is the God alike of Christians, Jews, and Muslims, is likely to take this conflict as a cue for (a) working out Christian hopes regarding the Second Coming—a reported reason for Christian support of Israel in this situation, (b) responding to Jewish hopes respecting an affirmation of the Covenant—a justification for their moves to take all of Israel and the West Bank, or (c) a response to Palestinian hopes that their fears regarding Israeli expansion and Palestinian expulsion will disappear. However, one should also ask how much good unqualified American support does the Israelis?

In the long run US support may be harmful. More likely, even in the short run, such unqualified support will be counterproductive. While it may always be good to have strong, influential friends, it is time to get to the real issues. First, would strong US support protect the Israelis from future suicide bombers or other terrorist attacks? It would not; even if significant US or other forces were interposed between the Israelis and the Palestinians. Unfortunately, whatever may be the final revelations about Israeli attacks in Jenin and other communities, the next two or three generations of potential suicide bombers have been created. There is no telling when one or more will decide to go critical.

Second, will strong US support for Israel make the Palestinians more likely to cooperate? The answer is unlikely. Moreover, as already has been indicated by Egyptian President Mubarak's snub of Secretary Powell this week, Arab governments in general will be offended by any such skewed US posture. They are unlikely to cooperate on the key issues of getting Palestinian leadership to the table and shutting down the violence.

Third, will the War on Terrorism be advanced in any degree by an unbalanced US posture on Palestine? Here the answer is clearly no. European governments are already visibly uncomfortable with our actions regarding Palestine. Middle East governments on the whole are unhappy. Some, for examples Iraq, Syria, and Iran, may be unlikely to help very much in any case, but they could be materially less unhelpful, if they thought we were taking the Palestinian plight seriously.

Most of those governments have signaled that the War on

Terrorism we are conducting in Afghanistan should not be equated with or confused with what is going on in Palestine. Whether their support for the War on Terrorism would diminish or disappear if we came out wholly for Israel is not a question we should put to them, unless we can live with a hostile response.

Finally, will unequivocal US support for Israel in any way speed the conclusion of the present conflict and creation of conditions for peace? The record shows clearly that our support has not been decisive in the past toward creating a stable or peaceful environment for Israel.

The parties themselves must fix this. But that cannot happen unless both parties are treated equally by each other and by outsiders. Each party must respect the other's rights. Until that happens, no amount of support from outside will be meaningful. The impasse will go on, as it has already for more than half a century.

PALESTINE'S SELF INFLICTED WOUNDS
October 2002

Almost every week the world watches the Israel Defense Force march, fly, or drive into a new area of the West Bank and Gaza and wreak new havoc. Not every week, but too often, the Palestinian reply is a suicide bombing. The Israelis claim is that the whole problem is caused by Palestinian terrorism. The Palestinian complaint is that they are being repressed and their people and their society are being systematically destroyed by Israeli military and intelligence operations. That charge is valid, but it goes largely unheeded.

At no time in recent memory has a well organized, equipped, and funded military force dealt so harshly with a virtually defenseless population. The obvious intent and likely outcomes of this Israeli effort are the destruction of the Palestinian state and the dispersal of its people. So far, the results have given Israel little satisfaction and much grief. Instead, both Israel and the Palestinians have been the victims of self-inflicted wounds.

By most accounts the Israeli economy has been imploding at a scary rate since the beginning of the Palestinian Intifada two years ago. It has declined even more since the IDF invasions of the West Bank and Gaza during the past few months. To be sure, Israel's economy was severely affected by the after-effects of 9-11. This was followed by the financial market effects of the Enron, WorldCom, and other corporate scandals. The Palestine conflict is a continuing and probably deepening drag on Israel's economic fortunes. And its consequences are much more the products of Israel's own actions than they are the results of Palestinian attacks.

The economic downturn is driven daily by developments around the conflict. Responsive to suicide bombings, tourist travel to Israel has been reduced by more than 50%. That amounts to 1.5% or more of the whole economy since the conflict heated up. Construction and agricultural sectors have slowed materially due to the absence of the more than 100,000 Palestinian workers (some say twice that number including non-registered workers) who fuel these sectors.

Unemployment in Palestinian sectors, the West Bank and Gaza, and the disruptions caused by military incursions and the imposition of curfews have cut Palestinian income and spending on most products, even on food and basic services. While unemployment in Israel is said to be approaching 10%, it is estimated at a much higher 50-60% or more in the West Bank and Gaza. Much of the Palestinian market is typically served by businesses in Israel or handled by Israeli pass-throughs, which benefit the Israeli economy.

Probably the largest economic effect has been created by diversions of national treasure to the IDF, estimated to be equivalent to more than ten billion dollars. This is robbing resources from all other sectors of Israeli economic activity.

All Israel has gotten for those heavy costs are self-inflicted wounds to the Israeli economy and to Israeli citizens. There is hardly any doubt remaining that the IDF incursions, and the excesses usually associated with them, have generated a continuing series of suicide bombers. These have killed civilians, not all of them Israelis, undermined safety and security in Israel, frightened tourists away, while shattering foreign investor confidence.

One Jewish source has suggested that Sharon knows he must have the suicide bombings to justify his brutal attacks in the West Bank and Gaza. Without the bombings, this source indicated, Sharon would face irresistible pressure from the US, other governments, and the UN to cease his campaign. That may well be true, and it raises a serious question as to whether the harsh attacks are deliberately designed to provoke Palestinian retaliation, mainly the bombings, to keep alive Sharon's program to expel the Palestinians from the West Bank. The unspoken price of this strategy would be the lives of a few Israeli civilians, including women and children. Those would be leadership-inflicted wounds.

While the Palestinian Authority is aware that Israel uses the suicide bombings as the excuse for harsh military reprisals and the occupation of the West Bank and Gaza, the Palestinians have no other effective defense. It is doubtful that, even with a hard line effort, Arafat could stop all suicide bombings. The prices Palestinians pay are occupation, curfew, harassment, attacks on civilians, frequent shootings, and arrests by Israeli forces.

Perversely, each bombing has unleashed more military incursions, leading to extreme actions such as the 1,000-pound bomb on a family housing compound in Gaza, which led to more Palestinian attacks. By now, the lesson is clear: Brutal military actions do not stop, but rather provoke small scale, devastating terrorist attacks. It is time to halt. The safety of the Israelis, the economic future of Israel, and the future of the Palestinians are all in jeopardy because of the continuing conflict.

There are more self-inflicted wounds. American Jews and others within Israel continue to go into the West Bank and Gaza to build or expand settlements. The current target is Gaza. This increases Palestinian anger and frustration, further arousing the prospect of terrorist attacks, either on settlers or on people in Israel. The Israeli victims need to know that part of the cause is the action of other Israelis. The Palestinians need to wake up to the fact that their strategy does not work either.

Calls for building a fence around the Palestinians recently became a popular idea among some Israelis and some prominent Jews in America. That fence, as noted, the 24 foot wall which is now being built, will do a number of things, none of them good. It will physically codify the pattern of enmity and distrust that exists between the two peoples. It will impose a responsibility and an expense on the Israeli wall keepers to be sure the integrity of the wall is maintained. It will impose an obligation on Palestinian extremists to thwart it. It will harden the resolve of Hamas and other extremists. It will disrupt a mutually beneficial commerce between the two markets. It will serve as a daily reminder to Palestinians that the Israelis consider them second-class people at best. It will re-impose a barrier between the Israelis and the people of the region that many Israelis and Palestinians have spent half a century trying to overcome. Finally, it will precisely define a long-term target for anti-Israeli terrorists. All of those represent potential but deferred self-inflicted wounds.

Over the past months it has become increasingly clear, by Israeli actions and policy statements of Ariel Sharon, that the aim of Israeli operations is to finish a process begun in the late 1940s—to drive the Palestinian people out of all areas of Palestine west of the Jordan River and perhaps beyond. If that strategy succeeds, the Israeli people for years to come can expect to pay for it through continuing exposure to random, destructive, and potentially deadly terrorist attacks. Those attacks will be the ultimate self-inflicted wounds, because Israel is unlikely ever to be at peace, and as 9-11 demonstrated, even the most powerful are not immune.

THE CHRISTIAN COALITION AND ISRAEL
An Open Letter
November 2002

This week you, the Christian Coalition of America, announced your intent to hold mass rallies across the United States in support of Israel. These rallies, you stated, are intended as follow-up to a reportedly successful rally in Washington DC in October. As your President stated in announcing these events, they are designed "to activate people more in support of Israel, because we do have a common bond with one another, and we want to show support".

This drive to show solidarity with Israel is supported, it is said, by interpretations of the Biblical predictions, mainly in Daniel, that the second coming of Christ will occur 7 years from the date that Israel acquires control of the Temple Mount. The Coalition, as would all of Christendom, would hope to be present and accounted for in that event. In current predictions, the starting date for that 7-year period was the 1999 agreement between Israel and Palestine on settling the status of Jerusalem.

The Second Coming has been long awaited by both Christendom and Islam. Because the event is much anticipated by both religions, and because adherents of both share the same prophets, save for Mohammed, the two religions ought to have much to share on this subject. In light of that shared interest, the Coalition and its members should ask themselves hard questions about the situation in Palestine before jumping into this alliance. Even more importantly, they should be prepared to answer the questions honestly and to assess the answers candidly.

The hard questions you should ask include: (1) In view of the Christian, Muslim and Jewish histories tied to the holy places of Jerusalem, is anyone entitled to exclusive control or ownership? When Israel became a state, the United Nations partitioned Palestine into three elements: The state of Israel, Palestine, and Jerusalem. The UN assumed that, in view of the many historic religious interests in Jerusalem, it should not be ceded to either the Israeli or the Palestinians. (2) Should not the 2 billion or more Christians, Jews, and Muslims of the world be guaranteed free access to the holy places? (3) Would you cede control to anyone who does not guarantee unimpeded access to and protection of the sites? (4) Is not the most reliable approach to the equitable sharing of the city with the adherents of all three monotheistic religions involved to assign its management to a neutral party?

(5) While we all must deplore the suicide bombing of Israeli people and places, how should the virtually complete destruction of Palestine by the Israel Defense Force be adjudged? (6) Is it morally acceptable for a heavily armed state to destroy the foundations of an unarmed society? (7) If you were a Palestinian, would you endure the constant repressions of an occupying army without fighting back by whatever means available to you? (8) If you were a world court, would you put three or more million people on trial and make them endure endless hardships for the violent acts of a small number or the threat posed by even a few thousand? That is what present Israeli leadership is doing to Palestinians. (9) Can you wholeheartedly support the Israeli cause with these facts staring you in the face? (10) Should you care, or is caring irrelevant to the purposes of the alliance?

In coming weeks there will be a national election in Israel to choose a new Prime Minister and a new cabinet. Present prospects are that hard-line leadership will prevail, and as a result the willful destruction of the Palestinian state will continue. More settlements will be built. Less space will remain for the Palestinians. More Palestinian homes and businesses will be destroyed to make way for new settlements. The de-facto repression of Palestinian Christians and Muslims will continue. Will it matter to Coalition leadership and members how this electoral process turns out? Should it make a difference to you whether the new leadership of Israel will be just and fair to all people?

Inside Israel, there are several distinct levels of society that are racially and religiously determined. The Central European Jews, the Ashkenazi, and their descendents are on top. The Sephardic Jews, the people or the offspring of people who lived in Israel before statehood or who came from surrounding countries, (in truth, the "people of the book") are second-class citizens. So too are the Jews who intermarry between Ashkenazi and Sephardi. The Christians are looked down upon and they are limited both in number and what they are free to do. So are the Muslims. Arabs are at the very bottom. This is an appraisal that is based on the observations and conclusions of both Israelis and American Jews.

(11) Do members and leaders of the Coalition wish to bless an Israeli leadership with unquestioning support if that leadership does not give equal status to Christians or adherents of other religions? (12) In your view is it all right to discriminate in this manner? (13) Would you willingly bond with people who think your faith is inferior to theirs? (14) Is the outcome of a gamble on prophecies that have existed for thousands of years worth taking part in violating so many human rights?

These comprise a short list of questions that should be asked before a decision is made on the proposed alliance. Equivalent questions must be raised regarding any alliance.

One would hope that the Christian Coalition will ask these and related questions, and that you will find answers that give your leaders and members a balanced outlook toward all peoples of the Holy Land.

IRAN—THE NEXT ISRAELI DOMINO
September 2003

According to Israeli Foreign Minister Silvan Shalom, "Iran is fast approaching the point of no return in its efforts to acquire nuclear weapons capability," and as reported September 2 by AFP, he considers this a "nightmare scenario". That could be so if, as Shalom appears to assume, the most likely target for an Iranian nuclear weapon is Israel. His solution is to call on the world community to use the processes of the United Nations International Atomic Energy Agency to pressure Iran into systematic inspections by IAEA of the country's nuclear facilities with the goal of deterring Iranian weapons development.

The whole world should view with concern the possible development of nuclear weapons by any new country, including Iran, and the possession of nuclear weapons by any country, including the United States. But the Israeli posture on the matter is a supreme irony.

Beginning immediately after World War II and the founding of their state, the Israelis began a nuclear weapons development program. Under President Eisenhower's Atoms for Peace program they acquired knowledge and technology that, contrary to the Atoms for Peace rules, they parlayed into a nuclear weapons program. With the help of the French, who built the Dimona reactor and up-graded it for them, and with the help of South Africa, the Israelis successfully tested a weapon in the late 1960s.

They have since accumulated a stockpile variously estimated at 200 or more weapons; how many nuclear and how many thermonuclear is not clear. Their nuclear facilities at Dimona in the Negev Desert are off limits to all visitors.

They admit nothing to the international community. They have not joined the Treaty on the Non Proliferation of Nuclear Weapons (NPT). With their not-so-secret weapons stockpile they have become the driving energy for nuclear weapons development programs by Iraq, Iran, Egypt, and others.

It is now obvious that much of the so-called intelligence about Iraq's nuclear program under Saddam Hussein was based on Iraqi exile and Israeli, meaning Mossad, reports. On the basis of such tenuous truths the United States launched an unprovoked war against another nation and put 150,000 young Americans, many thousands of Iraqis, and others in harm's way in Iraq. At the present rate, the US will spend many billions of dollars and thousands of American, Iraqi, and other lives to clean up the resulting mess. Given the record in Iraq, the neo-conservatives would be complete fools to attack Iran based on Israeli or Iranian exile information.

Since its acquisition of nuclear weapons, Israel has stalked aggressively behind a double standard. While refusing to take a position one way or the other on its own weapons and ignoring international criticism, Israel has successfully used its considerable influence in US and European affairs to get any development of such weapons by its would-be enemies on an international taboo list. The problem is that Israel has the weapons; everybody knows it. Other governments accept the possibility that, if provoked, Israel may use such weapons against them. Those governments seek to develop such weapons at least in their own defense. This is the operative formula for the long-term Middle East arms race.

Israeli nuclear weapons are at the center of this problem. It will not be resolved by efforts to suppress weapons development in Iraq, Iran, Syria, Egypt or any other regional country. It might be disrupted by an absolute ban on the export of nuclear related technologies to any of those countries, but do not count on agreement to, or enforcement of, such a ban.

If Israel succeeds in conning the United States, the European Union, perhaps the UN, and of course the Iranians into stopping weapons development in Iran, the next Israeli domino will be Pakistan, a Muslim country that already has tested weapons that are outside the purview of the non-proliferation treaty. The Israeli weapons are an attractive nuisance, and they will remain so unless destroyed.

The elephant in the room is existence of nuclear weapons anywhere. Israeli weapons represent a grown up offspring, because with 200 or more, Israel rivals China for pride of place in the nuclear club. However, the newest driving forces are the plans of the United States. The United States already uses UN-banned depleted uranium weapons and has "leaked" plans to upgrade and develop new battlefield nuclear weapons, including bunker busters to take out the deepest enemy safe-havens. As the history of arms races has shown for millennia, that plan will inspire others to the same excesses.

Israel's plan to keep its own weapons while using the international system to keep its potential enemies from developing them will not work. Rather, at least sixteen (some say more) countries will continue underground efforts to acquire nuclear weapons and delivery systems that fit protection needs against perceived enemies. Developed countries will continue to abet this process by providing either approved, e.g., electric power generating and research, or "dual use" materials and equipment.

Survival is a powerful urge. It appears, probably realistically, that Islamic countries perceive Israeli weapons as a greater threat than any or even all of the weapons in the official club. Since the Israelis deliberately advertised their preparations to use as many as 20 nuclear weapons on Egyptian and Syrian targets in the Yom Kippur War of 1973, even though that did not happen, the regional concerns are valid. That positions Israel at the vortex of a potential horrific storm. The bad news is that most people do not pay much attention to this problem. US officials, caught in this decades-old Middle East policy quagmire, try desperately to ignore it. The good news is that a growing number of Israelis are concerned about the future of Israel, and nuclear weapons are only part of the cloud over it.

WHAT'S WRONG WITH DEPOSING ARAFAT
September 2003

For the past two years, Yassir Arafat has been a virtual prisoner in his compound in Ramallah, West Bank, Palestine. Since founding Fatah in the 1950s and building it up to being the principal militant wing of the Palestinian movement, Arafat and Fatah and its offshoots have been the primary and most persistent thorn in the side of Israeli leadership. In more recent times, Arafat has struggled unsuccessfully with the fact that whatever current Israeli leaders might say they just want the Palestinians to go away. Arafat is one of the reasons the Palestinians have not given up and left to join the rest of the Palestine refugees abroad. But the strongest and, among Israelis, least appreciated reasons the Palestinians are still there is they believe fervently that Palestine is their home.

The Peace Process (which is political and media quick-speak for an effort that looks more like a Mexican standoff) has swirled around Arafat from the beginning. Starting with the creation of Fatah, an acronym for the Arabic words meaning national liberation movement, he moved upward from terrorist to spearheading the declaration of a Palestinian State, winning the Nobel Peace Prize for efforts to achieve a Middle East peace and ultimately to dominating the Palestinian Authority. There he sits in the posture often achieved by revolutionaries, a successful warrior unable to solidify the peace. He remains ill-equipped to pursue peace and probably unable to imagine or achieve a settlement that would recognize the essential objectives of both parties.

He has been unsuccessful for several reasons. First, he is able to exercise only partial control over Palestinian extremists, including Hamas and the Al Aqsa Brigades, because the Palestinian extremists have a well-earned distrust of the Israelis, and expect little from negotiation. Second, the Israelis provoke the extremists by targeted assassinations and arrests and confinement without trial. The Israelis then argue that since Arafat cannot control the extremists, he ought to be ousted. To diminish his power, the Israelis placed him under house arrest in Ramallah, a scheme that enjoys only limited success. Rather the recent resignation of Prime Minister Abbas and prompt selection of a successor shows that Arafat still calls the shots. In light of Israeli threats of the past few days, if asked, the Palestinians would re-elect Arafat with a landslide vote to continue running the Palestinian Authority.

This situation is frustrating to the Israelis and to the Bush administration. Both want to see their chosen counterpart across the negotiating table. The only reason the Israeli and US preferences count at all is that the Palestinians and their leadership remain too weak to fight back. How would Yalta have gone if Roosevelt and Churchill had insisted that the Russians send someone other than Stalin, whom neither liked nor trusted? Even as vilified as Saddam Hussein was by the US, Britain, and Israel, nobody proposed that negotiations before the war should be pursued with someone else. Constituted governments often have genuine scoundrels in charge, but the selection of their chief negotiators is, by widely practiced tradition, their call.

In truth there is little to choose between Sharon and

Arafat. Sharon is an old school terrorist out of the Stern, Irgun, and Haganah tradition. He was forced to resign as Defense Minister when he allowed the deliberate massacre of over 2,000 Palestinians at Sabra and Shatila in Lebanon in 1982. In those attacks and the other battles of his invasion of Lebanon, Sharon had responsibility for a larger death toll than 9-11, for which we have chased Bin Laden over much of Afghanistan. As head of the Likud party and the Government of Israel, Sharon has aggressively pursued a program of targeted assassinations of Palestinians that if pursued by any other government would be called state terrorism. His harsh applications of the IDF in the West Bank and Gaza, including the killing of innocent bystanders, and his wholesale destruction of homes and businesses look strikingly like terrorist acts. In a moral-ethical frame, his appropriateness as chief negotiator for Israel stems solely from the fact that he is the elected head of government.

Arafat began his violent career as a soldier fighting against the Israelis in 1948. He graduated to terrorism with the founding of Fatah in the 1950s. Hamas was promoted at times by the Israelis to oppose Fatah. Arafat, who has no army, no doubt has used Hamas and other extremists to fill this gap since Fatah was elevated to political status in the movement. Following the Israeli destruction of the town of Jenin, or the destruction of a seven-story apartment building to get one suspected militant, Arafat may not have wanted to restrain the extremists even if he thought he could.

By weakening Arafat, Israeli leaders have made it more difficult for him to control the extremists. They have also made the task of any successor enormously difficult. The continuing IDF attacks and targeted assassinations after Abbas was selected to succeed Arafat cut the ground out from under him and drove the Palestinian political center more toward Arafat than before Abbas took the job. So Arafat will have a seat either at the negotiating table or immediately behind it. Israeli actions have assured that outcome.

The selection of a representative in any negotiation is the

call of the Palestinian people. Anyone the US or the Israelis might choose will have difficulty demonstrating acceptability to the Palestinians. That alone could delay negotiations longer than good sense dictates. The more sensible approach is to recognize that Arafat remains a player to be reckoned with.

One aspect of the situation that is easily missed in the fury of political squabble is that both Sharon and Arafat are unique products of the Palestine wars. Sharon was born of Russian, Ashkenazi Jewish immigrant parents on a collective farm in Palestine. Arafat was born of Palestinian parents in Cairo. Sharon is a member of the European immigrant Jewish line that brought Zionism to Palestine. Arafat's family line traces back to the Mufti of Jerusalem, and he is a practicing Muslim. Both were very young when they fought in the 1948 war, Sharon for the newly formed Haganah and Arafat for the Egyptian army. Neither has been far from the conflict in the past fifty years. In fact, Sharon once commented, "My whole life has passed in this conflict." Arafat has been the dominant personality in the Palestinian movement since the late 1960s.

The frustrating fact for Sharon must be that Arafat refuses to go away. Sharon would be comfortable with someone on the other side of the table who might be dazzled by the prospect of peace, even if there is no substance in it. Arafat has never fallen for this, even when it was offered with ruffles and flourishes by Ehud Barak in the Clinton years. Sharon has made it plain countless times that he does not support any reduction in settlements in the West Bank or Gaza; he is unlikely to make any conciliatory moves, but if he did, they would most likely be a scam. He sees Israel extending all the way to the Jordon, and he signed on to the Bush "Road Map" without any attempt to hide his positions on these matters. Arafat knows Sharon's position, and only the removal of all settlements, preferably before any agreement is signed, would be acceptable to Arafat. Similarly deep-seated differences exist between the two leaders and their constituencies on Jerusalem.

This leads to the conclusion that neither Arafat nor Sharon is a logical candidate to lead Palestinian or Israeli negotiations unless the goal is merely to mark time. Bush, with an eye to the 2004 elections, might welcome such a temporizing outcome, but the Palestinians will not buy it and neither will a growing number of Israelis.

Sharon has devoted much of his life to forceful moves against the Palestinians. If that had worked, the Palestinian people would no longer be a challenge for Israel. But the Palestinians believe every bit as strongly as any Israeli that Palestine is their home and they refuse to give it up. Arafat embodies that conviction, and any threat to him is a threat to that outcome. Predictably, by threatening to remove him, the Israelis strengthened Arafat's hand and made it more likely that any negotiation will include him.

There is a perverse quality about the Israeli and US desire to remove Arafat from the scene. As a rule, diplomats want someone on the other side who fully represents the positions and needs of his or her following, including any possible room for concessions. Generally, that is because fools and ignoramuses make deals that seldom endure.

Arafat surely knows those things better than any other Palestinian. But the problem is he has been burned so often that he is not easily swayed.

The US position on this problem is not as unfeeling as it is politically driven. Many professionals in the Department of State, in CIA, the armed forces, and elsewhere know full well how destructive Israeli policies and actions have been of the Palestinians and their interests. They also know that the Israeli defense is a fraud bought by the American leadership group and the committed Israel partisans in the American public more than by anyone else. What the public may not know so well is that many an American politician is well paid through political contributions to support the Israeli position;

those contributions, in large part, account for a unanimous Congressional resolution in support of Israel last year.

Bush must contend with this American political reality, but he will be mistaken if he insists that the chosen leadership of the Palestinian people be removed from any future negotiations. The US, along with virtually every other government, has taken the correct public position on Israeli threats to expel or eliminate (read kill) Arafat by opposing them. Now, the task is to get both parties to the negotiating table in a frame of mind to make some progress.

The task is not easy for Bush but the requirements are clear: Back away from categorical support of Israeli positions. Give full consideration to Palestinian ones. Give the Palestinians room and encourage them to select a new generation of leadership. Insist that all Israeli settlements be removed from the West Bank and Gaza. Assure that the wall comes down, and that the boundary between Israel and Palestine be at least reasonably associated with the Green Line. Insist that such Israeli programs as targeted assassinations and the willful destruction of Palestinian property be terminated. Recognize that IDF destruction of Palestinian security personnel and infrastructure has created enormous problems for Palestinian leadership. Persuade Sharon that Palestinian control of their extremists will be much easier if the Israelis stop attacking.

Getting rid of Arafat will not change any of those fundamental issues. Sharon may hope that he—with US help—will be able to bulldoze some less determined personality into accepting an outcome more to his liking. Arafat—as well as any successor—has every reason not to trust Sharon—or any likely Likud successor—because Sharon does not project a constructive outcome from negotiations. Based on his statements about the Road Map, he is more likely to make a vague remark or to avoid any statement that might have negotiating value to the Palestinians. Moreover, in private remarks that show up outside mainstream media, Sharon makes it clear that he is tightly wedded to the positions of hard-line Zionists who have no intention of giving up any part of the West Bank or Gaza. So long as he feels the United States stands solidly with him, he is unlikely to budge from this position. These reports tell Arafat that little can be gained from negotiations with Sharon.

With or without Arafat, the Palestinians will not buy Sharon's formula. The region will return quickly to terrorism. Palestine's new Prime Minister, Ahmed Qorei, will experience evil days. In light of Islamic reactions to the Israeli threat against Arafat, notably in Saudi Arabia, there will be more regional support for Palestinian militants. Israelis will continue to lose the asymmetric war of terrorism. There will be blood in the streets, and the Israelis will be at least as guilty as the Palestinians.

There is no room here for American bias, indecision, or standing on the sidelines. It has been said that the political and spiritual will of George W. Bush to solve the Palestine problem would assuredly lose the next election, while probably winning him the Nobel Peace Prize. We won't know unless and until reality takes charge. But Arafat, while an obstacle, is not the problem. The central problem is that the Palestinian people have not been offered a fair or reasonable or honest solution.

Terrell E. Arnold

THE CHALLENGE OF ETHNIC CLEANSING IN ISRAEL
January 2004

In a recent interview on Israeli public radio, a prominent member of Ariel Sharon's Likud party said that the idea of ethnic cleansing to rid Israel of non-Jews had widespread support in Israel. This idea apparently was put forward with little to no public discussion as a "final solution" to the growing demographic fact that Palestinians could well outnumber Jews in Israel, the West Bank and Gaza in a fairly short time. In this climate of opinion, mass expulsions of Palestinians and assassinations of militants could easily morph into generalized ethnic cleansing to rid the areas west of the Jordan River of all non-Jews. Without going into the moral, legal, religious, or humanitarian failings of such a choice, it is worth examining the practical complications of deciding who is to be expelled or eliminated.

The first question is: Who is a Jew? The Old Testament answer to this question is quite simple: Jews are the descendents of Shem, Noah's eldest son. Shem's descendents became known as Shemites, a name that gradually evolved (probably more through Arabic than Hebrew) into the modern term, Semites. The term applies about equally to all Palestinian people. That appears a simple enough point of departure, except that over a period of several millennia (we have no idea how many) the sons of Shem were both prolific and adventurous. They traveled widely and married or otherwise mated with females in every place they ventured. Moreover, Shem's sons had daughters who did much the same.

By the time Moses led the children of Israel out of Egypt, the bloodlines were quite complicated, despite efforts to maintain purity. Moreover, on the basis of four to five generations per hundred years, any living Jew is at least several hundred generations from Shem, and a pure bloodline at this stage would be miraculous.

Therefore, perhaps the more operational question is: What is a Jew? Most of us who are non-Jews and hardly expert in ethnography or genetics are likely to say a Jew is someone who practices the Jewish religion or who identifies himself or herself as a Jew. People generally do not look behind these orders of preference and self-selection.

Just what do the would-be ethnic cleansers have to work with, here and now? The answer may seem crass, but they have only their preferences. Here is where an ethnic cleansing venture can go most egregiously awry.

The problems start with the simple fact that no one we know took a DNA sample from Shem. Moreover, a dozen or so tribes of the children of Israel were cast into the Diaspora, where a fairly strong Jewish tradition holds they still belong. Meanwhile, many of the sons of Shem, a large number of whom were not adherents of Judaism, remained to populate the eastern reaches of the Mediterranean with Christian and Muslim and Jewish communities. They were there when the Zionists, who bill themselves as Ashkenazi Jews, appeared out of Central Europe to begin their creation of the state of Israel.

A further complication was the dispersion of Sephardic Jews, many of whose ancestors were expelled in the late 15th century from Spain, all along the North African coast and around the Middle East. Even in the blackest periods of relations between Israel and Arab states of the region, such as the early 1960s, the Sephardic Jews lived in Arab countries, some still carrying the Spanish of Don Quixote as a spoken language in their households. Their ethnicity was also further diluted by centuries of living and of passage along the African coast. Additionally, in an effort to accelerate growth of the Jewish population, Israeli leaders sought migrants from Jewish communities in Iraq, Peru, Ethiopia, and elsewhere and these communities are now slowly being added to the pool of Jewishness that is Israel. In Israel, the Ashkenazi number 4 million plus and the Sephardics about a million; together they are 80% of the population. Palestinians and others make up the remaining 20% of the population in Israel plus (the demographically frightening part) the bulk of the population in the West Bank and Gaza.

This, then, is the gene pool that would-be ethnic cleansers must confront in the lands west of the Jordan that they want as Israel. Some of their likely preference is revealed in the elite and governing power of the country. The northern or Ashkenazi Jews are at the top, with Palestinian, Sephardic, and other regional or imported Jews at the bottom. This picture is further complicated by the probability that the Ashkenazi are not descendents of Shem, but from other, Central European stock whose ancestors were mere converts to Judaism.

It appears that an honestly pursued ethnic cleansing would have perverse effects on the Israeli power structure. However diluted the bloodline may be, the Palestinians, both Jews and non-Jews, appear most entitled to the distinction of being "people of the book", therefore, ethnic descendents of Shem as nearly as those can be identified. In that awkward way, ethnic cleansing could be a "final solution" in that it would give the land back to the people whose forbears were resident in Palestine in 1916-1917.

Of course, putting true ethnicity aside, ethnic cleansing could be pursued on behalf of the Ashkenazi majority, which appears to be what the Likud speaker cited above had in mind. That would codify elevation of the whiter, larger European Jews over the darker, smaller Mediterranean, African, or Latino ones, which is already the defacto situation. This result could have an ironic twist in that it would relegate the "people of the book", the genuine Semites, at best to the minority status of second-class citizens.

The history of the Jewish people denies the Israelis the luxury of a "final solution" through ethnic cleansing. They have three choices: One is to continue on the presently decaying path of Israel. That means sustain a hierarchical, Central European based oligarchy. The oligarchy would be supported by second, third and fourth class citizens (Sephardis, Palestinian Christians, Muslims, and others). These groups are increasingly dissatisfied with the arrangement, and some of them harbor deep-seated grievances and fight back. The second is to achieve a compromise by recognizing that all the parties have equal rights and interests. The third and best choice is to recognize that the power of Judaism is always greatest when based on spirituality and focused on the major contributions the tribes have made to communities as enclaves and citizens.

Biblical Jewish efforts toward purity and exclusiveness were always frustrated, either by God or by the human condition. A vocal minority of Jews suggests it should stay that way. God keeps his/her own counsel. The human condition appears no better disposed than it was. Outsiders can hope that realists among the Israelis will accept ethnic diversity, already the dominant human condition virtually everywhere else.

AGAINST THE LAW TO CRITICIZE ISRAEL
May 2004

Scholars and journalists who for years have studied, written, and talked about the Israeli-Palestinian conflict are facing a brick wall that almost daily grows higher. This wall, not unlike the concrete barrier now being built by Israel to contain the Palestinians, is designed to silence all discussion of Middle East issues that involves any form of criticism of Israel on any American university campus. The wall would be raised several feet by senators Rick Santorum (Pa) and Sam Brownback (Kan.) through an amendment to Title IX of the Higher Education Act. Deceptively to be called an amendment to include "ideological diversity" and "sexual equality" as prerequisites for federal funding, the real purpose of the measure is to require denial of federal funds to any university whose faculty or students, perhaps even guest lecturers, make statements that are in any way critical of Israel. The argument is that any action or statement critical of Israel is perforce anti-Semitic.

Among hardliner supporters of Israel and the Zionists, this type of censorship has been evolving for some time. Critics of Israeli treatment of the Palestinian people have been increasing in number and clarity. But in human relations there are always several ways to deal with criticism. One obviously is to ignore it. A second is to meet criticism head on with superior proofs and arguments. A third is to kill the messenger. A fourth is to assert that the critic is actually the problem. A fifth is to argue that the critic (or everybody) does the thing being criticized. A sixth is to assert that the criticism falls within a broad class of statements that are taboo, e.g., anti-Semitic. When all these essentially social control options prove unworkable, as they have in the Israeli case, the last ditch option is to suppress criticism by law.

Note that the optimum choice of dissenters is and always has been to modify the behavior being criticized. However, anyone listening to and watching closely what Israeli leadership is doing under Sharon and the Likud party knows that there is no intent to modify behavior. That would require acquiescence in creation of a Palestinian state and acceptance of the Palestinian State as an equal in the family of nations. This would require final determination of the size and shape of Israel. The Zionist dream of a Greater Israel would have to remain just that.

It may not be possible to persuade the Zionists and their supporters, Israelis, fundamentalist Christians, or well-wishers in general that the only solution to the Israeli-Palestinian conflict lies through recognition of the rights of the Palestinian people. It may not be possible for Israelis and their supporters to face the fact that denial of Palestinian rights and repression of their freedom are the taproots of Palestinian terrorism. Nor may it be possible to persuade the White House and the Congress, and the Democratic candidate for President that unconditional support for Israel is not and never has been a winning strategy for the United States. But they all must understand that continued insistence on this posture is courting a national disaster.

This proposed amendment is an echo of Nazi, Communist

and other totalitarian forms of censorship. If enacted it would provide cover for increasing Israeli excesses against the Palestinians. That will surely provoke more Palestinian resistance, including more terrorism. Every member of the Senate and House of Representatives who is worth the confidence we placed in them and the salary we pay them should vote against the Santorum/Brownback amendment. Their best strategy would be to prevent it from coming to the floor. Passage by the Congress would pervert our national laws, willfully corrupt our diplomatic relations with other countries, and undermine the intellectual freedom of our higher educational system.

Efforts to take a fair or neutral position on Palestine issues have been under attack since the partition of Palestine was first proposed at the end of World War II. Shortly after the Deir Yassin massacre of hundreds of Palestinian villagers by Israeli terrorists in 1948, Albert Einstein and other scientists raised objections to Israeli behavior through a letter to the New York Times. Another Jew, Alfred Lilienthal, delivered a broadside with his book <u>What Price Israel</u>, published in 1953. However, Zionists, their Israeli and Christian supporters responded by elaborating the far-reaching censorship tools outlined in the article, "An Outrageous Invasion of American Diplomacy" that concludes this section of the book. The Santorum/Brownback amendment was designed to close another perceived loophole on American university campuses. We call that "loophole" academic freedom.

George Washington saw the problem clearly, as outlined in his farewell address more than 200 years ago:

> "...a passionate attachment of one nation for another produces a variety of evils. Sympathy for the favorite nation, facilitating the illusion of an imaginary common interest.... and infusing into one the enmities of the other, betrays the former into a participation in the quarrels and the wars

> of the latter without adequate inducements or justification..."

The definition of national interest as Washington saw it has not changed. Nor has the stickiness of the fly paper wrapped around the proposed amendment. We have conceded to no other nation such a license to interfere in our internal affairs. The way for Israel to reduce or eliminate most of the criticism that is abroad today is to clean up its own act.

THE FALLACY OF EVEN HANDEDNESS
June 2004

On May 19, US representative, James Cunningham, abstained from voting on a UN Security Council resolution that demanded the Israelis halt demolition of Palestinian homes, mainly in the Rafah refugee camp in Gaza. Although the Israelis have destroyed thousands of Palestinian homes and businesses and rendered thousands of people homeless, in the process infuriating most of the world community, the US vote was typically at odds with world opinion, but it was progress of a sort. For the second time in less than two years, the US representative abstained on a resolution critical of Israel. That abstention permitted the resolutions to go into effect. Had the US used its veto, which it has done 38 times since 1972 regarding UN actions critical of Israel, the resolutions would have failed.

If it were to last, this US position in the Security Council would be significant because the United States appears to have moved from refusing to allow UN criticism of Israel to refusing to block UN criticism of Israel. However, the US delegation to the UN has yet to take a flat-out stand against anything the Israelis do, though the US is often critical of the Palestinians.

The United States stand on events in Palestine has always been pro-Israel. The US has refused to go along with any UN resolution that does not criticize, and as USUN Ambassador Negroponte has put it, the US opposes any draft text that does not include "robust" condemnation of Palestinian terrorism, regardless of the behavior of the Israelis. In 2002, the US refused to vote for a UN Security Council resolution calling for Israeli withdrawal from Palestinian cities, but it agreed to abstain once the text demanded that the Palestinians bring terrorists to justice. The May 19 vote is interesting because there is no clear-cut demand of the Palestinians beyond getting on with the peace process. For close watchers of UN language, the implied US disapproval of Israeli actions in Gaza, backhanded though it appears, may therefore be quite strong.

US verbal sleight of hand around Palestine includes slippery definitions. The Palestinians who fight back against Israeli attacks, whether in Israel or in the West Bank and Gaza are categorically labeled "terrorists." When twelve IDF soldiers were killed last week, their deaths were labeled acts of terrorism. Both the Bush administration and the Sharon government ignored the fact that those soldiers, in two groups, were carrying massive amounts of explosives in their armored vehicles into Gaza to blow up homes and businesses along the Egyptian border.

In reality, the IDF soldiers were about to carry out large-scale acts of terrorism against the Palestinians. The two IDF teams were going to blow up houses allegedly with entrances to tunnels leading into Egypt. However, Israeli intelligence on tunnels was apparently as poor as it was on WMDs in Iraq, since Israeli authorities admit that so far only one tunnel has been found. However, hundreds of Palestinian homes and buildings have been destroyed, and the IDF appears under instructions to destroy more. That means the Palestinians are in for more terrorism, IDF style.

Another abused term is "militant." In Israeli language, implicitly accepted by the Bush team, "militant" is generic for the bad guys. In this lexicon, anybody who refuses to lie down and take persecution, expulsion from their homes, destruction of their property, and assassination of their leaders, is a "militant" and if he or she fights back, a "terrorist".

In war, the winners write the history. In modern terrorism, the strong or even the stubborn states decide who is a terrorist or what is terrorism. All actions and personnel of the strong states are excluded from these definitions. The asymmetry of this struggle, as summed up by the Sharon government and largely acquiesced in by the Bush team is: Everything we do is appropriate (no matter how horrible) because "we have the right to defend ourselves." Everything the Palestinians do is bad (no matter how justified in terms of their self-defense or efforts to protect their interests) because the Palestinian militants are committing acts of terrorism.

The policy applies a perverse "even handedness" toward the two sides in the Middle East conflict. No matter what the Israelis do in the conflict, the US permits no criticism without having it paired with a criticism of or an injunction to the Palestinians. That is the extent of the even-handedness. That pairing of any critique puts the Middle East conflict into a moral, ethical, and legal no man's land. It simply preempts any detached judgment on the legal or humanitarian rightness or wrongness of any action by imposing the tit-for-tat logic of a child's game.

In that judgmental zone, the typical US official reaction turns the landscape into a free-fire zone for the Israelis. The Palestinians are in a position where anything they do to attack the Israelis will be condemned, while any attack of the Israelis on the Palestinians is likely to be glossed over. In the event of even the most egregious actions, such as the destruction of Jenin or recent destruction in Rafah, the White House spokesman, or the President himself is likely to repeat the usual litany of "the Israelis have a right to defend themselves", or in the case of Rafah, "We are asking for clarification."

The Israelis take such refusals to criticize as a US license to proceed, including the assassination of any Palestinian of choice. In that vein, the US has refused to join in UN condemnations of either Israeli threats to remove or assassinate Arafat, or the actual Israeli assassination of the last two leaders of Hamas.

To be sure, over the years there have been numerous behind the scenes diplomatic approaches to the Israelis to stop or moderate behavior in specific cases, usually when Israeli actions are particularly absurd. The problem with this so-called "quiet diplomacy" is that it holds up no public standard of behavior for the Israelis to follow. They know this all too well, and they act accordingly.

This broad public policy prevents the United States from ever looking squarely at where the most crucial faults lie in the Middle East problem. It is a bit like juggling balloons in an air duct. No room is allowed for critical judgment because US use of the phony even-handedness argument is always weighted against the Palestinians. US officials say basically they are not prepared to exert pressure on the Israelis until the Palestinians stop fighting back.

There is no map drawn yet that will take one around this roadblock toward any reasonable solution. The Road Map that now exists is defective because it views the problem and its solution through the optic of that official US evenhandedness which means no matter what the Israelis do the US always insists on holding the Palestinians accountable.

The effect of this policy is to make all Palestinians pay for the acts of any Palestinian who fights back against Israeli oppression. Last week Mr. John Dugard, the Special Rapporteur of the UN Commission on Human Rights, summed up the problem by saying that Israeli treatment of the Palestinians in Gaza constitutes a "collective punishment" and amounts to war crimes under the Geneva Conventions. Mr. Dugard went further to say that the UN Security Council ought to take action to stop the violence including possible "imposition of a mandatory arms embargo on Israel" such as occurred in the case of South Africa in 1977.

According to a report of journalist Mike Furner, US forces are using the same tactics on the populations of villages such as Abu Siffa in Iraq. A number of critics have said this is no coincidence, since US forces have been borrowing from the Israeli play book, as evidenced graphically in treatment of Iraqi prisoners at Abu Ghraib and other prisons. Several critics have pointed out that the United States violates its own laws by supplying weapons to the Israelis that they use to repress the Palestinians. Mr. Dugard said "it is impossible to accept the Israeli argument that these actions are justified by military necessity." That is a strong objection, because the IDF, a modern national army with modern weapons and an air force, is occupying a would-be Palestinian state that has no armed forces.

The Human Rights Commission conclusion is the strongest UN statement to date on the Israeli dehumanization of the Palestinian people. However, the important part of the statement is Dugard's conclusion that the Israelis have crossed the Rubicon on abuse of the Palestinians and stand in violation of the Geneva Conventions. Unfortunately, the bad practices antedate the Geneva Conventions because the pattern was actually set in 1948 with the massacre and expulsion of Palestinian villagers that resulted in creation of the Rafah refugee camp.

Underlying the problem is a ratcheting process of Israeli actions that slowly tighten Israel's hold on Palestinian territory. Because of settlements, the map of the West Bank and Gaza looks like a piece of Swiss cheese. Despite promises to remove settlements, the area embodied in Israeli settlements grows by accretion. That ratcheting process is a constant source of fear and frustration to the Palestinian people, and some of them fight back.

While the US asked for "clarification" in the Rafah case, no amount of "clarification" will make this kind of wanton destruction acceptable. In truth, no clarification will ever occur. The interplay between the Bush team (and earlier US administrations) and the Israeli leadership is a repetitive strategy, and it works. Because it works so well in the United States, this game gets played over and over. Moreover, because the Israelis have well-honed media support in the United States, they never get blamed. People ignore how much the Israelis offend and provoke the Palestinians and just focus on the Palestinian reaction.

The only time the Israelis even get called on something—ever so politely—is when Israel's behavior gets obviously out of hand, as clearly occurred in the gross destruction of Jenin and the bulldozer attacks that are now rendering thousands homeless in Rafah.

This cumulative pattern of abuse—expulsion from their homes, harassment in their communities, imprisonment, and recognition that there is no intent on the part of Israel ever to make any of it right—is what the Palestinians fight back against. But the US always says the Palestinian response is terrorism.

A double standard applies as well to outside support. The Israelis, and US supporters of Israel object regularly to support of the Palestinians from Saudi Arabia, from Iraq while it was under Saddam Hussein, and from other Arab countries. But the massive aid from the United States that makes the Israeli IDF terror and destruction operations possible is all considered quite proper.

The US is supporting a country that is systematically raping a society. We pretend that is ok, that the Israelis are only defending themselves against terrorists. When put this starkly, the US position on Rafah is easily as reprehensible as that ascribed by Mr. Dugard to the Israelis.

The Bush team approach to world terrorism is a creeping version of this concept of collective guilt and intent to punish that is directed loosely at the whole Muslim world. Attorney General Ashcroft in a press briefing last week reported an al

Qaida threat against the US, a statement of threat that appears to have been based on little hard information. Moreover, he spoke only of Islamic terrorists. He conveyed the view that all Muslims terrorists are affiliated with and guided by al Qaida, which is simply not true. He also ignored the larger terrorism universe in which the majority of terrorists are not Muslims. Nor are they affiliated with al Qaida. In addition, he and other Bush team spokespeople tend to use the terms terrorist, Islamic terrorist, Islamic fundamentalist, and al Qaida interchangeably.

Such statements about world terrorism charge all Muslims and Islam with collective guilt. They purvey a guilt-free versus guilt-ridden distinction between us and Islam that at root is racist. This is a deceptive moral trick. It is a deliberate way to dehumanize an intended enemy. While that may not be the US intent, it is a widespread impression of US intent. In the alliances the US has created with other governments for the war on terrorism, the same concept of collective guilt is being applied against minorities whose members are labeled militants, dissidents, or terrorists. This is a harsh implication of the Bush team assertion: "You are either with us or against us."

The sum of this thinking is powerfully destructive. It provides a constantly repeated cover for Israeli abuse of the Palestinians and their rights. It is now providing a destructive policy framework for US troops in Iraq who are trying to stay on top of a failing occupation. It provides the principal justification for the Bush team War on Terrorism. It feeds the Western belief that we are not only better than others but we are also free to impose our rules on others.

The accusations of collective guilt along with Israeli-style collective punishment are powerful generators of resentment, of sympathy for terrorists, and of recruitment for local terrorist groups and for al Qaida. Those perceptions are widely paired with the realization that very little in fact is being done worldwide to combat the causes of terrorism.

Meanwhile, the US policy of even-handedness shelters the persistent abuses of the Palestinians by the Israelis.

There is a growing worry about where all this leads. In many visible respects the US has adopted a strategy for Iraq that the Israelis have used for fifty years without success. A weird game has developed around which way the road runs between Baghdad and Jerusalem. As Zbigniew Brzezinski sees it in a recent article, "The US occupation of Iraq is now seen by most Arabs as a mirror image of Israel's repression of the Palestinians." Henry Kissinger has said the road actually runs the other way. However, the tragic flaw is not merely in the game plan. That flaw is in the attitudes of the key players toward the people they are allegedly trying to help. There are no superior beings in this picture, only superior egos. That, unfortunately, is what drives the even-handedness policy into the ground in Palestine.

MAKING THE WORLD LESS SAFE FOR AMERICANS
June 2004

Wednesday, June 23, the Congress of the United States passed an incredible resolution. By a vote of 407 to 9, the House passed Concurrent Resolution 460 to give total support to Israel's hard right Likud government's announced intent to annex the great bulk of Palestine and make it part of Israel. The Resolution, which appears to have been passed with little discussion or debate, expressed two main thoughts: It strongly endorses the April 14, 2004 George W. Bush letter to Ariel Sharon that gives US approval to Israeli Likud plans for the West Bank and Gaza. It supports efforts to build Palestinian institutions to fight terrorism that will "prevent the areas from which Israel has withdrawn from posing a threat to the security of Israel."

But the really devastating language of this resolution is in the "whereas" clauses, those statements made to justify the resolution. Those clauses in summary affirm that: President Bush and Ariel Sharon already have made a deal, and that the Palestinians, the United Nations, and all third parties no longer have anything to say on this subject. **"The United**

States will do its utmost to prevent any attempt by anyone to impose any other plan"** (emphasis added).

In light of 'new realities,' mainly because the Israeli settlements exist (they are called 'Israeli population centers' in the Bush letter) they have become part of Israel. The Palestinian refugee issues can be resolved only **"through the establishment of a permanent alternative and the settling of Palestinian refugees there rather than in Israel"**(emphasis added). "The United States remains committed to the security of Israel...and to preserving and strengthening the capability of Israel to deter enemies and defend itself."

Stripped of any polite language, this resolution is a total commitment of the President and the Congress of the United States to the creation of the Zionist dream of a greater Israel. To the Palestinians, this resolution says any territory they retain in this deal will look like a piece of Swiss cheese and include no more than 10% of their ancestral home. Israeli peace activist, Uri Avnery, called this plan "a recipe for continuing the war."

Particularly to Arab states, the resolution is take it or leave it: "All Arab states must oppose terrorism, support emergence of a peaceful and democratic Palestine, and state clearly that they will live in peace with Israel."

Moreover, the resolution leaves no doubt that the United States will continue to arm the Israelis. Arming them also means, as noted in earlier articles, that the United States will continue to look the other way while (contrary to US law) Israeli forces use modern, powerful, US supplied weapons to repress the Palestinian people.

Why would Bush and the Congress do this now? The Bush letter says the Resolution "will enhance the security of Israel and advance the cause of peace in the Middle East." Such an outcome is devoutly to be wished, but the Bush statement is pious nonsense.

In fact, even considering the chaos in Iraq, the Congress of the United States has just codified the most powerful terrorism generator that has come into existence since 9-11. While most signs have been at best ambiguous for several years, this resolution tells the Palestinians that they should abandon hope, recognize that their future will be worse than their past, but that they must fall in line, and cooperate with the inevitable. The prospect this paints for them is that they not only must accept loss of their homes and property, and the end of any prospect for a viable Palestinian state, but they should expect no compensation and they must look elsewhere for a place to live. Not only are Palestinian extremists strengthened by this, but their support bases will grow among the Palestinian people and among other peoples of the region.

On the day before this resolution, it already appeared clear enough that Osama bin Laden was having no problems recruiting new adherents to al Qaida. On the day after, bin Laden is probably ready to thank the Congress for making his job so much easier. What is most striking about the situation is that the Zionists have to know that the risks of Palestinian terrorist attacks, and attacks by sympathizers, will greatly increase.

Perhaps the Zionists are so dedicated to the idea of greater Israel that they do not care. But as several analysts recently have concluded, Sharon could not move ahead with his plans, and he certainly would not receive promised levels of US support if the terrorists stopped attacking.

Probably no members would concede that this resolution makes the President and the Congress of the United States responsible for coming rounds of terrorist violence and military reprisals in Palestine, and attacks on Americans abroad, but that is the simple fact. In a slavish bid for political support in November, both the President and the Congress have bought into Zionist plans. Neither seems aware that polls show the majority of American Jews oppose Sharon's plan but are too intimidated by the Zionists to object. In any case, in order to get themselves elected, Congress and the

President have guaranteed continuing violence in Palestine and they collectively have chosen to make the world less safe for Americans.

AN OUTRAGEOUS INVASION OF AMERICAN DIPLOMACY
October 2004

Last week Congress passed The Global Anti-Semitism Review Act of 2004. To dispel any doubt as to why this was done, President Bush immediately signed it and took his bragging rights on the campaign trail. This legislation requires the United States Department of State to monitor and combat anti-Semitism everywhere in the world (anti-Semitism is not defined in the legislation). The legislation requires creation of a special office in the State Department to oversee such activities and to make an annual report to the Congress. State would also be expected in any country where alleged anti-Semitic acts occurred to "combat" those acts and to publish country "report cards" in a document that is additional to the annual human rights report State already is responsible for publishing.

The legislation was passed over State Department objections as contained in comments of the State Department Spokesman, and in reported memos to the Congress and the White House.

Why this legislation now? This legislation comes at a time when a growing number of Jews take the position that anti-Semitism is not a global problem. The problems are Zionist extremism and the behavior of the state of Israel. As stated in an article this week by Gilad Atzmon, an Israeli: "there is no anti-Semitism any more. In the devastating reality created by the Jewish state, anti-Semitism has been replaced by political reaction."

In a recent writing on the traditional Jewish view, Rabbi Joseph Dershowitz says that the Zionists have "created a pseudo-Judaism which views the essence of our (Jewish) identity to be a secular nationalism." The thrust of these arguments is that (1) Jews and Judaism are not the same thing as the secular state of Israel and (2) the behavior of the secular state is the source of Jewish trouble in the world. Unfortunately, the many Jews who disapprove of what Israel does take the heat along with others.

Below the radar, Israeli leadership, supporters of Israel and pro-Zionist lobbying groups in the United States have worked for years to build a wall around Israeli actions in Palestine. Their principal charge against people who object to Israeli actions is that the critics are "anti-Semitic". The Anti-Defamation League (ADL) makes a continuing effort through a nation-wide program that is reported on the Middle East Forum website called Campus Watch. This site regularly comes down hard on academics who take a critical view of Israel, Zionism or actions against the Palestinians.

The site makes it clear that one aim is to stifle faculty, students, speakers, or groups on campuses who are likely to criticize Israel, to favor the Palestinians, or to make disparaging remarks about Jews or Judaism. A recent example occurred at Duke University in the past few days where an attempt was made to cancel a conference on Palestine. All of those approaches have been aimed at making Israeli treatment of the Palestinian people absolutely disappear from American awareness.

Those efforts have been accompanied by assurances

obtained by Ariel Sharon from George W. Bush, and by assurances obtained by US Jewish community leadership from John Kerry that, whatever the outcome of the election, the President of the United States will totally support Israel.

What is the immediate problem? It is important to note that the current rise in attacks on Jews, Jewish symbols, and Israel coincides in time with the current Palestinian uprising that began in 2000. That event was deliberately provoked by Ariel Sharon's visit to the Temple Mount. The Israelis could not allow a peace process to go forward, and they needed more excuses for continuing to expel Palestinians. The solution was to make Palestinians angry enough to fight back, class those acts as terrorism, and pretend that the Israelis are innocent victims.

Objections to Israeli behavior toward the Palestinians have been a major cause of anti-Jewish actions for more than fifty years. There are many countries where governments or private groups are sympathetic to the Palestinians, or where people simply object to Israeli violations of human rights. Objections to Israeli actions have increased in parallel with growing repression of the Palestinians through targeted assassinations, Israel Defense Force attacks on refugee camps and towns, wanton shootings of unarmed teenagers, conflicts between settlers and displaced Palestinians, destruction of Palestinian orchards and farms, construction of the so-called security fence—in reality a 24-foot high concrete wall whose main effect is to destroy any territorial integrity that remained for a potential Palestinian state and continued repression of Palestinians in Israeli prisons.

Why the apparent sense of urgency? In light of their anticipated increase in expulsions and repression of the Palestinians, Israeli leadership and supporters have every reason to expect that retaliatory attacks of the kinds that already have occurred in various places around the world probably will increase in the future. Thus, the likely purposes of the current legislative and intimidation drives are to head off future criticism by getting any and all complaints about Israeli behavior bundled under the heading of anti-Semitism. By this action, the Israelis hope to retain a claim on the moral high ground that now belongs significantly, albeit not entirely, to Palestinians. Moreover, they want to make every American diplomatic mission defend the high ground for Israel, regardless of who the true victims of repression in the reporting countries may be. The immediate urgency was to use the Jewish vote to assure passage of this bill before the election.

The act tells State to rate governments. The presumption is that any government that cannot account for an act of reported anti-Semitism or cannot control the actions of a dissident group is itself responsible for such action. That is a severe yardstick, one that the Congress or any other American institution would not willingly apply to events in the United States.

How severe is the problem? How much comment on Middle East issues can be defined as anti-Semitism, meaning as actions or statements against Jews or Judaism? The answer to this question is clouded. Blanket assertions by Jewish groups and defenders that all attacks against Jews or symbolic targets are anti-Semitic and unprovoked create an impossible analytical environment. That may indeed be the goal. It would certainly help the Zionists if no questions of Israeli culpability or provocation ever arise.

The reported rationale for the legislation is an asserted "alarming increase in anti-Semitism in several countries." The legislation cited several examples: (a) a speech of Prime Minister Mahathir Mohamad of Malaysia; (b) car bombings outside synagogues in Instanbul, Turkey; © anti-Semitic slogans (unspecified) burned into the lawn of Parliament House in Tasmania; (d) desecration by vandals of gravestones in a Jewish cemetery in Russia; (e) attack on a Jewish school by vandals in Toronto, Canada; and (f) a fire of unknown origin at a synagogue in Toulon, France.

Those incidents are deplorable, but what were the causes? The comments of the Malaysian Prime Minister were on their face provoked by Israeli actions in Palestine, but there is no handy way to know whether the motive for the others were actually anti-Semitism or political objections to Israeli actions. Nor is it possible to determine whether, in a world approaching 6.5 billion people, the present number of incidents is out of proportion with global incidents of vandalism and crimes against persons or property for other minorities or populations.

What is going on here? This legislation is only one piece of a comprehensive thought control process. Part one begins with the canard that Zionist extremists have created about Jews who object to what Israel is doing to Palestinians or what extreme Zionism is actually doing to damage or destroy Judaism. Jews who contemplate or make such objections are called "self-hating" Jews. That is a perverse but no less artful way of killing the messenger: The basic charge is "None of the things you, the self-hater, worry about are true, and you only think them because you hate yourself, or maybe you actually hate Judaism." That charge aims to shame the victim, and informed judgments are that it has silenced numerous potential Jewish critics of Israeli behavior.

The second thought control device concerns the Holocaust. No other event in history is exempt from scrutiny. In this case, however, there is only one version of the experience. To question any piece of the official version evokes a charge of "Holocaust denial". Coming out of the chaos of global war, many details of this experience are likely to be hard to know, but rigorous efforts have been made to keep investigators or interested historians from looking at it. The barriers include laws in such countries as Germany and France that prohibit any revision of the Holocaust story.

In fact, one writer, Ernst Zundel, who was not satisfied with the official version of the Holocaust and, after extensive research said so, has been in prison in Canada for many months, and it is by no means clear that he will ever get a fair hearing. A French critic of the official version of the Holocaust appears on the verge of losing his position as number two in a French political party and his job as a university professor. That is pretty persuasive killing of the messenger.

The third element is thought control on university campuses. Through a combination of legislation and intimidation via Campus Watch, a variously successful effort has been made throughout the United States to prevent detached and scholarly examination or commentaries on the Palestine issues or any other that include criticism of Israel. This was also discussed in the article, "Against the Law to Criticize Israel". The goal is to keep potential messengers nervous and silent on campuses country wide.

The fourth element is the charge of anti-Semitism. Here the effort is to include under the label any statement or action related to Israel, Judaism, Jewishness, or the Holocaust, and to make the entire set of subjects taboo at all levels of discourse. That is the unstated purpose of the legislation passed by Congress last week. The goal is to silence all criticism by anyone, anywhere, particularly of Israeli policy and actions toward Palestinians, through an elaborate construct of the shame sanction, in this case enforced by the United States through the State Department.

What is wrong with such a law? This law is an outrage because it forces the Department of State, perforce the US Government, to bias its reporting of human rights violations by concentrating on alleged anti-Semitism—as State objected in its submission to the Congress—by forcing focus on a single set of events. Americans in general did not seek this law or even know about its consideration. Since the pressure from ADL and other Israel supporting lobbyists who got this law introduced and passed will be to make any attack on Jewish targets or symbols acts of anti-Semitism, there will be no honest reporting on possible violations of religious freedom or human rights. A blanket label of anti-Semitism will foreclose any examination of the reasons for the attacks.

The current Zionist effort is part of a long process going back more than 50 years. The problems actually began with the League of Nations Mandate that required the Jews to achieve a majority in Palestine before the State of Israel could come into being. The only way that could be achieved was to remove the Palestinians and bring in more Jews from outside, because the indigenous Jews numbered only about 50,000 while there were well over a million Palestinians.

That process began in earnest with Jewish terrorists of the Stern and Irgun groups massacring the people of the village of Deir Yassin. Since that time over 400 Palestinian villages have been emptied, razed, or occupied by incoming Jews who became the new Israelis, and the displaced Palestinians have ended up in Gaza or West Bank refugee camps or abroad.

The Zionist party line is that beginning in 1948, without provocation, the Arabs took the position that the Israelis should be driven into the sea, and that all the Israelis have done since has been to defend their rights. However, the expulsion of 750,000 Palestinians from their homes and villages in the late 1940s early 1950s began the Palestinian problem.

The Israelis now say that a two state solution is impossible, and one proof of that is the unwillingness of Israeli settlers–a quarter million strong–to give up their settlements in the West Bank. Settlers appear to be a growing political force in Israeli politics, and their settlements, "promoted and subsidized by the Israeli government", are intended to scuttle the two state solution.

Many Palestinians, and many Jews, do not want a two state solution anyway. They want one state that is open to both. But that conflicts with the Zionist ambition to have an exclusively Jewish state. It is perhaps unfortunate that the idea of a mono-racist, mono-religious state is contrary to the needs of the case, out of step with events and with the leading philosophies of modern states.

What kind of reporting now and in the future? According

to media reports, State took the position in its objections to the new law that the Department is already charged with providing an annual report to the Congress on human rights and religious freedom, and that report requires collecting data and reporting on such actions, no matter who might be the victims. The new law says that State requires the right of Jews who may be the subject of such violations in some countries will be given priority in reporting. The position the legislation presents is that Jews are the most important potential victims of human rights violations in any country. As a matter of policy, not only will the law require State to single out those incidents for special reporting, State officials will also be expected to take action to assure that such incidents are not repeated and the perpetrators are punished.

In short, the actual working of the law, unstated of course, is that on behalf of the Zionists the United States will become the legal defender of Jews who may be the subjects of violent or offensive actions anywhere in the world for any reason. By this action, the US Congress has given Zionists, Jews, or Israel supporters in any country a right to petition the United States for redress of grievances, and the State Department is legally required to respond.

In objecting to this outrageous invasion of American diplomacy, one is at risk of being accused of Holocaust denial and anti-Semitism. That risk is part of the problem, because it is one of the accusations that supporters of this legislation will throw at objectors. On the one hand, one cannot and should not deny the massive human rights crimes that were committed by the Nazis against non-Aryan and non-supportive peoples of Central Europe during latter phases of World War II. But it is only a proper respect for humanity that we establish as accurately as possible the numbers and the racial, ethnic, religious, and national origins of the victims, and the perpetrators, and that we do an honest job of reporting on what we find. At this time, people of the world have neither an accurate nor a complete picture of Nazi crimes, and in the pervasive atmosphere of refusal to look at the entire experience, we are not likely to learn. The parallel of Palestine is more than metaphorical.

What kind of distortions will occur? In a world driven by the self-serving Zionist impulses behind the Global Anti-Semitism Review Act, we are likely to experience the same distortions of truth and perception that perturb history of the Holocaust. Ours is a time when, thanks to the mindset of the Bush administration, our people are overly preoccupied with terrorism and the people who commit acts of terror, and we are designing for ourselves a repeat of the Holocaust distortions. Bush and the neo-cons, aided by supportive media, have singled out Muslims and through careless use of language have brought our people and our government to focus exclusively on Islamic terrorists.

In the process, the Bush administration and cooperative media have committed a thought crime against the whole of Islam. They have simply ignored the fact that most terrorist groups and their causes are not Islamic. Most events are not in Islamic countries, and most of the victims are not Americans. That is a mirror image of Holocaust distortion, and it is the kind of story telling that the law just signed by Bush wants the State Department to indulge in worldwide.

State rightly took the position that such a reporting requirement will take diplomatic eyes off the ball in several ways. First, the human rights problems of countries with dissident elements are caused by governments and elites, and/or by extremists who are tolerated by them. A severe example is now occurring in Darfur. Secondly, under this law, American diplomats will be required to use their assets, their experience, contacts, and sources of influence to pursue charges of anti-Semitism that largely will relate to political objections to Israeli behavior. US diplomatic effectiveness worldwide will be impaired by this requirement, and countless peoples and causes will be done an injustice by it. The quality of American diplomacy, and the credibility and respect for American diplomats will be impaired by it.

State can and should add to its human rights reporting any conclusions, findings, or official comments in reporting countries about how and why the climate for anti-Semitism has changed. That would include observations such as in the 2003 report on France that officials attribute much of the problem to the Israeli-Palestinian situation.

What is a balanced view? It is important to make a distinction between sentiments or actions that are directed on the one hand against Jews as a matter of religion or ethnicity, and on the other hand against the visible manifestations, representatives, and symbols of Israeli policies and actions. An attack on the Israeli Embassy should not be viewed as anti-Semitic any more than an attack on the American Embassy should be viewed as anti-Christian. Israeli policies and actions are a legitimate secular area of potential discussion and disagreement, and they should not be sheltered from public view. They should not be protected from the objections of people who are affected by them or who simply disapprove.

The actions of Palestinians, Iraqis or other peoples who seek to repel and eject invading armies cannot legitimately be classed as terrorism. At the same time though, kidnappings, beheadings, and suicide bombings obviously cross a human rights line no matter how just the cause of the perpetrators may be or who may be the victims.

Protecting the Jews as Jews is not a problem for us. Protecting the Israelis as political actors whose treatment of the Palestinians is reprehensible is entirely another matter. In this light, the White House, the Congress, and the Kerry campaign are on the wrong side of the Israeli political issues; that posture is enormously costly to the United States virtually everywhere in the world.

How can we cope? As the State Department attempts to implement this law, officials can do the principal things required by continuing to report as they do on human rights in every country. Using France and Australia as examples, the 2003 report is indicative of what properly can be done.

Under the heading of freedom of religion, the report includes an enumeration of incidents and descriptions of the perpetrators where known and indications of any actions taken by government to deal with the incidents.

US diplomatic approaches might be appropriate, on behalf of American Jews, to protest a genuinely anti-Semitic incident. However, our diplomats should not fall into the trap of protesting French or any other private reactions to Israeli policies and actions. To protect the integrity of US diplomacy, State has to look behind the reasons for any incident to determine whether the motive of the perpetrator relates to Jewish religion or ethnicity or to Israeli politics. If the root causes are politics, the human rights report should make that clear.

What ultimately is the problem? The root problem here is an improper Israeli/Zionist extremist drive to force the United States to provide political cover for Israeli actions against the Palestinians. This is only a specific application of a much larger abuse of the American system. As stated by Alfred M. Lilienthal more than two decades ago, Americans really need to look at what is going on here. According to Lilienthal who took up this cudgel initially with his 1953 book What Price Israel:

"Our system of representative government has been profoundly affected by the growing influence and affluence of minority pressure groups, whose strength invariably increases as presidential elections approach. This makes it virtually impossible to formulate foreign policy in the American national interest.

This explains why the politicians have been mesmerized by fear of the "Jewish vote" in a hotly contested state. The inordinate Israelist influence over the White House, the Congress and other elected officials, stems from this ability to pander bloc votes. Few Jews appreciate the methodology employed by the powerful Zionist lobby in Washington to keep the politicians in line. It's not exactly pretty, and even in the declining morality of our day, I am certain that many would be revolted by what is done in their name to help the Middle East's "bastion of democracy."

That appraisal is excerpted from a much broader critical statement made by Lilienthal in 1981. Zionist manipulation of our leadership and our policies is far worse and even more open than it was two decades ago. Lilienthal's book and later writings on the subject earned him the Zionist epithet, "self-hating Jew". He was thoroughly castigated by Zionists and other Israel supporters for his views, but all Americans should take his words to heart and seriously fight back.

What must be done? Congress and the President have made it clear to the whole world that on any matters pertaining to the Middle East they are catering to Israel. They are prepared to buy votes and other political favors by protecting Israel from the consequences of continuing repression of the Palestinian people. In this instance they have enacted a law that provides American political cover for ongoing Israeli violations of human rights.

The law is an outrageous Zionist interference in American diplomacy and in the internal affairs of the United States. It should never have been enacted. It should not be applied. To protect our diplomats and our reputation abroad, The Global Anti-Semitism Review Act of 2004 should be repealed at the earliest possible moment.

For all reported cases, our diplomats should observe and report as required for the annual report on human rights. Americans should be diligent about dealing with any actual cases of anti-Semitism in the United States. However, the Israelis have their own Embassies. Let them explain themselves and fight their own battles. Hopefully they will listen, learn, and moderate their own behavior.

PART FOUR
IRAQ- INVASION AND OCCUPATION

IRAQ—THE CASE IS STILL NOT MADE
September 2002

Since President Bush addressed the UN General Assembly last week, Washington has descended into a swamp of confusion; misinformation and hard-headed opinion peddling that should scare Americans a great deal more than Iraq. It should be deeply disturbing to us that not a single new piece of information about Iraq has appeared in months. But if you take your cue from the noise level, you would think that Saddam Hussein controls a large meteor that is headed dead on for mid USA, and we must act strongly and right now to head it off. The known facts plainly do not support this judgment, but what are the facts?

Eleven years ago the United States led a coalition war to stop the Hussein expansionist scheme to control the Persian Gulf. That engagement was both short and successful in that allied forces quickly routed Iraqi troops and destroyed much of the Iraqi war-making capability. In succeeding years, UN inspectors discovered and destroyed significant parts of the war-making machinery our forces had failed to uncover during the Gulf War. Thus, when UN Inspectors left Iraq in 1998, there were still questions, but it was clear that Iraqi capabilities were a mere shadow of their former scope and power.

Those capabilities were by no means eliminated, and there is no doubt that Saddam has worked steadily to rebuild them. Moreover, studying the limitations of long supply lines and slow replacement schedules that cost him dearly during the war, Saddam set out to become self-sufficient in as many areas of armament—munitions, weapons and missiles—as his industry could achieve. That effort has given him more autonomy than he had a decade ago, but the best estimates available indicate that he is far below his pre-Gulf War strength in any area of military capability. Even at that, he may have achieved greater staying power by making his military industries more self-sufficient.

One must search carefully here for what is really new and newly frightening about Iraq. The answer is nothing. At the end of the Gulf War, we already knew pretty well what he was up to in the effort to acquire or make WMDs. Under UN auspices a great deal was done to slow those efforts and to derail them. Saddam did not stop trying. In such areas as Scud missile engines, tank guns and artillery he learned to make his own. Former UN inspectors assert regularly that he was not that successful in concocting WMDs, and he did not succeed in solving the problem of how to refine weapons grade nuclear materials.

That does not mean he could not have acquired weapons grade material for one or more weapons, or even one or more complete weapons. The accounting for former Soviet/now Russian weapons and materials is by no means reassuring. Even senior officials who had control, such as general Alexander Lebed, have expressed doubts that all are accounted for, and not too far back five kilograms of plutonium (enough to make at least one weapon) were discovered in the trunk of a Mercedes in Germany. That material could have been of interest to several countries. Iraq poses no unique WMD threat.

Just what is a threat? As defined by serious professionals, a threat is a capability to do harm that is combined with the intent to do harm. The capability itself is a risk, but the intent to use it is required to make a threat. As an example, we have more nuclear weapons than the rest of the world powers combined. They are not a threat, unless we decide to use them. As a second example, Americans own about 40 million shotguns. If the shotguns are a threat, then we are in deep trouble, because one person out of every six or so has one. But they become a threat only when someone is on the warpath, or possibly in the hands of a militia on the march. As a specific case, if possession alone of nuclear weapons and other WMDs by a Middle East power is a threat to the United States, then Israel is a major threat, because the Israelis have around 200 actual nuclear weapons and unclear numbers of chemical/biological weapons.

By the above definition, Bush has only half of a threat statement. We do know, at least we are told, that Saddam is trying to build or obtain weapons of mass destruction. In that search, he is a member of a fairly large club of 20 or more countries. But even if he already had WMDs, there is no evidence that he has the capacity to deliver them against the US. His missile program, while impressive, could not yet produce an ICBM. Although he had biological and chemical agents, he apparently had neither the capability of weaponizing them successfully nor of delivering them across thousands of miles. In short, he had nothing to threaten the US with, had he chosen to do so.

In any case, he has not threatened to use any weapon on the US. The most widely held view of the situation is that if he used such a weapon on the US, or on Israel for that matter, he would be obliterated. No one has suggested that Saddam has a death wish. I don't know where Chicken Little is today, but the cry sounds very familiar.

The bottom line: Iraq is part of a global problem of policing the capabilities and the behavior of nation states, some with extra-territorial ambitions. As noted above, there are twenty or more nation states trying to acquire weapons of mass destruction. Most seek such weapons to dominate or deter the actions of a neighbor, e.g., India and/or Pakistan, or as trappings of the power of autocratic leaders, e.g., pick pretty much any of the group. Over time, any of these may need to be reined in, moderated or even de-fanged by the UN and the leading world powers.

The clarity of this situation leads many observers to suspect that the group around Bush had a hidden agenda respecting Iraq. But if their objective is improved access to Iraqi oil, that problem can be solved when necessary by agreement among UN members to lift sanctions. If the objective is US company control over Iraqi oil, then it is too bad that the key players in Washington (from the President and the two think tanks involved down to the Undersecretary of Defense) are oil industry insiders. Maybe the national interest coincides with the interests of that group, but don't count on it.

Certainly, the US Congress should ask more questions than it has to date about the Bush agenda. And Congress should get better answers than Bush or his core team have provided to date before approving of any program for Iraqi regime change. They should be very wary of any program that would put US troops on the ground and in jeopardy.

SADDAM'S DILEMMA—HOW TO PROVE A NEGATIVE
December 2002

The latest threat from the Bush administration, articulated by the President himself, is that by Sunday, December 8, Saddam must produce 'credible' proof that he has no WMDs or face likely US attack. With that, Saddam Hussein faces probably the toughest challenge of his long and bloody career: How to prove that he has not done or does not have something. The only thing he has going for him may be the conventional wisdom that proving a negative is impossible. But the choice confronting Saddam is tough, because he faces a US President who chooses to put aside the norms of American justice and apply the Code Napoleon.

Under the Napoleonic Code, brought to Louisiana by the French, Bush does not have to prove Saddam is guilty. Saddam has to prove his innocence in a court that is predisposed not to believe anything he says. The Bush test is that the proof must be 'credible' to him. In short, the proof of nothing must meet a subjective standard of evidence that is likely to be revealed only after the fact by the President either backing off or, possibly, beginning the war without saying anything.

One can assume that Saddam Hussein, being a man of proven shrewdness, will give this his best shot. His life may depend upon it. Openness and candor may not be his strongest suits. But survival is. His ability to come out of the Gulf War, not only in one piece but with many of his capabilities intact or restorable, was a remarkable piece of footwork. However, his ability to do that depended on the fact that the Gulf War Coalition members lacked common goals, had no agreed game plan, were short of reliable intelligence, and made some bad decisions, e.g., letting the Iraqis keep their helicopters. Moreover, Coalition members sought post war futures that did not require Saddam's departure. If he can just figure out how to deal with the United States, Saddam's present situation is not radically different.

While it may not look that way from Pennsylvania Avenue, Saddam has played his side of the game very well. That doesn't mean he has 'fessed up as repeatedly asked. It means he patiently has used a mix of UN procedure, international misgivings, and homegrown devices to stay out of the crosshairs. Most governments do not see any need for a war with him: Saddam has merely had to watch as those governments nudged the issue into UN channels where it played out basically in line with his needs.

Bush did most of the work by threatening a pre-emptive strike and regime change, both of which disturbed even people who avidly dislike Saddam. In the meantime, Saddam did not threaten. Most of the bluster came from his subordinates. He timed his response to UN Resolution 1441 skillfully to maximize US official bluster, which further frayed the nerves of other governments. His production of a 60-plus page reply to the UN in Arabic was mostly for show, because the only words that could have mattered to the US were: "Yes, I have the following listed weapons", or something like that. "No" was not an option in the US lexicon.

Saddam is getting a fair amount of help from others to defer personal proof of the negative. Most of the world is skeptical of this whole venture, and the order of proof is not rigorous for most. The UN clearly wants to see the inspection process reinitiated by Resolution 1441 played out in a respectable manner. Governments opposed to war with Iraq, including France, Germany, and Russia, favor that outcome. For that to occur, the UN inspection teams must do their work in an orderly and methodical manner, because questionable procedure will backfire.

To flit about trying to surprise the Iraqis is not only irritating to Iraqis, it risks hasty and sloppy work that will not pass muster. White House impatience aside, the best result for all parties is a thorough and unchallengeable inspection, whatever it uncovers. That process takes time. So far, stretching things out has served Saddam well, and it may have served Bush better than he knows.

At this point, Saddam's options for proving the negative are clearly defined. He has been a crafty cat to herd, but he did agree to the conditions of Resolution 1441, and that limits his choices. The first test was cooperating with the inspectors, and there have been no problems so far. The second real test will come December 8, when he is required under the resolution to declare whatever is there in the way of programs, materials, or products for weapons of mass destruction.

He said Tuesday that he will report on December 7. That implies he is confident that the inspectors will find nothing because there was never anything there or because he has destroyed, hidden, sold or given away everything incriminating. If that proves to be the case, and the UN inspection teams are unable to contradict him with solid evidence to the contrary, then the game is over. So far as most people are concerned, the negative will have been proven.

What constitutes adequate evidence to start a war? That is a tricky question. In the past few days, inspectors found a few artillery shells containing a chemical agent. They had inspected these shells in their present location in 1998, but had not destroyed them. Do they count now toward a make-war bill of particulars? The UN resolution does not read that way. In principle, if Saddam has materials, capabilities, weapons, or delivery systems that he accurately declares on Saturday, he has complied with the resolution. If he does not make such a declaration, he must present proof of the negative.

Saddam may be confident that the inspectors will prove a sufficient negative, or that he has nothing to declare that is worth going to war over, but his worst nightmare has to be that someone or some group that hates him will plant a false flag piece of evidence. As US forces learned in the Gulf War, Iraq has a large and empty desert where it is easy to hide things. At least a few governments and a number of ethnic or tribal groups might plant evidence.

A plant of false evidence would play to the Bush team, because it is leaning forward so far that the team might not look closely enough at the evidence to discover the falsehood. Saddam's deficiencies are well known and not in dispute, but any evidence must be carefully gathered and validated to avoid any possibility of such trickery. This reinforces the need for a careful and complete inspection. It would be grim irony to fight a war that is not needed against an enemy who is not guilty.

WHY SHOULD WE FIGHT IRAQ?
February 2003

As international disagreement grows over any decision to invade Iraq, the United States is increasingly isolated on the issue. Moreover, as recent demonstrations indicate, opposition to the war is growing even in the United States where, at the beginning, President George W. Bush had substantial support. If the war had been fought immediately after 9-11, while public furor over those attacks was high, the Bush team might have pulled it off. However, as more than a year has passed, the flaws in the Bush case against Iraq have multiplied, and an awkward lack of integrity has emerged in case building, as Secretary of State Colin Powell learned when materials provided by the British Government were found to be bogus. Lack of official clarity and the passage of time have given critics the opportunity to examine many scenarios for war, but none so far is persuasive.

Numerous writers say that key members of the Bush team—Cheney, Rumsfeld, Wolfowitz, Feith, Bolton, and Perle (the only one outside government but closely linked through the Defense Policy Board)—were planning war on

Iraq before Bush entered office. Given their earlier writings and affiliations, that is highly probable. Immediately after 9-11, the war on Iraq took increasing precedence over the War on Terrorism, probably because some understood that the War on Terrorism is not winnable. Rather the focus turned to a pre-emptive strike to strip Saddam of his alleged weapons of mass destruction and to break up his alleged ties to al Qaida.

Neither of those reasons has survived close international scrutiny because UN weapons inspections so far show that Saddam has less of anything in the WMD line now than he may have had before the first Gulf War. Moreover, the link to al Qaida, still asserted by US officials, has yet to be proven. Maybe Saddam will oblige the US by having something that can be construed as a material breach of UN Resolution 1441, but he has been successful so far in retreating just ahead of the inspectors and staying out of range.

The second rationale for war on Iraq many critics say is oil. That argument has certain appeal because it at least brings an element of genuine pragmatism onto the table. Since we use about one barrel in every four produced globally, we obviously need oil. However, we have taken the lead in sanctions against Iraq that have limited Iraqi oil exports, and we have done that without harm to ourselves.

As the world's largest user of oil, we do not need to own the sources to command market attention; product prices are typically a good deal lower in the United States than they are in any other developed country. We get hit by lower taxes, but we pay the same import prices. Thus, fighting a war to get products that typically flow to us in any orderly market would not be rational. That fact may not keep some members of the Bush team from eyeing the Iraqi wellheads with envy, but that kind of lust does not translate into the national interest.

A third justification for war on Iraq is often cited by President Bush: To create a democratic government in Iraq and hopefully start a democratic transformation in the region. For that to work at all, however, thoughtful observers of Iraq have suggested that the present country should be turned into two or three. One of those countries could be the area now actually ruled by Saddam—the territory not covered by so-called "No Fly Zones"—meaning the area of his secular governance. The southern No Fly Zone could become a country for the Shi'a Muslims, assuming they do not wish to join Iran. The third country would be nominally the northern No Fly Zone, that area of Iraq that is a piece of ancient Kurdistan, along with parts of Syria, Turkey, Armenia, and Iran.

In effect, colonial era state building created an ethnic, cultural, and religious mess that is unlikely to respond in any short period to democratizing, and none of the countries involved want to give up territory. However well intentioned, Bush may not have enough time or shovels to clean out this stable. Meanwhile, democratic consensus building is arrested, to say the least, in all of the countries involved, and no outsider is likely to fix it.

A fourth rationale for war on Iraq that is increasingly discussed on the Internet is to do a piece of national security work for Israel. How will the Israelis benefit from a war on Iraq? To answer the question, one must have an understanding of the Zionist dream for Israel and the obstacles the Israelis have encountered in bringing the dream about.

A human obstacle, set in the Balfour Declaration that initiated creation of Israel, was a requirement that the rights of the Palestinians be protected. That dictum interfered with the Zionist ideal of a Jewish National Home. Palestinian discovery that the Zionists had no intention of observing the Balfour dictum, generated the second obstacle, because that perception, reinforced by repeated Israeli attacks on villages and expulsions of Palestinians, led to hostility and open warfare.

The largest and most persistent obstacle emerged with the annexation of the West Bank by King Abdullah of Jordan and of the Gaza Strip by Egypt in the 1948 war. Under the original UN partition scheme, those areas would have become part of Israel, and in line with the Balfour Declaration the Palestinians who lived there at the time had a right to remain there, just as those in the coastal regions had that right. Israel retook this territory in the 1967 War. However, by that time the land was occupied not only by Palestinians whose families had lived there for centuries, but also by refugees expelled from other areas of Israel. The so-called "Green Line" boundaries that nominally demarcate Israeli and Palestinian territory were established in the 1949 Armistice agreements.

Incremental accretions of this territory to Israel are being attempted with Jewish settlements, mostly with Jews brought from outside Israel. Despite the settlement activity, the West Bank and Gaza are still the home of 3 million Palestinians.

As Zionist hard liners and some more moderate Israelis see it, the main obstacle to achieving a Jewish National Home as originally conceived is the presence of Palestinians, in Israel, in Gaza, and in the West Bank. The Jewish National Home the Zionists have in mind extends from the Jordan River to the Mediterranean.

What does this have to do with a war on Iraq? It might be said that since Iraq never agreed to a truce with Israel at the end of the Arab/Israeli war of 1948, the two could be considered still at war. However, there are two more direct answers. One is about power politics. To carry out the program they had in mind, the Zionists needed a military arm. Initially that consisted of two terrorist groups, the Stern and Irgun groups whose early achievements were brutal attacks on Palestinian villages and the ultimate expulsion of the British from Palestine.

Over time, these capabilities evolved into the IDF. Israeli leadership knew from the start that their creation of the IDF was an attractive nuisance to other countries of the region, but remarkably only one country rose to challenge Israeli regional military dominance: Iraq under Saddam Hussein.

Israel also set out to acquire and now has nuclear weapons. Here again, the Israelis have tried to assure dominance. To that end, they carried out an attack on Iraq to destroy that country's reactor, thereby delaying if not actually frustrating Iraqi acquisition of nuclear weapons.

Despite Israeli success on that front, however, and despite the setbacks Saddam has experienced since loss of the Gulf War, Israel still considers Iraq a threat, because Saddam has the resources and the will to compete for regional power. That threat is increased by continued Israeli repression of the Palestinians, because Saddam is known to assist the Palestinian cause, mostly with money.

Another answer to why the Zionist hard liners want a war with Iraq concerns what some Israelis refer to as the "vexing demographic" of the Palestinians. As discussed in the article "The Challenges of Ethnic Cleansing in Israel", there are upward of 4 million Palestinians in Israel, the West Bank and Gaza, and at observed rates of increase the Palestinians eventually will outnumber the Jews. For the Zionists, that is an intolerable condition for the Jewish National Home. Since the Palestinians have shown for years that even under repressive conditions they will not leave voluntarily, the only answers are to learn to live with them, give the Palestinians their state, or expel them.

Zionists want to expel the Palestinians, and war with Iraq would provide the opportunity. For decades, going back virtually to the birth of Israel, the dream of the hard liners has been that a war will break out in the region and provide cover for expelling the Palestinians. While in normal times world opinion would rebel at the thought of expulsion of the Palestinians, the hope is that no one of importance would notice systematic expulsions under cover of a regional war.

US leadership fought hard during the first Gulf War to keep the Israelis out of it because Israeli entry would have destroyed the coalition of Gulf states that supported war against Iraq. The same problem exists now, so the US is likely to insist that Israel abstain from any second Gulf War. However, given the all too polite US criticism of harsh Israeli attacks and repression of the Palestinians in the name of a War on Terrorism, the Israelis might gamble that no one, especially not the United States, would object if the Palestinians were forced into Jordan at the height of attacks on Iraq. By the time that war ended, Israel would have its National Home, and we, with Jordan and the UN, would inherit 3 million, maybe 4 million refugees; as the French say, a fait accompli.

Under this scenario, as a result of its war on Iraq the United States will have inherited management of two large ethnic and cultural nightmares: the Kurds who would not wish to join any Iraqi government, and the Palestinians who would be out in the cold. In essence, the United States would take over two refugee problems, neither of which regional powers have shown any willingness to solve on their own, and the US could solve them, at best over a long time, only by going head to head with the several regional powers involved on matters of policy, governance, and national territory.

Assessed in this manner, a war on Iraq looks like a bad foreign policy investment for the United States, no matter who joins the coalition. We would make enemies of a billion Muslims, most of whom are at least neutral toward us now. We would trample on long-standing alliances with European nations, and convince many others that we have abandoned our democratic values. We would inherit by default two intractable sets of refugee problems, and we would have taken on unilaterally the adjustments to nation states that likely are needed to make any peaceful future work. We could end up doing all of that for the dubious reward of making Israel the unchallenged power in the Middle East, and we would have facilitated the largest of the humanitarian crimes the Israelis will have committed against the Palestinian people.

Meanwhile, Sharon told a visiting US Congressional delegation in Israel this week that after Iraq he wants Iran, Libya, and Syria disarmed next. He appeared confident he could get the US to do it. That would make four countries whose leaders we will have overthrown, even though they are not threatening us. Then the Zionists could think about expanding into Jordan, looking for land and water, and expelling the Palestinians to where? How about Saudi Arabia and Egypt, or even Iraq, since the new Israel would be Iraq's neighbor?

Why doesn't George W. Bush just tell Cheney, Wolfowitz, Perle, Feith, Bolton, and other strong Iraq war supporters in his administration that this game is not in the US interest? Most of our friends and allies and many of the world's Jews would applaud that decision, despite the screams Bush surely would hear from the Zionist lobbies. Some argue that losing face would keep Bush from backing away from war on Iraq, but how could he lose face at the same time so many people will applaud his good judgment?

DEMOCRACY ON TRIAL IN IRAQ
May 2003

How do you transform a society that has been under the rigid control of a tyrant for decades? How do you get people who are ethnically, culturally, and theologically fragmented to head in the same direction to build a unified state? Who has the final say in the outcome? Will any or all of them be content with the outcome? Who is available to guide this process? What do the guides themselves want? Will any system the guides impose be enduring? What happens if the guides give up in disgust and leave? What happens if their guidance is rejected and they are asked to leave?

Baghdad is a uniquely interesting place to seek the answers to such questions, because it has been a power center of varying importance for three thousand years. It is in the territory of Biblical Nineveh, and boosters say that somewhere there was the Garden of Eden. This is not impossible, given that the human history of this region goes back thousands of years before Baghdad. Iraq has been in the middle of the road for millennia for reasons of location and endowment. It was a way station on ancient trade routes that slowly tied Asia, the

Middle East, Europe, and North Africa together in patterns of commerce. But more important it possesses two of the great rivers of the Middle East, the Tigris and the Euphrates, known locally as the Dijlis and the Furat.

With that illustrious past Iraq never has enjoyed a singular culture, a society with common values and goals. In fact, Iraq as now bounded did not even exist until the British cobbled it together in the early 1920s out of Kurdish, Turkomen, Arab, Iranian and other tribes who happened to have occupied their parts of the present Iraqi space for centuries without getting together.

A succession of leaders of modern Iraq struggled with those disparities in their human landscape. In the past 100 years, the country has been ruled as part of the Ottoman Empire, as part of the British Empire, as a monarchy, as a republic, and under Saddam Hussein as a brutal autocracy. Bloodletting has been a common feature of the political landscape, and while conspiracy was not invented here, it was certainly refined.

Aside from the persistent problems of political confusion and external domination that have plagued Iraq, the most persistent drag on human development has been scarcity. Scarcity of food, shelter, health care, safety, raw materials, and opportunity cause the ethnic, cultural, and religious groups to circle their wagons and depend on strong internal loyalties and relationships. Saddam's rule made these tendencies even more pronounced and part of any exultation from his fall is due to release from the severe hardships his rule imposed.

However, much of the fear and uncertainty that now pervades Iraq stem from the other scarcities that still dominate, and cause the Iraqi people to depend on imports for much of everything they need except oil. Unless these scarcities can be overcome, the chances of creating sound and solid relations among Iraq's main groups will be limited.

It is worth recalling here that much was done in the late 1940s and 1950s to initiate the modernization of Iraq.

During the last days of the British sponsored monarchy, an Iraq Development Board (IDB) was created and undertook major projects including flood control/ water management for both the Tigris and the Euphrates rivers and the development of a national power grid, a highway system, and a modernized national railroad. These projects were of great long term significance, but many common people felt the projects benefited mainly the tribal and political elites, and they objected because the projects yielded little immediate improvement in the quality of life for Iraq's impoverished masses. This popular dissatisfaction contributed to the overthrow of the monarchy and the launching of political events that led to the takeover by Saddam Hussein. He may have turned the system's energies to creating palaces and monuments, but much of IDB infrastructure remained, at least until the 2003 US/British invasion.

In this setting, the problem is not what form of government to install in Iraq but how to get the majority of people in Iraq to sign on to a consensus. The solution to that problem is not likely to be a democracy with majority rule, but a hierarchy of tribal, ethnic and religious leaders who effectively represent their own constituencies. They will have to reach agreement on protecting each other's free space and on exploiting the benefits of modern technology for the society as a whole. Those leaders have to be chosen by their own communities by a process acceptable to that community. The Iraqi Shi'a are certainly the largest group and have a narrow statistical majority. Indications are however that if they were to obtain political control of the place their decisions could be a serious backward step causing Iraq to descend into the anarchy that bedevils much of its history.

There are specific risks in this situation for the United States. One of those risks lies with the fact that our democracy is faltering in important respects. Two criticisms are immediately manifest. One concerns the surge in political power of the Protestant religious conservatives whose views on Islam are jaundiced to say the least. At home their effort to push the nation toward compliance with fundamentalist Christian beliefs is a problem, especially for a society as diverse as American society now is. But more than that, it is a bad example for Islamic societies.

The second criticism concerns the power of the political, media, and economic elites whose icons regularly rotate among each other's chairs and missions and whose actions largely ignore the will or the interests of the American people. If representatives of these leadership groups are allowed to dominate US decision-making on the political future of Iraq, then Iraqis will once again face the reality of domination by outsiders. US-led occupation will drive severe militant and insurgent activity against the Coalition.

The model of American democracy, as defined by critics, exports reasonably well to the extent that most other countries are ruled by established elites who know how to work the system. However, the pure form that is being talked about for Iraq does not fit the Iraqi case and almost certainly would not work even in the United States. There are several reasons for this. One vital precept of our democracy is majority rule, and our founding fathers were well aware that it would not serve us, as indicated in their crafting of the tripartite system of checks and balances and the Bill of Rights.

Moreover, as our society has diversified, we have had to find satisfactory ways to amend and limit the system conveyed by our founding fathers to properly reflect the rights and interests of a growing pool of minorities. We have come a long way in that process, even though some minorities would argue that we are still not there in terms of equality of representation and participation.

The clear danger in Iraq is that an idealized or even ideological concept of American democracy, based on majority rule, will backfire. To start with, the Shi'a majority ethnically is a mix of Arabs, Kurds, and Iranians. The Sunnis, the second largest group, are split between Kurds and Arabs. Turkomen, many of them Muslims and Assyrians who are mainly Christian, plus a few others make up the rest. Rather than serving to bring people together, it has served to keep them apart politically. Moreover, tribalism and ethnicity appear to have mattered at least as much as religion. However, the adoption of majority rule on a national level could cause the Shi'a to come together on religious grounds, creating a situation in which an internal majority of conservative Shi'a could drive the larger Shi'a community toward fundamentalism. That outcome would cause many modernizing and westernizing attributes that began much before the Saddam era to be lost or repressed.

Meanwhile, the 35 years of Saddam's dominant role in Iraqi affairs, and a century of exposure to the rest of the world, have generated a sizeable middle class and secular element in many areas of Iraqi society. Ironically, Saddam himself promoted a secular leadership class, but its power in a political process has not been tested due to the repressive weight of Saddam's rule. Moreover, women, who prospered in many areas under Saddam's rule, could conceivably have a key role in making the secular element dominant in an electoral process. If that were to occur, and various religious, ethnic, and tribal clusters could be assured of their free space, a new era could truly be launched in Iraqi political life.

Whatever the outcome, the decisions on how they will be governed and by whom must be made by Iraqis. Developments since World War I and the emergence of Iraqi nationalism have begun to turn a fragmented collection of people into a nation. Instead of identifying with their cities of origin as in the past, Iraqis generally identify themselves today as Iraqis. For this purpose putting aside antecedent tribal, ethnic, and religious differences, Iraqis have agreed on only one abiding goal: to get rid of foreign domination.

Objections to rule by the Coalition are already widespread and obvious. The way to harness that energy in rebuilding Iraq is to show that Coalition leaders understand the situation, but also that the sooner the Iraqis can agree on a suitable representative form of government the quicker the Coalition will withdraw. The US should also recognize that it could greatly enhance the credibility of the process and its chances for success if, at the earliest feasible moment, the Coalition were to hand electoral oversight authority over to the United Nations.

IRAQ—DEALING WITH SADDAM'S LEGACIES
May 2003

While American television audiences watch the gleeful destruction of Saddam Hussein statues and the willful looting of anything that is not nailed down in government, academic, and leadership buildings and residences, war continues to rage in many pockets of Baghdad. Officially, Baghdad has fallen because no one appears to be in charge, but Coalition troops do not dare turn their backs on buildings, side streets, and byways that are not under their immediate control. According to observers on the scene, uncertainty and risk prevail in much of Baghdad and Iraq outside the areas under Coalition control, and outside those areas the Iraqi people remain fearful.

Iraqis have several worries that so far do not appear to have penetrated Coalition pre-conceptions: What will happen to us when the lid Saddam imposed is lifted from traditional patterns of conflict among major groups, e.g., Shi'a, Sunni, and Kurdish clans and families? Saddam was brutal, and he may have improved on them, but he did not invent any of the extremes that some Iraqis had visited on others for generations. Keeping that lid on by reserving the uses of violence mainly to himself was one of Saddam's legacies, but there are other regressions Iraqis may fear.

The US media picture of life under Saddam has been narrowly focused on issues related to the Bush team justifications for war. That picture displays an Iraq that is cowed by Saddam's brutality, victimized by his large and small tyrannies, limited by his egocentric behavior, rendered threatening by possible weapons of mass destruction, and destabilized by the desire of many people to get out from under his rule. Like any other black and white picture, much is left out, including all of the color. Just what did Saddam do to Iraq, and what is he leaving behind?

While we focused on Saddam's dictatorial and repressive actions, in his two decades plus of power he almost brought Iraq into the 21st century. He was a secular leader who lived well himself, moving as he wished among palatial homes around the country, but he also used oil money to develop the only really secular society in Islam, and he further developed the largest middle class in the region. He provided free education, clean water, an advanced medical services system, and a food distribution system that the United Nations Food and Agriculture Organization called "a model of efficiency". In the shadow of repressive and largely male sexist practices toward women elsewhere in the region, the Iraqi women were liberated, many holding prized and important jobs in government.

The flaw in all those achievements, except possibly the public administration ones, is that Saddam achieved his social advances not by modernizing Sunni, Shi'a, and Kurdish habits and attitudes but by suppressing opposition to those steps. Shi'a and Sunni clerics and followers could object at their peril to the liberation of women, the adoption of secular government, the almost gleeful import of advanced technologies, and such other Islamic anathemas as imbibing alcoholic beverages. Saddam also suppressed vocal and/or violent expressions of the differences among Sunni, Shi'a, and Kurds, and other clan differences in Iraq. He came as close as any leader in the region to achieving a modern state. There were many flaws in the infrastructure; Iraq was not yet a modern economic state, but the main flaw may have been that it was uniquely Saddam's toy.

Coalition forces, for whatever reasons, did not understand and plan for the kinds of situations that would exist when Saddam's authority collapsed. Similar failures occurred in Serbia and Kosovo when US and other peacekeeping forces failed to see the need to immediately transform their mission from military roles to civil law enforcement ones. The irony of that failure in Iraq during the past ten days is that since Baghdad and other Iraqi cities were occupied by Coalition forces the infrastructure of those cities has been vandalized and looted. A largely modern system of government operations and public services has been destroyed.

Only now do Coalition forces seem to have grasped the fact that an immediate switch to law enforcement was essential. That realization may be too late because the damage to public services already has been done, and those systems must now be rebuilt at large costs of time, money, inconvenience, and delay in restoring the viability of Iraq's economy. The Saddam legacies that could have been a boon to postwar administrators must be recreated mainly because of a hiatus of good sense, good planning and common sense governance on the part of Coalition leadership, a condition fostered by exaggerated, over-riding Washington control. Because of those failures, there are simply not enough experienced Iraqi and other experts in law enforcement, public administration, utilities management and other key areas of governance in place. Until those gaps are filled, conditions in Iraq can be expected further to deteriorate.

The promised transition to a democratic Iraq will be rendered infinitely more difficult by the patterns of chaos that have been allowed to prevail for several days in much of the country. But the technical problems are not likely to be as serious as the human ones. Herein lies Saddam's final legacy. To the extent that peace existed under Saddam among the contending Sunni, Shi'a, and Kurdish factions, and throughout Iraq, that peace was enforced by Saddam's police, not by mutual consent. How much rancor, suspicion, anger, grievance, and hatred may now emerge remains to be seen. It could be that everybody learned something from the Saddam era experience. However, it is most likely that given a choice, the essence of a democratic system, each group will revert to its historic habits. Assassination of two leading Shi'a clerics in Najaf in the past few days may be the bellwether of some very bad times.

Any occupying power could expect difficult times with the Iraqi situation. However, for the US, with an announced plan to impose if not inspire democracy, the hurdle can be even higher. In any democratic model each power group will expect considerable autonomy in selection of leadership and in pursuing basically self-interested goals. If granted fully, such autonomy could turn Iraq into at least three countries, as many experts have already noted. This could also create/exacerbate underlying international problems in Turkey, Syria and surroundings. However, to avoid conflict, certain categories of religious, ethnic, and cultural conflict may have to be ruled out from the beginning, forcibly if necessary. Saddam, behaving at times like an occupying power, recognized this from the beginning and obviously did not flinch. In the end, an American or Coalition administrator may have little choice but to be about equally forceful.

The solution here is to give the chief peacekeeping mission to the UN and to create a genuine UN command. With the onus of its actions over the past several months, including actual conduct of the Iraq war, already on the table, a bad Iraqi occupation experience can turn the US into a total pariah, literally making a US administrator the successor to Saddam. Despite the obvious temptation of the oil barons in and around the Bush team, a bad occupation experience is not in the US interest.

Given the visible facts of the situation, the US should distance itself as quickly as possible, and so should Britain, from any long-term occupation or Iraqi recovery management role. Despite the harm the US and Britain have done to the credibility of the UN system, the UN is still the only organization with enough integrity, detachment, and patience to carry out what will need to be done in Iraq to retain the good and erase the bad features of Saddam's legacy.

REFORMING THE MAJLIS—
IRAQ'S NATIONAL ASSEMBLY
May 2003

Reports indicate that the Iraqi people grow more restive every day under Coalition management. The handwriting is also on the wall that decisive actions on several critical issues such as food supplies, housing, jobs, restoration of public services, and assured public safety must occur with a speed and precision that so far has been lacking. The new US civil administrator, former Ambassador L. Paul Bremer, and his team have been in the region only a couple of weeks, but they already must know that what awaits them in terms of restoring and refining Iraq's operating system is a daunting task.

At the same time, there are dark political clouds on the Iraqi horizon as groups maneuver for positions in any new framework of governance. Indicative of the seriousness of that process, Ayatollah Mohammed Baqer al-Hakim, leader of the main Shiite faction in Iraq and head of the Supreme Assembly of the Islamic Revolution in Iraq (SAIRI), upon his return from 23 years of exile in Iran, threw down his faction's gauntlet by saying on Sunday: "We refuse imposed government. So how can you expect us to be governed by the

Americans?" That assertion from a leading cleric of half the Iraqi people is itself daunting.

A further daunting situation exists with the Kurds in that both main factions, the Barzani and the Talabani, are expelling Arab populations that were relocated into their territories years ago by Saddam Hussein. Their efforts already have resulted in the displacement of thousands of Arabs who now are a floating population without homes, jobs, or means of support. This kind of localized ethnic cleansing or, perhaps better, tribal sorting was a predictable feature of the situation, because Saddam had maintained the living arrangements created to support his regime by force, not by mutual consent.

That political cacophony introduces an ironic twist and a significant opportunity into a rapidly deteriorating situation. There clearly will not be time to design and install a brand new operating system in Iraq. As much as is possible must be retrieved and restored from what is already there. Now that the party that dominated Iraq for four decades is no longer in control, it is simply not smart to throw out Saddam's whole baby with the Baath.

For example, following the first Gulf War, Saddam developed a food distribution system that, as noted earlier, was admired by the UN for its effectiveness. Something like it would be easier to restore than to reinvent, provided that these institutions are directed by new people. Bringing other systems back to where they were before the bombings began also looks like a good way to restore some order of confidence. But as the Shiite Ayatollah's comments suggested, the most telling and probably the most reassuring moves can be made in the political arena.

Here the new team could find some promising shortcuts. The first and perhaps the most impressive shortcut could be restoration of the Majlis, the Iraqi National Assembly. This body has had a checkered career in Iraq's political history. First formed with establishment of Iraq's constitutional monarchy in 1953, the assembly was dissolved by Prime Minister Nuri Said the following year. It was brought back but abolished following a military coup in 1958. Saddam used, abused, distorted and usurped the legislative functions of the Majlis, but he did not disband it. It appears that the present membership was elected in 1989, before the Gulf War, and no elections have occurred since. Moreover, while Sunni Arabs actually represent about 20% of the Iraqi population, Saddam contrived to have them hold 53% of the 250 seats in the Majlis, and of course to dominate all Iraqi governmental institutions. In truth, the various Shi'a elements form the dominant group, amounting to more than half the population, while, as noted, the Sunni Arabs are about 20%, the Kurds (most of whom are Sunnis) are also about 20%, while Turkomen, Assyrians and others make up the remainder.

Those numbers indicate that, even with Saddam's distortions, the Majlis represented a practical political means to provide representation at the national level from all areas of Iraq and from all political, ethnic, or religious factions. Creating an alternative to it looks to be a tougher task than the case requires.

It would be hard to invent an alternative with any standing, particularly given the open hostility of Iraqis, both elites and ordinary people, to an outside government. Iraqis have experimented frequently with representative governments, but the period from the 1930s to the late 1950s was plagued by coups and countercoups led largely by military officers who formed the majority of Iraqi nationalists. The picture changed with a coup carried out by a group of officers on July 14, 1958—Iraq's revolution—that expelled the last of the Hashemite monarchs, launched the Republic of Iraq, and installed the group's leader, a low-born Iraqi, Brigadier Abd al Karim Qasim, as the country's home grown leader.

Iraq's revolution changed society by destroying the power of the landowners and advancing the situations of the peasants and urban workers. Being one of them, Qasim gathered great support among the poor and worker groups. He courted Iraq's Communist Party as a counter to the growing Baath Party, a move distrusted by the US and other western powers, but he did little to develop political institutions. A group of officers led by Saddam Hussein first tried to kill Qasim and, when that failed, they overthrew him in 1963.

Qasim and his followers started something important for Iraq with the revolution of 1958. A new constitution, launched at that time, made a promise of government for and by Iraqis. Unhappily, at Qasim's overthrow five years later, Iraq was going in several directions at once. Political party activity was growing among the Baath, other nationalist parties and the communists. Increasing urbanization and modernization were breaking down Iraq's traditional social structure. Clan, ethnic and religious hatreds were resurging. Iraq was increasingly involved in foreign affairs. Class antagonisms were growing. The Iraqi revolution had failed mainly for lack of interest on the part of nationalist leaders in the welfare of the people.

When he took over, Saddam basically put a lid on it. He suppressed disputes among clan, ethnic and religious groups, focused political life on the Baath, gave increasing control of governance to Sunnis and his Tikriti—Saddam's home region—clansmen. When in 1970 the country adopted a new constitution that called for a National Assembly, the Majlis, it looked again as if real progress would be made. However, elections were not held for the Majlis until 1979, after Saddam Hussein's rise to total power. Two further elections were held in 1984 and 1989, but in the meantime the body had been made a captive of the Baath and Saddam.

Because much of the Majlis experience occurred under Saddam, It has been easy for US officials to dismiss the Assembly as a Hussein rubber stamp. That was the official US reaction to unanimous rejection by the Majlis of UN Security Council Resolution 1441 (in brief, affording Iraq a final opportunity to comply with its disarmament obligations...") in November

2002, despite Hussein's son's reported recommendation to approve, and Saddam's own eventual approval. If Saddam had wanted a Majlis rejection, he had a clear Baath majority that the mere rubber stamp theory presumably could be counted on to take care of it. However, by crude count there were 75-80 members of the Majlis who were not Baathists and need not have signed on. The Majlis also contained 30 women. Majlis action on this issue, therefore, deserves closer examination.

Was the rejection mere kowtowing to Saddam showmanship or was it one of the rare opportunities during Saddam's rule for the Majlis to make a clear statement of Iraqi nationalism?

Whatever the case, with a newly seated panel of members in any post Saddam election, the Majlis would have its first opportunity to behave as a freely elected legislative body. In any new Iraqi framework of governance, the Majlis could have several things working for it. First, it is genuinely Iraqi. Despite Iraq's rocky experience with representative government the representational framework is still useable. The essential first step of breaking the Baathist stranglehold on it is already in process.

Second, a system exists for selecting representatives and the system can be made more representative. Although the Majlis electoral system has not been exercised since 1989, it could be re-launched with appropriate alignment of seat allocations to fit current population demographics. The earlier system used 18 geographic electoral districts. Two decades later, maybe that is still a good number, maybe not; it needs to be tested. If the old district system is kept as a basis for elections to federal offices, no nonsense election oversight will be required to assure that the interests of all parties are represented.

Third, there is a strong argument for restoring the Majlis and holding new elections for it without the Saddam overlay. This action would tell the people that after three false starts under King Faisal and Prime Minister Nuri Said, Qasim and Hussein, they finally have their own legislative body and a voice in government.

This message can begin to have beneficial effect from the moment new elections are scheduled. Given the current restive state of Iraqis in general, and the likely behind the scenes maneuvering of all elites and sects to gain positions of influence, re-launching the Majlis could be a pre-emptive strike of some force. Its first value is that it would be a decisive step forward. Its second and maybe main value would be that it tells the Iraqis the Coalition really means business on restoring power to the Iraqi people. That would reduce the toxicity of Iraqi mood that presently shows signs of getting out of hand.

A fourth value is that recreation of the Majlis could commendably shorten the occupation. This could reduce the foreign policy and money costs, and casualties of the Iraq war.

The process of arriving at a new Iraqi federal system of governance involves a clear sequence of events. Step one is the creation or revitalization of local/community representative organizations. Some working concept of self-selection has to be called into play or established for the leadership of all factions and regions. This is a process that the Coalition can encourage and promote, so long as outside intervention in the candidate selection process is confined to keeping the system from being perverted by extremists. These representatives would then become the participants in a constituent assembly that would be charged with building a genuine federal system of governance.

The situation poses a bit of a quandary for an occupying force that may prefer to impose its will on a conquered people. But the Iraqis have been told they were liberated, not conquered. The first signs of direct foreign intervention in the election process will tell them otherwise. If the Coalition begins, as it has, by promising free and fair elections by the Iraqi people, and then the Coalition intervenes to select the parties and the candidates who may or may not participate, the Iraqi people will see themselves returned to square one, back under a foreign dominated leadership that separates them from their government, as they always have been.

In this regard, while decapitating the Baath is likely to be approved by a majority of the Iraqis because it removes the Saddam legacy, it will at the same time tell another story that will be taken as intervention. Eliminating the Baath is not the answer anyway; people of that nationalist persuasion will just put a new label on it, change their platform a bit, and re-emerge. A scary version of the future has the Baathists driven underground and formed into an insurgency that will do what the Baath has spearheaded before: pull off a coup at the first opportunity. They will be easier to watch and to contain if they are kept in the open and encouraged to take part in a new government, not driven underground.

At about this point, and possibly sooner, the whole process should be turned over to the UN. No member of the Coalition has the credentials for this kind of work, and none has either the detachment or the credibility. UN officers can monitor and intervene to assure integrity of the process, because they have those credentials. The Iraqi and international standing of the results will be far superior to whatever the Coalition might achieve. In any case, it would have to be a long, well-managed, and compassionate occupation for the Coalition to acquire the trust and confidence needed to carry out this assignment. The sooner the UN can be placed in command of the electoral process the better, and those consultations between the Coalition and the UN should be going on, openly and widely known, right now.

IRAQ MUST NOT BECOME AN AMERICAN PALESTINE
June 2003

If you are an American, the news from Iraq cannot be good. Each day on average we lose one or more soldiers, or Marines, or airmen. Fifty Americans have died since Bush announced the end of the war on May 1. Each day several Iraqis of uncertain militancy are killed or wounded in skirmishes with Coalition forces. The war is said to be over, but US forces this week launched Operation Desert Scorpion involving thousands of troops in the so-called Sunni triangle of northwestern Iraq. Meanwhile, the Kurds in the north, given their heads by the Coalition, are slowly consolidating their hold on the region, pushing out non-Kurdish peoples wherever they get in the way, thereby increasing the homeless population. In the south the Shi'a are basically in charge and are consolidating their hold on the region with the apparent support or at least non-interference of the British and with the alleged support of the Mullahs of Shi'a Iran. While not intended, Iraq is coming apart.

US authorities are blaming much of the trouble on disgruntled followers of Saddam Hussein, particularly

Baath party members and displaced military personnel. But several analysts of the region—European, Middle Eastern and American—label that model as too simple, and some have carefully put the nasty word "insurgency" on the table, meaning guerrilla warfare by organized resistance to the Coalition occupation. The uglier truth is probably that there are several emergent insurgencies, each reflecting the tribal, regional, religious, or political aims of the players.

There was a moment, about eight weeks back, when this evolution of the situation might have been avoided. As indicated at the time by Coalition spokesmen, power might have been turned over to Iraqis. Even carried out on a limited scale, that gesture could have told many Iraqis that the promise of getting their country back was real. But the Coalition leadership postponed any action to turn power over to Iraqis, while making a show of blacklisting the Baath, forbidding party members, especially officials on a roster of 30,000 or so, to take part or hold jobs in any new government. The speed and apparent lack of thought with which such command decisions were made may hide a deceptive truth: Ready access to secure telephones made it easy for Rumsfeld and White House leadership to micro-manage decisions on the ground and, in some cases—such as blacklisting the Baath—they reportedly permitted no discussion.

One result is that the Baath have been driven underground, and they have taken their guns with them. Some of the more disgruntled, it is reported, have threatened to undertake suicide bombings. The odds are that all the people choosing to go underground are not Baathists, but they are probably increasingly committed nationalists.

There is a familiar feel about this situation. It is moving toward relatively small clusters of extremists supported by larger surrounding communities. The extremists and less hard line militants are becoming embedded in communities and neighborhoods.

Based on reporting from sites such as Fallujah, US and

other Coalition troops who go into these areas to roust out extremists are themselves hard edged, ready for bloody action, willing to fire at shadows, frightened and insecure, and unprepared to take chances. Those feelings, as natural as they may be in the circumstances, are a recipe for disaster.

Meanwhile, the Israel Defense Force has been operating in that manner for more than a year in the West Bank and Gaza. In many instances, such as Jenin, the IDF virtually leveled whole villages. They have fired into crowds, used a combination of tanks, bulldozers, gunships, and indiscriminate shootings and missile launchings to kill individual militants or members of Palestinian groups. But they have not stopped the suicide bombers. In fact the IDF operations generate more angry Palestinians, help the recruitment of suicide bombers, and justify to Israeli hard line leadership the next round of IDF destruction and killing.

There is no simple way to shut down this self-perpetuating cycle of violence, but the initiative is with the strong. Countless times over the past year the IDF has conducted sweeps, "targeted assassinations", or a heavy-handed destruction of homes and businesses. Both US officials and the Israelis behave as if there is no connection between these patterns of harsh Israeli military operations and the suicide bombings that inevitably follow. The poundings Bush took from conservative supporters and Israeli lobbyists for criticizing IDF attacks this week, and his prompt retreat, show that denial of Israeli wrongdoing is well-established, high-level political blindness.

Mirror-imaging the Palestine situation, the problem for Coalition, mainly American forces in Iraq looks more and more like a Palestinian catch-22. Soldiers who go into an area to kill or capture extremists will inevitably over-react with the result that innocent bystanders will be killed or harmed. To limit American casualties US soldiers will shoot first, and that means Iraqi civilian casualties are likely to be far more numerous than American military ones. They already are.

That pattern breeds frustration and anger, generates more militants, and makes the surrounding communities less likely to be helpful to Coalition forces. This is a natural pattern of escalation that will deepen the rift between American forces and Iraqi civil populations. Matters will get materially worse, unless the patterns are broken now.

US officials and forces are slipping into an IDF mode in Baghdad and elsewhere in Iraq. It is probable that many of the excessive uses of force by American or other Coalition troops are situations brought on by the extremity of encounters. However, a growing number of Iraqi citizens are being injured, and it is not enough to blame the incidents on former Saddam supporters. Repressing or bullying thousands of people will not stop a few from taking revenge on their oppressors. That fact is well-established. The experiment does not need to be run again.

It may be that the US does not have enough troops in Iraq to occupy and pacify conquered spaces, just as the IDF cannot afford to station large numbers of troops in the West Bank. This limitation forces both to use hit and run tactics which may be optimally destructive while only minimally productive. The lesson of Vietnam was that if pacified spaces were not protected they had to be retaken. Protecting the pacified enclaves demanded more troops. Retaking the spaces cost more lives. Force limitations in Iraq appear to permit only hit and run—a deadly choice for all concerned. The deplorable costs as recorded in cities such as Fallujah are being repeated over and over in Iraq.

There are no easy answers for this situation, but there are good ones and they work. Somebody simply has to back off and keep the next incident from happening. If American authorities in Iraq really want to show the Iraqis that they have a future as a free people, our forces cannot be allowed to fall into the Israeli pattern of shooting anyone who moves or throws a stone or stands in the wrong place. We will have to take some unanswered hits and severely limit retaliation to bring the situation under control. If we do that, many more Iraqis will see what we are doing and they will help—provided they see that we are moving to give them back their country.

These initiatives are with us. The failure to take them will show up in increasing Iraqi rebellion and growing losses of American troops.

BAGHDAD AND WASHINGTON—IRAQ'S GUERRILA WARS
July 2003

Senator Robert Byrd of West Virginia, who sees the mounting tragedy of Iraq with greater clarity than anyone else in the United States Senate, chose in his latest analysis to draw on Lawrence of Arabia. Some eighty years ago T.E. Lawrence summed up the British situation in Iraq with "We are today not far from a disaster." Lawrence was looking at Mesopotamia where at the time the British were only recently embroiled, and they barely understood the people, their practices, problems and preferences. Britain would be expelled before they figured them out. Only a few of our people in Iraq today have more than a limited understanding of post Saddam Iraq or its people, and they are already experiencing the guerrilla tactics that ultimately toppled British rule. At least half their problem may be the fact that Washington is locked in a guerrilla war of recrimination over the information, analysis, and motives that propelled us into Iraq in the first place.

Each battle will be prolonged and complicated by the other. Our people in Iraq may be left to their own devices to design and apply a satisfactory exit strategy, or they may be micro-managed from Washington and handed a strategy that is irrelevant. Meanwhile, the growing roster of American and other Coalition casualties will sharpen the Washington debate about how and why we got into this mess. United Nations, European, Middle Eastern, and other relationships, already disturbed by the habits of current US leadership, will be rattled by events in both battles. In both places, people are in for a long and often bloody conflict.

Both wars are unique in our history. To be sure, little more than a decade ago we fought Gulf War I, but that war was not accompanied by the extreme doubts and misgivings of the current engagement. That war was not complicated by prolonged debate—there seemed to be sufficient agreement on the need to overturn Saddam's invasion of Kuwait—and it was not followed by military occupation of the country. Americans and others were agreed on finding someone to punish for 9-11, but the run up to Gulf War II was murky from the start because international agreement on the need for war never existed.

There was immediate disagreement about the facts of the situation and the need for action. Pointed, even aggressive, US determination to go it alone discouraged full and proper examination of the issues. Moreover, plans to occupy and run the country after the brief war were either ignored or not well thought out, or non-existent. As recent reports indicate, they were products of uncoordinated planning in Washington, and they have proven difficult to implement.

In real time the entire Iraq venture has been assiduously tracked in print and electronic media and on the Internet. But the Internet has added depth, complexity, candor, and directness to public participation in the Iraq discussion. Until recently those qualities were largely missing from print and electronic media.

On the Internet, much that is said or written is of uncertain reliability, but little can be hidden, and every new development or thought is quickly circulated. Both truth and fiction are transmitted at light speed. Error is enormously difficult to filter out. Interactions of mainstream media and the Internet are increasingly rich.

The result is an entirely new kind of national debate. The Internet provides fertile ground for soft (anonymous) and hard (declared) whistle blowers. Would-be presidential candidates, especially Howard Dean, are discovering that the free-spirited Internet has a power that is denied to managed media, because publication is often not driven by editorial policy or indispensable advertisers.

Emergent guerrilla warfare in Iraq and at home will be watched with excruciating sharpness on this national screen. Americans now know about and feel each US casualty every day in a way that never occurred before, even though pictures of flag-draped coffins arriving at Dover, Delaware have been largely forbidden. With that awareness will grow demands for accountability by American leadership. Failure will be defined by how events play on this wider stage and not by the merits of cases. Iraq has already seen rapid changes in battle and occupation management. There will be others if Iraqi guerrilla resistance persists. Washington ability to justify this war will become increasingly limited.

In the guerilla war of Washington, truth will be the most frequent casualty. Much is at stake in the eighteen month run up to the 2004 Presidential election. The hawks who led the President into Iraq with a dearth of knowledge plus hasty and faulty logic now find themselves having to reinvent all their arguments. The President is finding that his popularity, which always was based on the flimsy underpinnings of the War on Terrorism, is rapidly shrinking. Further shrinkage of his popularity will be a key goal of all Washington guerrillas, not only Democrats. Mainstream media already have turned on leadership and are hammering away at the factual basis for war on Iraq. Well ahead of mainstream media, the Internet was out front, pointing to the flaws and falsehoods in the Bush administration case.

The wars in Iraq and Washington share an overarching tragedy. 9-11 brought a unity of purpose and community of interest to the American people that had not been seen since World War II. Bush administration unilateralism was already chipping away at this foundation before the war in Iraq, while deepening "post-war" guerilla warfare is likely to be more divisive than unifying in Washington. The war at home unfortunately continues to be more about how we got into it than about how to extricate ourselves gracefully and prudently from it.

Both the conduct of an exit strategy from Iraq and the proper focus on a range of domestic issues such as debt, taxes, employment, and health care will suffer. Ultimately, we will be stuck with a war we did not need and a political debate that, where real national interests are concerned, is often beside the point.

The simple fact is that even if the entire rationale for our presence in Iraq was a colossal Republican hawk deception, we now have a very real American presence there. What the US does there not only places many young Americans in harm's way and continues to erode our country's reputation, it also affects the lives of millions of Iraqi people.

It will truly be a disaster if Washington remains so unfocused that it cannot effectively support our civil and military forces in Iraq. On the Washington end, the US effort is dominated by a narrow Pentagon militarist mindset, when civilian outlooks and people are required. In the opinion of many informed and knowledgeable observers, we have a far too small cadre of Americans and coalition supporters in Iraq doing the vital work of extricating us from the situation. Various reports indicate they are finding some success among the Kurds in the north and the Shiites in the south, but the Sunni Muslim tribes, not necessarily all devotees of Saddam, are yet far from pacified. Even worse, the Kurds and Shi'a will stay on board only so long as they think their goals are being served.

The resulting numbers define the challenge for our civil and military forces. Most estimates place the number of Sunni Muslims in Iraq at about 20% of the country's population of about 27 plus million people, or roughly 5.5 million Sunnis. Recent reports indicate we have about 600 civilians in country administrator Paul Bremer's team, and about 150,000 US and coalition military forces in country. The ratio is roughly one coalition force member for each 200 Iraqis in a territory a third the size of California. If the Iraqis are cooperative or at least passive and the forces are well supported, that is no problem. If they are not, the situation can be difficult, if not hopeless, and it will involve constant American and Iraqi casualties. As Palestine has shown repeatedly, a few extremists can do real damage, while maintaining an enemy's civil population in a constant state of anxiety.

As our summer and the Iraqi situation settle into dog days, we must keep these facts in mind: If our civilian and military forces in Iraq are to have the dual mission of maintaining order and restoring the infrastructure of civil society in Iraq, we do not have the right people or enough people there. No matter how large our numbers, extremists will take a toll. This puts an enormous premium on finding ways to pacify the Sunnis, but it puts an equal priority on elaborating an exit strategy for earliest possible departure. Bremer's team would probably appreciate being left alone to figure out how best to carry out these two missions; thus they may well welcome Washington's internal guerrilla warfare.

IRAQ—DECEPTIONS IN THE WAR ON TERRORISM
August 2003

Deputy Secretary of Defense Paul Wolfowitz just returned from an extensive visit to Iraq to make two incredible suggestions: One is that the "central battle in the War on Terrorism" is now in Iraq. The other is that American families will tolerate the continuing loss of their sons and daughters in Iraqi conflict, in effect, that the US will not be deterred by continuing deaths and injuries in Iraq.

In light of the growing doubts about the integrity of the Bush administration because of the way it led our country into the Iraq war, both Wolfowitz propositions need careful examination.

First, Bush stated two months ago that the war in Iraq was over; yet now Wolfowitz asserts that Iraq is the "central battle in the War on Terrorism." How did that come about? When the administration tried to make the case that Saddam Hussein was collaborating with Osama bin Laden and al Qaida, they failed dismally. The administration tried to make the case that Iraq posed a clear and present danger to the US because it possessed large quantities of chemical and biological weapons and was well on its way to acquiring nuclear weapons. None of that has been proven. Moreover, at no time did Hussein threaten the US, despite constant threats and frequent "no fly zone" bombardments by the US and British. We went into Iraq anyway.

The first shots of the war were attempted decapitation strikes against Hussein's hiding places. We still don't really know whether that succeeded or failed. The war itself was over quickly because the reported estimates of Republican Guard and other Iraqi force capabilities proved to be less than expected. In addition, a rumor sprang up that, all along, Saddam planned to have his troops retreat to fight again in another way. In any case, because the Iraqi military forces and equipment proved to be no direct threat to the US, the administration lost yet more credibility.

There are reports that terrorists from outside Iraq have been coming into the country, but so far, evidence of an Iraqi terrorism infrastructure has been non-existent. In the three months since the war ended, efforts to find terrorism connections, especially to al Qaida, have led nowhere.

These reports provide no basis for a shift in focus of the War on Terrorism to Iraq. However, Wolfowitz implies that our troops will not be coming home soon, because they are being staked out, not merely to face a growing Iraqi insurgency, but also to deal with a growing prospect that international terrorist groups, including al Qaida, may find Iraq more fertile ground than it ever could have been during Saddam's repressive years. As one writer put it, Iraq could become a "terrorist magnet."

Here one must listen carefully for verbal sleight of hand. Deputy Secretary Wolfowitz has stated that the central battle against terrorism is now Iraq. Iraq is where we are presently concentrating our forces, but it is verbal legerdemain to call the Iraqis who object to our occupation terrorists; they are trying to take back their country by whatever means they can. Even if our forces eliminate the visiting terrorists and effectively suppress Iraqi guerrilla warfare, the global terrorism threat will be virtually unchanged. The War will have to be fought again somewhere else, or we may just have to add Iraq to Afghanistan as places where the War on Terrorism goes nowhere.

By whatever mix of falsehood, ambition and hubris we were led into Iraq, we are there, and our forces are in harm's way. They face whatever is the mix of indigenous insurgents and imported terrorists. To change that situation, people on both sides (mainly the Iraqis and the US forces) have to be convinced that the battle is over, and in Iraq they are not. Iraqi resistance often makes our troops trigger happy, and the resultant mishaps only worsen the situation. People who might have gone along peacefully start fighting back when they lose families, friends, property, and livelihoods.

It is not given that American families will put up indefinitely with random killings of their sons and daughters in a war that had no provable purpose and has no foreseeable positive outcome. Rather, they might, and indeed should insist that the Iraq campaign be cut short, our forces be withdrawn, and Iraq's future be turned back to the Iraqis. A few more weeks or months of the present daily losses or injuries of US troops, and indications that the war is going downhill, will likely increase public pressure for an early end to the occupation.

FACING REALITY IN IRAQ
September 2003

Murderous explosions this week in the holy Shi'a city of Najaf said with brutal clarity that it is time to examine the utility of the occupation of Iraq and the American role in it. With at least 95 people killed and more than 150 wounded, this is the worst killing spree in a violence prone post-war Iraq. It most likely was an act of Iraqi Shi'a extremists against Shi'a moderates, but it could have been a Sunni Baathist scheme to frighten Shiites away from the Coalition. It should also have been a loud and clear message to the US Coalition leaders that, in rejection of the occupation, at least some Iraqis feel strongly enough to kill their own people. The Shiites are the most diverse cluster of Islamic opinion, but the root cause of the bombings was not about doctrinal differences within Shi'a Islam; it was about Shi'a support for the occupation.

Mohamed Bakir al Hakim—the target of the incident—was a leading Shi'a cleric and probably the only one who could have led the majority Shi'a community into at least a moderately secular Iraqi government. Because of the importance of Najaf in Shi'a Islam, Hakim's decision to support a cooperative process with the Coalition would have carried weight both within and outside Iraq. Whoever replaces him must contemplate the horrifying lessons of the bombings and decide in light of them how far he can push the center of Shi'a opinion and tolerance of the occupation.

The most obvious prospect is that Shi'a tolerance of the occupation will diminish. If it occurs, that shift will be a disaster for occupation designers of a new government. There is already resistance to Coalition, really US insistence on an American style democracy that, if created, would minimize clerical influences on Iraqi governance. That resistance appears to be shared by the Sunnis who appreciate outsider lectures about the role of Islam in government no more than the Shi'a. The coolness to an American style democracy would also extend to the Kurds, who are both Sunnis and Shiites.

A clear and unmistakable message emerges: The move to install an American style democracy in Iraq should not only be dropped; it should be obviously and publicly abandoned. The critical question is what should be put in its place. The most workable answer is whatever the Iraqis themselves can agree upon.

In the evolution of its political system, where is Iraq at this time? From the era of the Ottoman Turks, until expulsion of the British after World War II, Iraqis were ruled by outsiders. Their experience since then has been determined by strong men, the most enduring of them being Saddam Hussein. In short, while among the peoples of the world's oldest seats of civilization, the Iraqis have little experience with self-government. The emergence of the Baath party and expulsion of the British showed some promise of political maturing, but that promise was suppressed by Saddam and his immediate predecessors. Because their operations remain almost wholly military, the American and British occupiers are contributing nothing to Iraqi political enlightenment.

The message of Najaf is that the American/British role in designing Iraq's political future must be redefined and reduced. That is critical because Iraqis who ally with the coalition are being treated by other Iraqis as outsiders. In fact, some of them who fled and remained outside Iraq for many years are outsiders. The other meaning of Najaf for Iraqis is that cooperating with the Coalition is dangerous to one's health. The suggestion that the bombing of UN headquarters in Baghdad was really an attack on the Coalition is another indicator that major changes in the occupation must occur and occur quickly.

Both the needs of the Iraqis and the need of the United States to rehabilitate itself internationally can be met by turning the entire task over to the United Nations. That is no simple matter, because the UN has been badly burned in Iraq by the attack on its headquarters and the loss of one of the world's great nation builders, Brazil's Sergio Vieira de Mello. Change will not be easy for the United States because the neo-conservative advocates of the US presence in Iraq have an inordinate ego attachment to going it alone. But much good could come of the change.

Because the Bush team has not leveled with the public, and team members are not agreed on the facts, the costs of Iraq have become major political liabilities. The dollar costs are obviously ballooning. In the words of Iraq program administrator, L. Paul Bremer, they will be "tens and tens and tens of billions" more than the $4 billion monthly now being spent. Daily death and wounding of American troops are generating a wave of public dismay and worry with the occupation. Iraqi refusal to take the American presence with good will increases pressure for early departure. Lack of major foreign participation presages mounting US costs and prolonged exposure of US forces to violence. The two ways out are to attract others in and to end the occupation as soon as possible.

While the Bush team has struggled to avoid it, turning the problem over to the United Nations is the only reasonable answer. As former Ambassador Richard Holbrooke observed in the September 2 issue of <u>Newsweek</u>, there are command arrangements that could make that shift a reality. The shift first requires US recognition that nation building and peacekeeping are global missions for which the United States has shown itself ill prepared. Part of the problem is that the Bush administration vigorously opposed getting involved in nation building. Another part is that the US does not yet realize that it desperately needs help. It next requires abandonment of obvious biases such as Rumsfeld's objection to UN blue helmets in the forefront of the task. It then requires US recognition that the weaknesses US hardliners object to in the UN are in reality mirror images of the lack of US support for UN operations. Ultimately, it requires that the US define and carry out its purposes for being in Iraq in ways that are acceptable to the international community.

Finally, asking the UN to take on the task requires that the US, at the same time, move back to the position of respectable world leader, a position it recklessly abandoned in the post-9-11 rush to Iraq. However difficult it may be for the Bush Administration to swallow, it is hard to see any losses for the US in adopting this new course.

IRAQ—PAST TIME TO MOVE ON
September 2003

In his address to the UN on September 22, 2003, George W. Bush muffed the supreme opportunity of his presidency. For weeks the situation in Iraq had been deteriorating. European powers, especially France, Germany, and Russia, whose leaders opposed the war, nonetheless saw the problems and were developing alternative strategies that might have provided more money and troops to deal with the decaying Iraqi scene. Increasing numbers of influential Americans and the public were questioning the wisdom of the venture into Iraq, while looking for ways to support American forces in the field where they are confronting increasing danger. The UN organization and leadership were looking for ways to accommodate a US request for help.

At that moment, the US budget deficit was headed for historic highs. In fact, the International Monetary Fund had issued a rare warning about the waning strength of the US dollar. Despite all that, the portents of the UN session on the whole looked pretty good, but Bush waded in as if his main task was to justify the war.

The problem that day was not to justify the war but to

convince other nations to help manage the peace and extricate the US from a badly conceived military engagement. Instead, he repeated the charges about (a) Saddam Hussein and WMDs, (b) Saddam Hussein and al Qaida, and (c) Saddam Hussein and 9-11, all of which are now almost universally viewed as false. That was not the way to convince anyone.

On that ground Bush missed his opportunity. He should have stepped up to that podium and candidly addressed the present situation. He should have hooked his audience on the challenge of deciding what to do now.

Our country is in more trouble than it has experienced since the end of World War II. We do not have a global confrontation with any country, even though we struggle to convince Iran and North Korea to cease and desist from nuclear weapons development. We do have non-nation state enemies, some of whom are dangerous merely because they are serious and can command dangerous weapons.

We have a leadership cadre that behaves as if the opinions of the whole world are irrelevant to our interests and our decisions. Consequently, our leaders are squandering the diplomatic achievements of half a century on a narrow and aggressive neo-conservative agenda.

We have an economic elite that commands enormous power over public decisions. With White House and Congressional support, this group is radically distorting public budgets in their own favor while undermining the very concept of democracy.

We have a society that does not really think much about where things come from and spends well beyond its means.

We are spending blood and treasure on a military venture that should never have been. But the foremost problem, as Bush stood before the General Assembly, was how to extricate ourselves safely and successfully from Iraq.

Iraq cannot be fixed without serious and concentrated international help. With limited Coalition support, the US has learned the hard way that nation building as an occupying power is a nerve-wracking task, if it is not entirely hopeless. The US team in Iraq simply cannot overcome the Iraqi belief that the team is there only to serve purely US interests, and that image is making enemies for us as fast as we are making friends in Iraq.

The official explanation is that the trouble spots are all in the Sunni triangle of northwestern Iraq, basically the zone to which the pre-war No Fly policy tried to confine Hussein and his activities. That is where the US-led occupation is failing, because it is where Iraqis feel most under attack. That is where the most detached and non-military international support is essential, because the relationship with the Sunnis must become non-confrontational as quickly as possible. To be sure basic security is a problem where people live in poverty and fight for survival. However, those problems are likely to fade with improved overall economic conditions.

What the US needs from the UN and from individual national governments is focused attention on dealing with the problems presented by Iraq in its present condition. That requires money, skill and most of all dedicated presence. It means that the US has to recognize its limitations: It simply cannot do this alone. Going it alone or insisting on remaining dominantly out front means killing and wounding more Iraqis and getting more Americans killed and wounded. It means a stretched out and costly occupation.

Iraq cannot and must not be managed as an ego trip. It needs the best care and attention the international community can give; the US needs to help that happen. In principle, the UN membership appears ready to help, but on Tuesday Bush focused on justifying US actions to the American people, not on making a candid appeal to the UN membership for help in putting Iraq back together.

UN members are likely to remain ready to help because they have a realistic view of the effects of failure in Iraq. But to get that support, the Bush team has to adjust to sharing control, authority, and responsibility. There was no apparent interest on Tuesday in helping pull US chestnuts out of the fire. It is time for Bush and his team to recognize that reality and move on.

THE ENEMIES IN IRAQ
November 2003

As the weeks and months have dragged on after Bush declared, "Mission Accomplished" in May, and while even his neo-con mentor, Richard Perle, now concedes that the Iraq war was illegal, the administration faces an ever more deadly Iraq security landscape. Bush himself is unlikely to concede that the war was illegal, but several experts say the US is now bogged down in a quagmire, and that situation may well demand more careful and intensive management of the extraction than a totally legal engagement might entail.

Attacks have grown in number, seriousness, and location. Most security incidents appear to occur in the so-called Sunni triangle that is north and west of Baghdad, or in Baghdad itself, but incidents are occurring with growing frequency in essentially Kurdish areas of northern Iraq and in essentially Shi'a areas of the south. Bombings in and around Baghdad and the shoot-down in the last two weeks of three—with the Mosul incident Saturday, maybe five—American helicopters bespeaks a seriously escalating pattern. Meanwhile, American casualties in November alone have risen well above forty. But who are the enemies?

Published guesses of who the culprits are in each region have not fingered a singular enemy, although the most popular ones officially are Saddam loyalists, followed by imported alleged al Qaida adherents or other outside/foreign terrorists. There is substantial agreement among observers that the attacks have become more sophisticated; they have certainly become more numerous. Some reporters are talking insurgency, while one writer, Robert Fisk, makes a convincing case for a "resistance" movement, harking back to the French underground in World War II.

There is still no concerted statement either of who the enemies are in Iraq or what their motives are. The situation suggests a growing diversity of people who object or who support objectors to the American and Coalition occupation. Either an "insurgency" or a "resistance movement" will work to describe it.

The lack of a clear definition is not because of some locked-in word preference. Rather, what politicians call the enemy makes a difference. In simple terms, an insurgency is mounted by a national group that opposes an occupying force or a constituted government. An insurgency with a popular base, e.g., such as the Sandinistas in Nicaragua, may even have some international standing. It may also have some prospect of succeeding, even without outside help. However, as Jonas Savimbi and his group UNITA demonstrated in Angola, an insurgency—even with US support—can go on for years without deciding anything politically for a country while delaying indefinitely any national progress.

The problem facing the US is that insurgencies often acquire strong international followings and sources of support. That process, for better or worse, appears underway in Iraq. If all or a significant number of the violent clusters in Iraq actually coalesce into a functioning insurgency, the US faces several potentially painful developments. First is the likelihood that in the present Iraqi situation the insurgents will acquire a substantial popular following. Street reactions to the shooting down of a military personnel laden US helicopter suggest that such a popular following could be easily acquired. Second, if the nascent insurgency survives and pulls off a few more spectaculars, less decided dissidents, and plain Iraqi nationalists will commit themselves to it. Third, if the insurgency shows itself to represent a significant part of the population, international, government level recognition and sympathy will flow to it, initially within Islamic countries, but eventually from others including in the western world as well.

Such developments will mean, among other things, that external funding will flow to the group. Moreover, political acceptance, if not official recognition, will grow among UN members and other international organizations, both public and private. The net effect of such developments will be a smart curtailment of the already limited global tolerance for the US and Coalition presence in Iraq. Pressure will mount for an early departure from Iraq. Paralleling that will be a growing reluctance even of friendly powers to commit forces to Iraq. Continuing intense attacks on a daily or weekly basis are likely to move the situation in that direction.

The key to this situation is not merely to fight back. This may only worsen the situation, moving it more rapidly toward the painful developments cited above, polarizing Iraqis against Americans and the Coalition. Some effective way has to be found to reach the Iraqi enemies, and that means they must be effectively identified and dealt with somehow. Part of the task may involve recapture and imprisonment of all the felons that Saddam is said to have let out of prison five days before the US forces moved into Baghdad. But that is likely to deal more with public disorder than with the insurgency.

Current efforts are being made to classify the enemies on the ground by immediate affiliations or points of origin. That effort will be insufficient because who the people are is not as crucial as what they want and what they are prepared to do to get it. In this context, it is misleading to exaggerate the importance of reported al Qaida and imported freelance terrorists because few published analysts consider them critical components of this situation. The outsiders are not nearly as important to potential outcomes as what the Iraqis think is happening among their own people and what they feel driven or inspired to do about it.

That chemistry on the ground is what must be changed. But other enemies now operate in Iraq against improving the situation. Right now it appears that the US and its Coalition partners have several major enemies.

The two most serious enemies are ignorance and time. Much can be made of US lack of recognition of the lessons of British experience. There is no sensible explanation for the fact that the Bush administration ignored, even dismissed out of hand, the solid work of the State Department and other national security agencies in planning and predicting (accurately, as events have shown} likely situations in Iraq following an invasion. There simply may not be enough time to recover from those failures, because the situation is now so soured that stringing matters out while trying to fix things can only make matters worse. Meanwhile, Islamic and European and Asian governments look as if they could be more tolerant and helpful if the US timetable were better known and materially shorter than now appears.

The third most serious enemy is asymmetry, the differences in sizes and capabilities of opposing forces. Smallness, lack of visibly structured organization, and dispersion across Iraqi territory and society all work to present enemies who are invisible until they strike. This factor will make it disastrous to allow the Iraqi resistance groups to grow, because they can hide easily in Iraqi society. That indeed was one of the deadliest enemies in Vietnam. Asymmetry beat us when brute force could not.

A fourth enemy may well prove to be a misplaced and ideological drive to plant democracy in unready soil. The Iraqis threw the British out because they did not want a

British externally imposed form of governance. Many of them now appear to be reacting in a similar way to an American attempt to impose democracy. The Iraqi people obviously want to evolve their own forms of representative government. We do not know enough now to predict what forms that might take, and under present conditions we are unlikely to be given enough time to learn. Exiles such as Chalabi may know some things about Iraqi society and thought that could help in the transition, but they unfortunately are now too closely identified with the United States.

A fifth enemy is the Americanization of Iraqi oil and the selling off of Iraqi economic activities. While there is no official information on this, the grapevine has it that a scramble is occurring among Israelis and others to buy Iraqi industries and potentially profitable businesses that Saddam had largely nationalized. This kind of raiding, basically rape of Iraqi economic sectors while the Iraqis have neither law nor organization to stop it, is likely to turn even moderately disposed Iraqis against the Coalition and the Americans who are permitting these activities to occur.

A sixth enemy is the fact that American motives are badly tainted by big oil and private contractor exploitation of the Iraqi situation. Aside from the greed on display, news reports indicate that many Iraqis are angered by the domination by foreigners of activities they feel entirely competent and legally entitled to run.

Enemy number seven is clearly the illegality of the war. As Bush, now in Britain, Powell in Europe, and Rumsfeld in the Far East all are finding, the fact that most nations do not believe this war was necessary or legal stands in the way of their financial, moral or military support. Contrary to having improved the world security situation as President Bush claims, many think that global security is worse since the invasion, and multiple explosions in Turkey in the past few days tend to affirm that conviction. Thus, the US set out to go it alone as a matter of choice in attacking Iraq, and now finds itself uncomfortably isolated.

The sum of these enemies is that the Coalition and particularly the US will be given little or no margin for error. The insurgency-like animosity toward the United States is being driven in some degree by each of these enemies, and they are all there to be exploited by Iraqi dissidents, whatever the dissidents may be called. There may have been some high ground back in May that could be occupied for deposing Saddam Hussein, but that ground was not taken, and it probably no longer exists. Rather we have forces on the ground whose reactions to opposition are knee jerk and harsh.

The eighth enemy is a mismatch: The US is fighting a war against people it allegedly set out to help. US approaches alienate them at every turn. This is neither a time nor a place therefore for high-blown political agendas. There simply is no short order transformation of a society that is in chaos and agony. The people who created this chaos are unlikely to be able to clean it up. Those people must leave. Others, mainly the UN, untainted by invasion and occupation must take over the process. The ultimate enemy may be the blindness of the Bush team to this need. Only time will tell.

THE FALLACIES OF AMERICAN DEMOCRACY FOR IRAQ
November 2003

This week US civil administrator for Iraq, L. Paul Bremer, was called back to Washington for consultations on the worsening security situation in Iraq. Bremer's return was accompanied by grumblings from the Bush core team (Powell, Rumsfeld, Rice, and Bush) about the ineffectiveness of the Iraqi Governing Council. Since the beginning of November more than forty American combat deaths have occurred; U.S. forces have lost three helicopters: American forces have gone to a warlike footing in the Sunni Triangle, and at least two direct attacks have been made on Bremer's headquarters. Meanwhile, the CIA predicts that the situation will get worse, an appraisal that Bremer is reported to share. It appears indeed time to review the bidding.

One hopes that in this hastily called review, the situation and outlook for Iraq would be looked at squarely. Up to this point, the chances for that occurring have appeared slim, because the administration, and by extension Bremer's team in country, has appeared fixated on carrying out the Bush scheme for transforming Iraq into an American style democracy.

On the face of things, the US agenda has changed several times already, from (a) protecting the US from a monster with weapons of mass destruction, (b) ridding Iraq of a brutal tyrant, (c) "liberating" the Iraqi people, and finally (d) creating a democracy in Iraq as the first stage in (e) democratizing the entire region. This transition, perhaps better called a policy retreat, has convinced many people that the US does not know what it is doing. The notion of quickly or ever transforming Middle Eastern countries into western democracies bespeaks at best a superficial appreciation of the peoples and the problems involved. Perhaps even worse, it reveals a severe lack of understanding of how our system actually is working these days.

American democracy today is in serious trouble. At the national level, the process of electing a president, or representatives and senators, has become so expensive that only the wealthy or candidates supported by them can play. The process has been co-opted and corrupted by increasingly concentrated ownership of media and business. That includes banking, transportation, manufacturing, information systems, health care, and energy. Legislative programs and goals largely focus on catering to the large organizations and the wealthy contributors. Meanwhile, deceitful congressional redistricting has produced a collection of "safe" districts which eliminate the first locus of political compromise in the American system: a frequent change of blood.

Our system was designed to work on a basis of majority rule. However, control by a shrinking pool of elitists, who also control both parties through contributions, has led to a situation in which powerful minorities decide any important issue.

In the meantime, majority rule has become an obsolete concept of governance in any complex society. Majority rule was a great step forward from absolute monarchy or despotism, but it is an inadequate concept for our time. Consultations downward are weak and often superficial. Many minority and even majority interests are being pushed aside for benefits to elites.

In effect, what we are trying to export to Iraq is really a theoretical concept that does not work in this country. How can we expect it to work in Iraq or elsewhere in the Middle East? Majority rule poses special problems in Iraq, and these have already been well identified. Since the majority of the people (around 60%) are Shiites, the fear of Sunnis, Kurds, Christians, Turkomen, and advocates of secular governance is that rule by majority, especially a fundamentalist one, would result in suppressing their interests and beliefs. Saddam Hussein sidestepped this problem by running a secular government, but he also played a preference game that made his Sunni compatriots (about 20% of the population) a defacto majority for governing purposes.

Bush's administration is behaving like a minority government with majority acquiescence. Conservative Christians, media, and business elites, and the Israelis are setting the tone and calling the tune. The resultant government is systematically bent on undoing generations of social legislation that was targeted on the American population at large. This approach, more than any other posture of the Bush administration, makes it clear that neither he nor his key team members understand or necessarily care to know what the problems of instability and conflict in the world are actually about.

The Bush argument is that "democratizing" Iraq will make the world a safer place. He offers no evidence for this assertion. Indeed, there is none. People who are left out of the political and economic mainstreams in countries such as the Philippines, Indonesia, Egypt, India, and numerous others are the principal sources of the world's terrorists. A system of governance that depends on the will of the elite that elected it, and therefore focuses preferentially on the needs and wishes of that elite is exactly the troublemaker we already have. People who are not served by the system fight back however they can.

In our own system, key players have become totally preoccupied with the process. If you watch the President, you will see that his main business is keeping his party in power and raising money for the next election. Since election, even in a time he avers is a crisis, he has spent easily a quarter of his time as President cultivating funding sources for elections. American taxpayers footed the bill for this President to raise money for his re-election and for his own party by providing the best equipped airplane in the world, Air Force One, and the staffing infrastructure to support him, and of course his presidential salary while he is at the ranch raising money for the party. Other presidents have done this, but not as fulsomely as Bush.

The point here is that our system at present is too occupied with the process of getting people elected, and not nearly enough with the business of running the country. The two are not one and the same. No other country should copy this process, because it is fundamentally flawed in ways that make it incapable of providing government of all the people, by all the people and for all the people.

Our system grew up to meet the needs of an essentially white European society with differing religious and political views. Over time it learned to cope moderately well with the diversity the country now encompasses. But democracy by fiat has never been the principle of our system. Forcing our system of government on another state is a peculiar application of the idea of popular governance.

Iraqis in particular have experienced centuries of rule by outsiders from the arrival of the Osmanli, the Ottoman Turks, in the 16th century to the departure of the British in the 1950s. Iraqi nationalists threw out the British to form their own government only to discover all too soon that they were under the thumb of an indigenous tyrant.

The Iraqi Governing Council is handicapped because it is tagged as a US tool. As such, it is unlikely to prosper unless it hands authority over to leaders chosen by the Iraqis. The longer that handover is delayed the more violence will occur, and the lesson of early this week in Nasiriyah with the death of 17 Italian soldiers will be repeated. The CIA Station Chief in Baghdad appears to have delivered this message loud and clear.

The real meaning of the situation in Iraq is that broadly representative government, most likely chosen by traditional tribal and other community means, is the next vital step. The situation is simply too toxic to embrace most outside ideas. Some new representative forms of governance are also needed to deal with Iraq's ethnically, educationally, religiously, and economically complex society. Ironically, the secularism introduced by Saddam had that potential and still does. But new forms or accommodations of each community's wishes must grow out of the traditions, customs, religions, felt needs, and preferences of the people seeking to be governed. The forms cannot be transplanted en masse or quickly.

There is no one-size-fits-all, e.g., western democracy, solution to the problem. Thus there is no real solution the United States can provide other than early departure and a will-from outside-to help the Iraqi people find their own way. The argument against early American departure is that, if we leave, chaos will reign. With conditions as bad as they are, that is a hollow argument. Since outsiders and associated nationals are among the main targets of much of the violence, things could actually calm down if the Coalition withdrew. In that event, perhaps the United Nations—with US and broad international support—could be persuaded to take on monitoring and development support functions, if those were acceptable to the Iraqi people.

Obviously the US can and should promote representative government in the Middle East. But it is incapable of directly providing a workable model for Iraqi governance. The growing chaos shows clearly that US attempts to do so are unlikely to be accepted.

A FIFTY YEARS WAR IN IRAQ
December 2003

Put a razor wire barricade around a village. Block all entries and exits except one carefully guarded by armed troops. Make anyone who leaves or enters the village show a special identity card that is only in the language of the occupying force. Trash any building that appears involved in attacks on citizens or military forces. Hold members of any suspected insurgent family hostage until the insurgent turns himself in. Assassinate anyone who is suspected of being the leader or a follower of an insurgent cell. Deny any culpability for the resulting sorry state of affairs.

All of these hard-line approaches have been taken by the Israelis to vanquish rebellious Palestinians. Many of these tactics have recently been adopted by US forces in Iraq. US officers have gone to Israel to study them. Israeli "consultants" have gone to Iraq to help implant these new tactics. Reports from military officers in the Sunni Triangle, north and west of Baghdad, suggest the troops are satisfied with the results.

There is a perverse quality about this development. It can be taken as given that military forces under attack will try whatever methods are available to survive and achieve their military objective. It can also be taken as given that insurgents opposing invading forces will take whatever steps they can to stay alive and still do harm to their enemies. The tools on both sides, however, must pass acid tests of workability. This forces all of the players to ask: "Why are we doing this?" Typical answers to that question are all short term: We need to stop suicide bombers. We want to keep potential shooters out of range. We want to deny insurgents access to weapons. We want our people to feel safe. We want the people to stop resisting us. We want the occupiers to leave. The perverse quality is that nobody looks at the big picture.

The big picture in this case is harsh: The Israelis have been using these tactics for half a century and they are nowhere near success. They have displaced, killed, imprisoned, abused, hassled, and rendered countless Palestinians homeless with these tactics. The political promise of Israeli leadership to the people is that the tactics they use will make Israel safe and end the Palestinian struggle. That has not happened. All they have really achieved is enrichment of the common pool of Palestinian anger and the will not to submit. The Palestinians have never had equal capability to pursue this engagement, but they have pursued an equally bootless struggle. Neither side is victorious. Neither admits defeat. The relative sizes and capabilities of forces are immaterial.

American and Coalition forces in Iraq are moving toward this same dubious outcome as they concentrate on trying to squeeze the resistance out of the Iraqi people. Rather than quelling resistance, harsh measures are generating new pools of hate and determination to frustrate the occupier. It also generates new groups, in country and abroad, who offer sympathy and support to the insurgents. The prevailing result is a moving pattern of resistance that takes on new dimensions with each engagement. The "enemy" is not a fixed quantity, therefore defies containment. For the US, this situation is especially dangerous. Convincing the Iraqi people that we have their interests at heart was never a slam-dunk prospect. Invasion by its nature is hostile. Proving this invasion is not hostile to the Iraqi people can take more time than the Iraqis will allow. Increasing the harshness of tactics will only shorten the time to general disillusionment. The worst result of widespread resort to harsh tactics, however, will be a growing Iraqi conviction that there was never any intent to help them.

Capturing Saddam, if indeed he was captured and not bought, does not help this picture. Now that he is in custody and the Baath is in a manner headless, many Iraqis will believe that there is no threat from that source. Therefore there is no justification for harsh tactics against Iraqi civilians. With Saddam out of the picture in any military sense, the disillusionment of Iraqis will increase sharply unless the conflict environment improves. Insurgent groups can see this and outsiders, and Coalition forces should expect them to be deliberately provocative. Smart insurgent leaders will look for ways to increase the Coalition error rate.

Osama Bin Laden is probably looking on this situation with some glee. He can see that the situation contains the seeds of an American disaster. He would probably welcome, even provoke US adoption of Israeli tactics, because he knows how destructive of Iraqi belief in American goodwill those tactics can be. Use of those tactics will likely be publicized in Arab media, and the parallel to Palestine will become a common criticism in Islamic countries. Already damaged American credibility will be the main victim.

At this point, it is obvious that the exit from Iraq will not be easy. But any chance to make a graceful exit requires that American forces rise above the urge to make clever and immature military responses that undermine any effort to find a satisfactory political outcome. Restraint is called for now more than ever before, unless, of course, our forces and the Bush administration wish to repeat the Israeli experience of a fifty years war that goes nowhere.

ONLY A FEW BAD APPLES
May 2004

Hardly a Washington scandal begins without those closest to the problem reflexively asserting "this involves only a few bad apples." Or maybe even only one. And the best of resolutions will keep any proven guilt, or just the smell confined to one person. The White House initial reaction to the Abu Ghraib prison scandal started down this path with the assertion that President Bush knew nothing about this horror story until he saw the pictures on 60 Minutes. It could be that this statement is true and that his handlers and advisers in the White House and the Pentagon knew about the time bomb for weeks but did not tell Bush. However, the notion that the President would not be informed about a human and public relations debacle of this scale is just not credible.

Informed or not, Bush tried to talk his way around the Abu Ghraib horrors by telling Arab audiences on television that America is "a compassionate country that believes in freedom" and "cares about every individual." That was perhaps a fair statement about how Americans see themselves, but it explained nothing about torture and abuse of prisoners in

Iraq. And as the writer Michael Massing states in an <u>LA Times</u> article, "The rest of the world is not having it." Rather, others see recent actions as "part of a pattern of American arrogance and brutishness." What the President's apology suggested to listeners was that he was doing the politically needful while not facing the portrait of America being recorded and purveyed by digital cameras and laptops in Iraq.

As the story unfolds, senior Pentagon and US officers in Iraq knew about this problem before Christmas 2003, because they launched not only one but at least three investigations. As stated in its February 2004 report, the International Committee of the Red Cross reported numerous incidents to US military commanders in 2003. It could be, as Seymour Hirsh asserts in a May 5 <u>New Yorker</u> story, that both civilian leadership in the Pentagon and military leadership in Iraq thought they could keep this bombshell from exploding by keeping it quiet while looking into it. That might have been possible in the past for a screw up that involved only a few misdeeds in one Washington office, but not now. In the US military services where even the youngest buck private may sport a digital camera, a cell phone and a laptop, the actions of the "bad apples" in the middle of a barrel can be revealed to the whole Internet universe.

That happened. For better or surely for worse, the awesome images are either on the street or on the way to it. But what really went wrong here? The fiasco at Abu Ghraib stems from a combination of civilian leadership and military command failures. These began with the decision not to recognize the civil liberties of combatants captured in Afghanistan or elsewhere and confined at Guantanamo.

The Abu Ghraib frame of mind was fostered in Iraq by top-level decisions to treat any Iraqi who fought back against the occupation of his country as a terrorist. The label, "terrorists" was applied by L. Paul Bremer and military commanders and personnel. It fed a mindset of prison officials and staff to treat prisoners as basically a criminal element. The scandal that became Abu Ghraib grew in a series of decisions (a) to "prep" the so-called "high value" prisoners, meaning those who allegedly knew specifics of the insurgency, for interrogation, (b) to use methods well-developed in Israel and already in use in Guantanamo for this purpose, (c) to farm out responsibilities for these activities to civilian contractors, and (d) to send numerous cases to other countries where torture was commonplace. The resultant patterns of abuse set the stage for the digitally captured episodes that followed.

In short, Abu Ghraib is mostly about a failed chain of command, a failure that stretches upward to the top senior leadership of the Pentagon. It is also about a massive loss of perspective and high level abandonment of principle. Overall, the problem actually is with a few bad apples. Some are people. Some are behavioral. Some are institutional.

For those involved in battle, it is virtually impossible to switch abruptly from "shock and awe" bombings of civilians and an assault on weak military forces to error free management of an occupied country. Several thoughtful analysts have noted that it is a mistake to use the conquering troops as occupying forces. People simply do not switch suddenly from killing to caring.

They do not turn quickly from demeaning the enemy in words to establish a mindset for killing them to treating them with the respect due other human beings. The search and destroy instincts are essential to survival in warfare. If the occupied people resist, the search and destroy instincts of conquering troops are not likely to be turned off. The images from Abu Ghraib and reports from other prisons in Iraq and Afghanistan show that in the minds of prison guards and interrogators their Iraqi prisoners are sub-human.

The behavior that flows from considering a conquered people sub-human is too well documented to doubt. The horrible history of Nazi concentration camps, the allied bombing of Dresden, the American and Vietnamese tactics of the Vietnam War, the Israeli treatment of Palestinians, the actions of Palestinian extremists, the conduct of the Iraq war itself, and the treatment of prisoners in Iraq are all chapters in this sad story.

Many people have taken the lessons of those experiences on board. But it is equally clear that in the heat of combat, especially repeated and bloody skirmishes, the enemy will be de-humanized.

Military commanders know this, and they also know that to end a conflict they must either shut it off or bring in new people who never turned it on. In this instance Rumsfeld's insistence on a lean, mean fighting machine in Iraq is simply out of step with reality. This leaves us in Iraq with the wrong people with the wrong skills and the wrong outlook.

There were at least two avoidable mistakes: First, one of the ringleaders in the Abu Ghraib fiasco was a National Guardsman who was a prison guard in civilian life and had a well-known reputation for sadism. Sending him to Abu Ghraib was either deliberate or willfully stupid. In either case, it was avoidable. Second, from the beginning, top military commanders in Iraq, right up through General Sanchez were under enormous pressure, due to escalating casualty rates, to find information to combat an ever more deadly insurgency. Willingness to bend or even ignore the rules is a predictable result of that pressure, and necessary civilian oversight was not provided. Part of that problem, of course, was the fact that the orders came from top level civilian leadership.

It is difficult to say at this stage whether a new team with appropriate occupation skills could salvage the situation in Iraq. The American image in Iraq was badly frayed before the Abu Ghraib story broke. Discoveries of prisoner abuse at the prison, which seem to have already been widely reported and talked about among Iraqis, obviously have changed the climate for political transition.

It is likely that if the US tries to stay and to limit the scope and authority of any successor Iraqi government, the insurgency will get a new lease on life. An active insurgency is likely to prevent US forces from changing their habits: They must stop being combatants and become successful designers and implementers of an exit strategy.

AMERICA'S OIL PROBLEM
Iraq Is Not the Answer
June 2004

In the 2002-early 2003 run-up to the invasion of Iraq, US officials and media discussed several reasons for attacking that country. Weapons of mass destruction, a Saddam alliance with al Qaida, Iraqi involvement in 9-11, Iraqi support for terrorism, and implanting democracy in Iraq were all advanced as justifications for unseating Saddam Hussein. Note that Iraqi oil was never one of the officially advanced reasons, but on the Internet from the beginning the leading suspect was oil. Apparently, before he was fully in the loop on Bush team and neocon plans for Iraq, Secretary of State Colin Powell responded to suspicions about oil by stating that Iraq's oil belonged to the Iraqi people. Since the invasion, refurbishing Iraq's oil industry has been turned over to major US companies, and where that may lead is a question of great concern to Iraqis. How much difference Iraq will make to American oil needs is another question.

What are the leading issues? The leading issues for Iraq's oil future center on how substantial are Iraq's oil resources (potential oil) and active oil reserves (known developed oil), and what role those reserves can play in world oil exports, versus the constrained and harassed position Iraq has occupied since the first Gulf War. An interesting additional question is just how that role, with the US directly involved in production and exports would differ from the one a self-governing Iraq would play in the world oil market. The answers will be provided by the degree of sovereignty the designated Oil Minister Thamir Ghadbhan and his ministry will be able to exercise over oil industry decisions in the coming months. How well or whether Iraq will be able to reassert its role in OPEC will provide some of the answers.

How did OPEC come about? Before 1960, with the exception of the Soviet Union, world oil discovery, drilling, production and distribution were in the hands of large international companies, mainly American, British, French, and Italian. Prices for crude oil were quoted ex-Caribbean, at the gateway to the largest oil consuming market, the United States. In 1960, however, the Arab producers and the Venezuelans, whose countries contain most of the world's developed oil reserves, got together in Cairo, Egypt in an effort to take national control of their petroleum assets. Their solution was to form the organization now called OPEC, the Organization of Petroleum Exporting Countries. At the time western observers thought OPEC was not important. However, the founding of OPEC actually heralded the end of a colonial chapter in the Middle East.

Apparently only one of the founding fathers of OPEC is still living. He is Adnan Pachachi of Iraq, now the senior statesman in the Coalition Provisional Authority who just declined the offer to become President of Iraq.

What were OPEC goals? The overall goal of OPEC members was to take over ownership of their oil industries. But their first objective was to gain control over oil prices and the distribution of oil revenues. It took OPEC about a decade to get off the ground, and even a bit longer to have real impact, but in the early 1970s it began to assert itself. A succession of OPEC moves brought OPEC country shares (the tax) to 55% of the crude oil price in the early 1970s and sent crude prices toward a spike of $38 a barrel in 1978. Prices gradually drifted down from that peak to around $27 a barrel for Saudi Light in 1985, when supply manipulations by the Saudis caused prices to plummet to around $12 a barrel and lower. Prices since have fluctuated widely, going as low as $10 in the late 1990s, rising toward $30 per barrel in the reactions to the invasion of Iraq, and most recently going above $40 per barrel in reaction to chaos in Iraq and terrorism in Saudi Arabia. That compares with about $2.50 to produce a barrel of Saudi crude oil, and about $1.50 or less to produce a barrel of Iraqi crude.

What has changed? The entry of OPEC and the progressive nationalization of their individual country oil operations by OPEC member countries, and addition of countries such as Indonesia and Nigeria to the organization did not really change the international side of the oil business. It still remains in the hands of the major companies that are closely identified with transportation, refining, distribution, and marketing in the major markets. They were pushed out of their ownership positions in the national companies but retained control of the international business while themselves undergoing national and international reconfiguration. The international companies also became contractors to the new national oil companies because they had the relevant technologies and skills. But the big change was that OPEC members gained a major role in decisions respecting the quantities and the prices of their oil exports.

What is OPEC's present goal? Over the past several decades, literally since the Oil Shock of the early 1970s, OPEC and others sometimes allied with it have experimented repeatedly with the answer to a simple question: Just what will the traffic bear? The answers are crucial. It is important nationally for oil producers to satisfy their people that they are getting the best price for their national asset. But the answer most sought goes well beyond mere fairness. It has nothing to do with production costs. How aggressively can oil exporter countries raise the price? How much income can be transferred from buyer countries to seller countries without (a) starting a war, (b) provoking a diplomatic or financial crisis, or (c) encouraging the development of substitutes?

The same questions apply to the international companies who rule world oil trade. The answers are not fixed, because tolerance varies with economic conditions in oil consuming countries. Those conditions fluctuate separately and not necessarily in the same directions from place to place and, of course, the speed with which supply changes occur is always a factor. Price speculation in OPEC, oil company, financial, and share market circles only add to the uncertainty.

What leverage does OPEC have? In supply terms, OPEC members have most of the proven oil reserves outside oil importing countries. As domestic shares in oil consumption decline in the importer countries, OPEC leverage increases. The 95% dependence of the United States on oil for transportation is probably OPEC's most powerful weapon, because in the short run at least it is an inelastic area of our need, while US oil use is about a quarter of world demand, and OPEC—including Venezuela—provides about 40% of US oil imports. Thus OPEC oil export price decisions get immediate attention because they show up quickly in market behavior.

What do we want? Our long-term goal remains stable supplies and prices. The decline in US domestic oil production since the late 1970s—to less than half of supply—and growing total demand for oil, both for transportation and petrochemical uses, mean we must look more and more to imports. How to keep the US, with persistent and foreseeable heavy demand for imported oil, out of the oil exporter crosshairs is a major item in the national agenda. Every President of the United States and every leader of an oil importing country must attend to the day-to-day answers to this question. Oil alone represents more than one percent of US national product; the oil import account is the largest in US foreign trade; and it is a far bigger matter than that in our lifestyles.

How will Iraq figure in this? To put US companies in charge of the Iraqi oil industry sounds reassuring. But international companies, American or others, are just that. The temptation of US companies, if they run the Iraqi industry, would be to take a lesson from OPEC, in short, collect the same "tax" as OPEC, whatever may be the oil production cost. In the Iraqi case this could mean that at least alongside the Iraqi government, foreign-based American and other international companies will be playing the game of how much income can be transferred or how much can be kept abroad in their coffers. In supply terms Iraq is now exporting about 2.5 million barrels per day; the pre-invasion peak was 3 million barrels a day. Greater output appears unlikely in the near term, and significant expansion is likely to require heavy investment in oilfield development.

What is the outlook? "How much profit can we take without upsetting the market?" is the critical question asked by OPEC, and unless the players allow the market to descend into chaos, there will be only one set of prices for all the oil that moves in international trade. Thus American consumers stand to lose the same amount, that is, pay the same overhead in income transfers abroad, no matter whether the exporter to us is a foreign government, or an American/international company operating abroad, or a cartel in which those two groups of players are working together.

There are strong indications that the international oil outlook is worse than consumers generally suspect. There are differences of opinion among industry experts, but the most sober opinions are emerging right now from the group called the Association for the Study of Peak Oil now meeting in Berlin. This group includes OPEC and international company representatives, geologists, academics and others who know their subject.

Their view is that global oil production is about to peak. When it does, an inescapable pattern of shrinking supplies and rising prices will begin. Assuming that present oil users do not reduce their dependence, the Association message is that we face the end of what we know as cheap oil. In that case, the threat of terrorism will pale by comparison with the impact of shrinking oil supplies and rising costs. It means we will need to change our oil use habits, find alternative energy sources, change our lifestyles, or all of the above.

Is OPEC really in charge? Whether OPEC is in charge actually depends on whether OPEC members are working together or are operating separately as Saudi Arabia did in the early 1980s, at one stage driving the posted price of oil below $10. In that game, a major problem for OPEC is knowing just when and for how long to pursue a strategy. If prices go too high, the customers complain, even go to war, and begin to look for alternatives both habitual and material, while exporters may break ranks and increase exports to take advantage of the windfall. If prices go too low, the members of OPEC must act as a group to reduce exports, because they are losing money, but then so are all other exporters and producers.

What about energy alternatives? Up to now, change, as we have seen, has not occurred quickly in this realm. The urgency of the search for energy alternatives obviously grows when prices are high. However, the pace of searches by either governments or consumers for alternative remedies also slows when prices decline. As a matter of public policy, higher average fuel prices would force feed the search for alternatives and, based on experience, would achieve permanent changes in energy use. These tendencies represent a potentially powerful market mechanism for reducing oil dependencies, and greenhouse gases, but politicians have to have strong stomachs to force their application so long as oil remains available at tolerable prices. Moreover, serious analysts are pessimistic about alternative sources doing very much or very soon about the liquid fuel needs of the transportation system. Technologies to increase fuel mileage already exist, but adoption has been slow and the changeover can be expensive.

Who can manipulate the market? With the reserves of Iraq more fully developed and able to come on stream on fairly short notice, US companies could challenge OPEC for the price setting role. With some excess productive capacity they could also challenge Saudi Arabia in the last resort supplier role. However, non-traditional OPEC players have entered the game; in one instance both Norway and Mexico added their reserves to OPEC's bargaining strength. Others, including the Russians, can do that if they so choose. The main challenge device, increase exports, and cause prices to fall, appears an option with limited appeal, and OPEC countries can still limit price cuts by reducing exports

The appeal of the overall situation is that any gains OPEC makes in the level of international oil prices benefits all other oil exporters. Thus if the US companies in Iraq try to go off on their own they may suddenly discover they are something of a spoiler but lack sufficient clout to thwart OPEC with interested third parties in the play. This situation would be only a somewhat larger version of what has happened to OPEC before, i.e., members behaving independently to frustrate OPEC price manipulation gambits, or destabilize markets and cause prices to fall by offering excessive crude to the market. OPEC performs most effectively for its members when they work together and especially when OPEC goals coincide with those of other exporter countries. To be optimally involved in this play, therefore, US companies would have to join OPEC in the role of Iraq, or at least follow the OPEC model. What an ironic outcome!

The OPEC price band—Struggling with the problem of how to maintain their oil income streams while (a) keeping the members together on production and (b) still not driving the importer countries up the wall, OPEC established a price band mechanism on January 1, 1987. Under this arrangement, the prices of a basket of crude oils from seven different sources are used to police world export crude oil prices within a band between $22 and $28 per barrel. The rules of the game are as follows:

If the price of the basket of crude oils falls below $22 a barrel for 20 consecutive trading days, OPEC is supposed to reduce output/exports by 500,000 barrels per day, and if that does not bring average prices back within the band, output/exports would be cut another 500,000 barrels per day and so on. Conversely, if prices rise above $28 per barrel for 20 consecutive trading days, OPEC is supposed to increase output/exports by 500,000 barrels per day, and so on.

However, the basket price went above $28 per barrel on December 2, 2003 and the basket price remained above $28 per barrel up through the recent climb above $40.

If the Peak Oil group is right in its projections, prices may be soft for a little while at or below $40 per barrel. However, prices are most likely to rise, and one estimate places possible increases at a multiple of present prices. The prospect for oil exporters is that they will get more for less but still face long term shrinking income. The prospect for consumers is that they will pay more, potentially a great deal more, for less while facing growing scarcity in total supply. There is a real question right now as to whether the combination of demand growth in main user markets and supply uncertainty due to conflict conditions in the Persian Gulf and in Venezuela leave OPEC any room to maneuver. So the opening knell of future oil scarcity is already tolling.

Who benefits from the game? On its face the idea of managing oil prices within a range of acceptable fluctuation sounds like a good world market management tool. People everywhere adjust, one way or another, to stable prices. However, while it does have a supply stabilization effect, this mechanism is not being run for the common good of consumers. It is designed to protect the earnings of the exporters and the international companies. That this is surely so is reflected in the relationship of the price levels in the price band basket ($22-$28 per barrel) as compared to average worldwide crude oil production which is profitable at or below $10 per barrel. For Iraqi crude, as noted earlier, the production cost was about $1.50 per barrel before the US invasion.

Thus the export of crude oil at any price within the price-band provides substantial windfall profits to the exporter countries. At the same time, since US oil product prices are pegged to the costs of imported crude oil—currently more than 55% of US demand and rising—domestic producers and refiners receive a significant windfall on their domestic product. Consumers worldwide pay the price for this neat arrangement without ever knowing it exists.

Who is being had? It is argued that the price band is essential to assuring that producer exporter countries continue to keep the oil flowing. In fact, it is possible only when OPEC members work together as a monopoly. Certainly a rate of return that is two to three times the average cost of production represents a substantial incentive. On the other hand, however, if profits were merely fair, what would the exporters do? Keep the oil? Not likely. Seen in this light, we are all involuntary contributors to sizeable year-to-year windfall profit taking by the exporter countries and by our own suppliers in the oil industry, since our suppliers quite sensibly benchmark the price of their product on the landed price of imports.

Being sad sacks, we consumers just drive up to the pump and pay whatever it says, and we pay the price of truck and air transport on most everything we buy. We therefore make all of the oil pricing and profit taking possible because we do not examine the business in any critical way. Nor do we make any demands of the industry other than keep it coming at affordable prices. We do not run far enough in front of the problem to reduce our oil needs or restructure our energy use.

But we are not being had as much as some. There are two main reasons we do not change our habits. Because taxes, both federal and state, are lower, oil product prices in the US are lower than in virtually any other oil importing country. The US price for a gallon of regular gas today is nationally averaged at less than $2.50. In Britain it is more than $5.00. Moreover, gasoline prices in the US today are lower in real terms than they were 20 years ago. Of course, in a rising oil price situation, that gasoline pump price advantage will evaporate.

What next? Things have to change, because it is no idle threat that we are running out of oil. Around 1956, an oil geophysicist for Shell Oil, King Hubbert, predicted US production would peak in 1970 after which our actual output would decline. It was a bit delayed, but US oil production has peaked, output has declined, and increases in demand result in increases in imports. Moreover, expert estimates suggest that potential output from exploitable sources under US control will at best slow the rate of decline in US output. It is ironic that new US fields could be enormously profitable to the exploiters, but are unlikely to change the US dependence on imported oil or to deflect the rise in prices consumers will have to pay for it.

What about competition? While the United States still leads the pack, new economic miracles are rapidly moving up on it. As discussed in the final article, "Another Look in the Black Box", China, India, Brazil and a number of smaller economies rapidly are increasing their demands for oil. They are showing up in leading sources countries such as Venezuela and Iran, the rest of the Middle East, Nigeria, Sudan and elsewhere, seeking to tie up oil supplies. This competition is disorderly and, on the part of individual countries, necessarily self-serving. It is now asserting itself seriously, and it will eventually become a dominant fact of life for the US in planning its energy future.

Now what about Iraq? Where does Iraq fit in this international oil picture? The answer does not depend on who owns Iraqi oil. It depends on what role Iraqi oil can play in world supply and for how long, and, of course, on how world exportable supplies are allocated. As noted earlier, Iraqi oil reserves are now thought to be second only to Saudi Arabia, and since three-quarters of Iraq's expansive sand trap remains unexplored or at least under-explored, there may be more. As it is drawn down by anticipated consumption, however, world oil output is expected to peak by about 2020. Some say the peak is approaching now. But the point is there truly is a decline in sight, and we had better get on with the task of finding/developing alternative energy sources, not tomorrow or next day, but now.

Isn't it time to shed illusions? Iraq is a factor in any US strategy for exiting virtual complete dependence on oil for transportation and for shifting to alternative energy systems. But the Iraqi role is not decisive. Actually, Iraq has more impact on oil supplies and prices as an unstable conflict zone than it is likely to have as a stable oil producer. Its present role in setting OPEC prices has to be questionable. But any notion that control of Iraqi oil promises long term satisfaction of US energy needs is an illusion. And the notion that US control of Iraqi oil versus Iraqi control of its own oil makes any real difference in American supply or pump price prospects is also an illusion. That prices may come down again is certainly an illusion.

It is not an illusion that the supply situation is getting worse. It is an illusion that this prospect would be significantly altered by drilling for oil, and even finding it, in environmentally fragile areas of our national parks.

What is the bottom line? The big picture is clear enough. Either we get with the task of developing alternative energy sources, many of which are already known to us, or we prepare our country for long-term and possibly sudden increases in energy costs that will bring on severe economic decline. There is no ducking the costs of the needed changes in energy systems. Nor can we duck the difficulty—both cost and convenience—of changing our liquid fuel dependent transport system to non-oil energy sources. It is simply true that we can bear those costs most easily while our economy is growing. The costs will be most burdensome if we wait until the economy is in decline. The cumulative damage to our environment caused by delays may or may not be reversible.

Here then is our simple set of equations: We begin paying now for the technologies needed to move us into alternative energy sources, and we pay that as a tax on what it costs us now for oil-based energy. Let's say we pay a modest 5 cents a gallon, meaning between 75 cents and $1.00 per tank of gasoline into a dedicated fund for alternative energy development. Last month US refiners were producing and selling about 9 million barrels of gasoline per day. That is about 380 million gallons, and the tax revenue would be $19 million per day. Multiply that by 365 days a year and you have raised about $7.0 billion in alternative energy development funding. You could double that if you add airline and truck fuels.

On the other hand, we can continue to pay the rising costs of oil and make no investment in our energy future. But we will pay higher prices for shrinking supplies of fuel and industrial feedstock along with a high price in economic stagnation or failure. The countries that actually work to solve the alternative energy problems will take over from us. We may alter the curve a little by taking pre-emptive military action, but we will make many enemies while using much of our energy to get and keep supplies of energy. Iraqi oil may influence the timing a little bit, but Iraqi oil will not change the outcome.

SEEING OUR WAY OUT OF IRAQ
August 2005

During the past two weeks more than 30 American servicemen died in Iraq, and this month is shaping up to be the deadliest month of the entire war. The casualties add to a dismal reckoning that now exceeds 2,000 Coalition dead and 15-20,000 wounded. The unofficial count, by knowledgeable people who say the Government is not telling it like it is, amounts to more than twice that number of American dead and wounded. There are more than ten times those numbers of Iraqi dead and wounded, who are not included in any official tally. That is to say nothing of the thousands on both sides who already are or will become psychological basket cases from this experience.

The statistics for Gulf War I, tabulated by the Veterans Administration in 2002, suggest that, while initial casualties were light, the casualties of that War ultimately exceeded 30%. Gulf War II is and has been a far more hairy experience. Fighting has been heavier and much more prolonged. Many tons more of depleted uranium (DU) weapons have been used, along with other toxic devices. Thus, a long term casualty rate for American forces of 40-50% appears realistic.

Has the engagement been worth it? Should we stick around to see how it finally turns out? In the end, will we be able to say that the outcome was worth 60-70,000 damaged, distorted or destroyed American lives, to say nothing of the effects on their families and communities? Will it have been worth hundreds of thousands of Iraqi casualties, many of them women and children?

Available facts today are against a positive answer to those questions. Based on everything we have learned from real experience with the invasion and occupation—from the Downing Street Memo and following publications and admissions—neither the Bush team nor the British leadership either could or chose to see clearly into Iraq on the first day.

Are they able to see the way out? The view at this moment suggests they cannot.

Start with the global security situation. The most blatant indications of failure to see that situation is the thought, expressed by Tony Blair on the day of July 7, 2005 London bombings, and echoed by George W. Bush, that we are under attack because of our way of life. That is true only in the grimmest form of the observation: What we are doing in Iraq and Afghanistan, tolerating in Palestine, and perpetrating in Guantanamo and numerous other prison locations looks like our way of life, and that way of life is deeply resented and opposed by millions of people. We are fortunate only that so few of them choose to react violently. The attackers are not trying to wreck our way of life. They want us to stop destroying theirs.

Will the situation improve quickly? So long as there is a shooting war going in Iraq and Afghanistan, and so long as the human rights and dignity of thousands of men and women are abused by the United States as they now are, the prospects of peace are virtually nil. And the chance that some of the people who are now angry enough to try to kill some of us will cease and desist is zero. Having created a new generation of terrorists, we will experience more terrorism.

We won't necessarily know who some of those people are until it is too late, but the disturbing truth may be that there is now no turning back for some of them, no matter what we do. We will pay, and no war on terrorism can prevent that from happening, somewhere, somehow, sometime.

Can we do something about it? There are many things that would help. For example, several members of Congress, including John McCain and other Republicans, are pushing legislation to restore American observance of international law and our own military regulations on the treatment of prisoners. Ominously, the regulations are said to be in the process of being rewritten in the Pentagon. Provisions to restore US observance of international law and our own well-established practices have been added to a major spending bill that Bush has threatened to veto if they remain in the bill. Supporters of the President on this say basically that he is above the law, anybody's law. That announces to the world that the failures reported at Abu Ghraib, Guantanamo and elsewhere were not due to a few bad apples, but were brought on by the highest levels of American policy making, and US leadership remains unreconstructed on this issue.

Is presidential prerogative really at issue here? There is nothing in the Constitution or the United States Code that says the President is above the law. As the Chief Executive of the United States, one of the leading responsibilities of the President is to see that the law of the land is carried out. His oath of office says he faithfully will do that. In effect, the President's position on observing established US laws and treaties on torture says he willfully abdicates his responsibility as President of the United States. Under his "You are either with us or against us" rules, "combatants" are "against us", and Bush wants to be the nation's chief advocate of cruel and unusual punishment for people who have not even been brought to trial. The President's attitude on this and that of his supporters makes a moral and legal travesty of the American presidency. It simply cannot be a prerogative of the President to ignore established laws.

How does that bear on getting us out of Iraq? One of the hardest things about making peace is persuading the protagonists that the time for battle is over. People do remember that they were mauled, their homes and towns destroyed, their family members confined, tortured, and denied human rights. The longer that goes on, the more vivid is the recall. And if some die, others tend to remember for them. The peace, if it comes, is always troubled by such recollections, and the people who recall are seldom ever able to go after the real perpetrators. Thus, they go for softer targets. Communities, families, individual victims pay for the failures of leadership. The resultant instability makes it appear to leaders who are disposed to think that way anyway that they have no choice but to "stay the course" to "maintain the peace." They refuse to concede that they may be the reason peace does not prevail. That illusion sustains enduring occupation, which feeds enduring conflict.

Bush reiterated that position this week. Faced by a growing, but only morally armed group of Cindy Sheehan supporters outside his gate at Crawford, Texas, and surrounded by his war cabinet, Bush called the growing mayhem in Iraq "a grim reminder of the brutal enemies we face in the war on terror." And he pleaded with an increasingly skeptical America to support his "stay the course" strategy.

But what is the Iraq reality? Both President Bush and Britain's Prime Minister Tony Blair keep pushing their basic theme that there is no connection between chaos in Iraq and attacks or risks of terrorist attacks in the west. We went into Iraq allegedly to liberate a people who would be grateful for the freedom from Saddam Hussein. From the beginning, our people on the ground found that few Iraqis approved of the invasion. That disapproval gradually morphed into an insurgency in and around Baghdad that now covers the bulk of northwestern Iraq and breaks out sporadically in both the south (Shi'a territory) and the north (mainly Kurdish territory). A certain number of outsiders also disapproved and went to Iraq to fight with the insurgents, perhaps in some instances to make their own mayhem.

The effort to liberate Iraq bogged down. More Iraqis joined the fray, by some reports, creating not one but several insurgencies potentially numbering many thousands of adherents. The US set out to train Iraqi forces to take over the task of defeating the insurgencies and maintaining public order. The US lead in this effort, however, never diminished because the Iraqis did not seem capable of or, for that matter, willing to fight their own people, unless the situation turned to outright communal violence. Now the US has more than a mythical tar baby to deal with. Because the US remains in the lead, the Iraqis being trained, as well as officials who are running the interim government and drafting a new constitution, are widely if not uniformly tainted by the US connection. The insurgents attack them as well as the Coalition—mainly the American—forces. US efforts are then strengthened to train more Iraqis to take over, and in the meantime, American forces are stuck there, under siege.

A US promised democracy has become Iraqi against Iraqi. The US is training Iraqi forces to defeat Iraqis who do not want the American or other Coalition forces there. What this does is deepen and reinforce divisions among Iraqis that, in the Iraqi ethnic triad, were already simmering, and in some locations appear to be coming to a boil. In effect, people the US injured, tortured, killed or insulted by occupation increase in number every day, and the objectors, including the living victims and the relatives of the dead, take out their anger and frustration on Americans and on the Iraqis who are visibly affiliated with Americans. The Bush team is now saying the US can see itself withdrawing—at least partially—from Iraq when and if the Iraqis are able to contain the insurgency. Since the insurgency is fueled by the US presence, that withdrawal condition simply locks Iraq into enduring conflict.

The chances that the insurgency will abate while the US remains in Iraq are nil. It is hard to see your way out of a situation if you will not face the real nature of the situation. Bush and Blair have thoroughly confused the issues in their own minds, and they are increasingly at odds with the people of their respective countries. But the tragedy of it is that training Iraqis to kill or punish, i.e., imprison, other Iraqis, or Afghans to kill or confine other Afghans is merely setting these societies against themselves.

The situation needs to be turned as quickly as possible into one in which the US is not fighting the Iraqis, and neither are Iraqis. Expecting the Iraqis to bludgeon themselves into a democratic society is preposterous. The present conflict can be resolved only by turning the whole matter over to a UN peacekeeping force that does not contain any Americans, and that does not continue to set the Iraqi people against each other.

THE OUTLOOK

ANOTHER LOOK AT THE BLACK BOX
August 2005

On May 10, 2005, a federal appeals court in Washington, DC dismissed a lawsuit brought by the groups Judicial Watch and the Sierra Club to force disclosure by the Bush administration of the participants and the decisions of Vice President Cheney's 2001 energy policy task force. According to a May 11 report of The Washington Post, a Cheney adviser said that the decision will "preserve the confidentiality of internal deliberation among the president and his advisers that the Constitution protects as essential to wise and informed decision making," thus, the adviser continued, "further solidifying the President's power to deliberate and seek advice behind closed doors without disclosing details."

Candor is seldom the preferred stance of governments, but the Constitution does not contain language that certifies the alleged Cheney need for secrecy. Rather that document contemplates more openness than secrecy. By Bush team preference for a paranoid level of secrecy, we have a leadership that operates almost totally "behind closed doors".

Thus there is an enormous gap between government plans or actions and public understanding of them. The gap means that most people have no awareness of the specific problems our government confronts, or of the solutions—or failures to reach solutions—that will affect everybody, now and in the future. The gap also means that the public is outside the loop on what the problem really is and what solutions might be the most effective, least costly both politically and financially, or most desirable.

Many of the articles in this book concern decisions and actions that are surrounded by missing, incomplete, or even false justifications. A citizen trying to judge the purposes or benefits of such activities is severely handicapped. Maybe we can get some sense of what Bush and his advisers, or their successors, are doing or are likely to do by examining closely the most critical issues that require attention. What is going into the black box, now and in coming years?

The global issues – Several articles in this book talk about the global issues, those matters of common concern to people everywhere. The list is short, but frightening: Growing population, shrinking resources, increasing competition, resurgent militarism, the growing gap between rich and poor, degradation of the environment, including global warming, and the lack of a common set of answers to any of these challenges. To be sure, one can find enormous amounts of information about all of the issues on the Internet. That does not discharge the obligation of leadership to level with the people, and to engage them in making the decisions that affect everybody. But at the same time, neither we nor the Third Estate, the media, are asking enough questions and insisting on enough answers. We need to look at the issues in a future oriented way with a view to judging what the most serious issues are, and how closely current policies fit our necessity.

All the big issues are global. No issue is new, but some have grown more acute since the turn of the new century. There are signs that the global political and economic operating system faces rising pressure for change in the way those issues are managed. The 20th century began with a few more or less wealthy countries, mostly European except for the United States and Japan, and a mass of poor countries and colonial appendages. As the 21st century began, the lead was in basically the same places; the truly poor had increased in number, but the middle, led by China and India, was rising to challenge and perhaps even to take the lead.

Population—On May 1, 2005, the world population clock hovered at about 6.441 billion people. Population had more than doubled since 1960. More than a third of them lived in two countries: China and India. Over 60% lived in 11 countries, while the remaining 39% or so lived in 181 countries, ranging from the Philippines with 87 million people to Samoa with 177,000, plus a number of islands and enclaves. Only China has exercised significant state limits on population increase, but the Chinese model of one child per family has begun to decay as urban family incomes increase. At present rates of growth, world population could reach or exceed 12 billion people by 2050. That means at least two people standing everywhere you see one standing today.

While the already visible pressures on global resources show an urgent need to reduce population growth, the Bush administration, responsive to conservative Christian supporters, takes the view that nature should be allowed to take its course. The US has withdrawn all assistance to family planning, most importantly contraception, and has taken a position strongly against the abortion of unwanted pregnancies that, in the absence of contraception, have greatly increased in number, along with child abandonment by poor parents.

On a global scale, the Bush position is not only impractical, it is inhumane. Bush and his Christian conservative backers may revel in the morality they ascribe to this policy, but millions of families pay and will pay for it with reduced ability to survive an already harsh existence. Life, indeed, may be sacred, but forcing the creation of life without plans to assure its healthy survival is surely blasphemy.

Resources—Over the past century and even earlier, global resource use has been heavily concentrated in a few places. The production and use of key resources—coal, oil, natural gas, metals, food, building materials—have focused on the leading economies. Individual country shares of global income and wealth are heavily concentrated in those countries. The United States, the European Community, and Japan account for more than two thirds of global domestic product. At the other extreme, more than 300 million people—equal to the entire population of the United States—earn an income well below the US defined poverty line. China, India, Brazil, and a few others are advancing rapidly, but for at least a third of humanity economic prospects are stagnant, locked in at low levels.

More than half of the world's primary energy—the developed and distributed forms being oil, coal, and gas—has been consumed by the United States, Japan, and the European Community. The three also have produced or imported and used most of the iron and non-ferrous metals such as copper, and much of the world's timber harvest.

Up to the present century, competition for supply of such resources was largely in those developed markets, and known supplies generally exceeded their demands so that prices tended to stay reasonably consonant with production and distribution costs. However, demand has been growing at a rate approaching frenzy in the increasingly active and competitive markets of China, India, Brazil and several smaller countries.

No globally agreed strategy exists today for allocating scarce resources. Market forces have worked in the past to allocate them to the strongest economies. That worked so long as supplies were adequate to effective demand. It clearly will not work unaided where supplies are not adequate to demand. The emerging need is to allocate the impact of scarcity, meaning to assure that some equitable distribution of supplies takes over from the old system that was driven by sales to the highest bidder.

The outlook is shaping up as highly competitive and probably contentious. World material resources are being allocated by each contender independently bidding for a corner of available supplies. As long as there is enough of any key resource to satisfy the market, the principal result of this competitive arrangement will be increasing prices to consumers as extraction costs rise with increases in energy costs. However, what will happen when absolute supply limitations or prohibitive costs due to scarcity set in? At that point agreements to share limited supplies on an equitable basis will be needed, or the markets will descend to various levels of cutthroat bargaining.

The neo-con image of America's future, as contained in the work of the Project for the New American Century, is focused on making the US strong enough militarily to dominate the globe. While apparently military in focus, that prescription for strength also positions the United States to win the coming battles for resources. The basic neo-con move is to embrace a pre-emptive strategy that depends on superior military power, including nuclear weapons. In this manner, the battle for economic resources will fuel a perpetual arms race.

The scramble for energy – Energy must be at the leading edge of the pre-emptive resource strategy. The actual scope of world energy resources is generally known but still hotly debated. US coal has been mapped and looks sufficient to support coal-powered activities for at least another 200 years, if the environment can stand it. Advocates of the so-called "peak oil" analysis say that the United States reached peak potential output around 1970, and indeed the country has imported increasing amounts ever since, now buying more than 60% of its oil abroad. Promoters of the non-biological origins of world oil argue that it did not result from the decay of vegetation but from earth-forming processes, perhaps such as those recently shown in satellite images from Saturn's moon Titan. Therefore, they claim there is much more to be found. In essence, the non-biological oil advocates say, we have plenty, and "peak oil", they claim, is a conspiracy of big oil to retain control of supplies and prices.

Whatever the case, normal demand growth in advanced countries plus recent explosive increase in demand for oil in China, India, and Brazil, has driven the world price of a barrel of oil above $50, and that sets the price even in countries such as the US, where it costs a great deal less than that to produce and refine. Such obviously windfall profits from oil, plus belief that the near term prospect is for shrinking supplies, has driven the Bush administration to put virtually all of its energy development resources into the oil and nuclear baskets, leaving little for advancing renewable energy sources such as solar, water and wind or for new developments or discoveries.

The Bush team obviously views the assurance of American access to oil and natural gas as a critical matter; uncertainty indeed poses a threat to economic growth, national income and finance, national security, and the American lifestyle. That threat is likely to grow, and it may not really diminish until the American economy/life style has switched successfully over to alternative energy systems. Thus, present policy is to position in the Middle East, in Afghanistan and in countries along the northern frontier of the region to assure American protection of its energy supplies. Being placed to acquire and defend energy sources at this moment are at least fourteen bases in Iraq, bases in Afghanistan, Uzbekistan, around the Caspian Sea, and at points along major pipeline and supply routes, all to make certain that the flow of oil and natural gas is not disrupted, and that drilling and oil/gas field operations in those regions can be pursued without interference.

The world economy needs oil and natural gas at this stage on an unprecedented scale. Thus, efforts to assure discovery, drilling, production, and distribution are in the common interest of everybody. If one reads the neo-con agenda carefully, however, it is clear that the aim of all the energy related maneuvers is not to serve global needs even-handedly, but to preempt supply, to assure that the US economy does not suffer severe shortages, regardless of how the rest of the world fares. Short term expediency is driving this train. Other countries are taking a less visibly aggressive but obviously a self-interested view of how to serve their own resource needs. China, for example, is chipping away at most US oil import sources.

That competitive focus is defining the resource struggle for the whole world for the indefinite future. It assures that the battle for resources will be contentious and combative. It assumes that the only way to assure US supplies of these scarce and critical resources is to control them from source to the American market or to limit flows to the markets for other leading contenders.

Increasing competition—Global resource allocation issues that grow every day more urgent are being left to competitive market practices that have served to sustain American economic demands up to now, but the rules are changing. China not only has become the key US supplier of imported consumer goods, it has become a thirsty competitor for oil. Chinese mines are producing coal at a reckless rate, as shown in virtually daily mine accident fatalities. At the same time, China is a voracious user of imported coal and iron, especially from Australia. If current leadership thinking prevails, the next stages of Chinese growth will depend largely on greatly increased coal use for power production and creation of synfuel from coal to reduce oil imports. Given present mining practices and absent pollution controls, this model will result probably in an environmental nightmare. However, near term growth depends on successful competition for available world oil. That means higher prices and/or scarcity driven switches to alternative energy sources.

This story repeats in great measure for each of the world traded materials used in manufacture, many of which—platinum for example—are held by only a few source countries. The unwanted effect of rapid economic growth is increasingly acute scarcity of key materials, leading to increasing competition and rising prices, and rising money and energy costs for materials recovery. Moreover, the energy shortage presents a potential crisis across a broad range of material needs and production processes.

A new plan is needed. The planet needs urgent and transparent examination of how key resources will be allocated in the future. Since the key resources—energy sources, metals, timber, non metallic minerals—are critical to economic growth, each country will strive to acquire what it needs. At the margin, the methods used to deal with shortages can be cooperative or competitive, sharing or conflicting. Up to now, competitive market strategies have worked—not entirely without conflict, but the biggest single attribute of a successful competitive resource allocation system has been the weak demand of most of the world. The resource base worked best when only a small portion of humanity made heavy demands on it. When, as now, key resources are dwindling and half of humanity is in hot pursuit, new rules clearly are needed.

New scientific thinking can help. In a sense, the black box is being reinvented and perhaps greatly improved. Instead of simply trying to predict the future, a new generation of thinkers seeks to model alternative futures, to postulate possible configurations of future inputs and developments and then to plot positive and negative outcomes. Such analytical exercises can be run for a variety of situations and time frames to determine what may be the best starting lineups and patterns of future inputs, given what is known now. The analysis has been enhanced with computer simulations that speed analysis, identify gaps and weaknesses, and sharpen judgment. Governments and business planners could and should use such techniques to weigh the future utilities and consequences of present or planned resource use patterns. A great deal of future conflict might be avoided if they did.

Where does terrorism fit in this environment? A number of experienced analysts think that the War on Terrorism is a non sequiteur. Not only does the War fail to deal with the global problems of violence in society, it also fails to deal with the underlying causes of terrorist violence. Our country simply does not have enemies who are avowedly or visibly dedicated to taking what we have away from us. But our country faces a battery of increasingly effective competitors whose goals must be to assure coverage of their own resource needs. As the Bush/neo-con team may define our situation publicly, the War on Terrorism is the only immediately plausible/politically defensible reason for arming to the teeth.

Resurgent militarism – In the context of the coming scrambles for resources, the Bush/neo-con conception—indeed perhaps the long term Washington conception—is that military strength is a crucial bargaining tool. Being absolutely the strongest is essential, while revealing nothing about plans is probably vital. Viewed in terms of pre-positioning, the Bush posture on several issues is revealing. On a global basis, the key to successful bargaining is power—the more the better. That makes nuclear weapons, including newer and better ones, an important part of US preparation for the future. It makes heavy expenditure on defense systems a vital part of the posture. It means playing to the maximum the bargaining leverage represented by the US contribution to global economic performance. All of the above provide a rationale, if not legitimate justification, to expect others to acquiesce in allocations of scarce resources that favor the United States.

If those efforts succeed, what comes out of the black box is a severe drag on the development prospects of at least half of humanity. Whether alternative energy sources will come along fast enough to meet transitional requirements is questionable. How much individual and business decisions to install alternative systems will free up existing oil and gas supplies is unknown. It is impressive that business is booming in the solar energy systems and hybrid car arenas, even though the price of a complete system could equal more than 10% of the value of a medium priced home, while a hybrid car may cost much more than its gas guzzling predecessor. The near term prospect is that the wealthier countries will outbid the rest of the world for scarce resources. The big new contenders—China, India, and Brazil—can compete because they have the cash flow to bid successfully for supplies. That portends a pattern of limited supplies and high to rising prices that will penalize everybody, but will hurt the weaker countries the most.

The new colonialism—The future has a colonial era caste to it. Before and during the first half of the 20th century military power was used often to prevent intrusions into colonial spaces; e.g., efforts to interfere with control over areas and key resources such as copper in the Congo. Colonial ownership of the sources no longer being possible, the use of superior force to preempt supplies, set favorable prices, enforce a preferred position, or deflect competition look like the future habits of mankind.

As often demonstrated in the past, the military power that was generated to avoid losing colonial possessions had the effect of generating competition among colonial powers. Such power always has had economic purposes: To obtain or control key material sources, intimidate competition, protect supply lines, ensure key markets, assist allies.

The irony of it, however, is that the game is self-perpetuating. By insisting on being militarily number one, the US is encouraging the evolution and growth of number two, number three, and so on. It is a heady business to make expensive things for dropping, blowing up, propelling or throwing away, and then doing it all over again to sustain a lifestyle of exaggerated consumption. Colonial military powers have lived that way for centuries.

A further irony is that the United States has used its rich mixture of consumer buying and military expenditure/waste to fuel the global economic system to the tune of a third of global domestic product. It has hitched its wagon to a global economic star, because all other world economies are vitally interested in the health of this operating system. While they may not like the military side of it, they are vitally interested in keeping this system healthy, even to the tune of financing the excessive US external debt, and tolerating our profligate consumption habits This is not the first time a colonial/imperial power has lived off the neighbors.

The emerging model – China and India are in a process of challenging and reinventing this model. While their military tools may be less powerful and likely to remain so, they both have the enormous attraction of large markets, new sources of demand for goods and services, large and literate labor forces, all likely to be associated with firm to rising prices for all goods and services. Meanwhile, Brazil is moving to pose a similar challenge in the Western Hemisphere.

The model that led to US, European and Japanese preeminence is faltering, and the dispersed concept of global economic growth that is emerging will undercut it through various devices: larger markets, larger labor forces, greater needs for materials, the ability to field larger armies, greater pollution, and each country's will to serve its own needs, even if that involves conflict.

The tragic flaw—Economists long ago identified the flaws in the guns/butter economy, but up to now their understanding has failed, even with the help of explosive new service sectors, to provide an alternative economic model for continuous growth and prosperity. The driving rationale for the guns/butter economy is the fact that it underpins the concept of full employment. That, in turn, permits large and diverse populations to enjoy lifestyles that are often far removed from survival necessity. The downside is that it is voracious, requiring continuing growth and commitment to the burgeoning waste associated with military systems and forces. Since World War II, as President Dwight Eisenhower warned in his farewell address, the providers of military systems and their increasingly powerful political support have parlayed this model into a bonanza for themselves, while offering a shrinking share to the people who do the work and provide the services.

The dominant flaw in this system in our time is that it cannot be made non-threatening. No country at this time, except Iraq, has a declared military antagonist, but no country can arm itself to the teeth without suggesting to all other countries that they, under unclearly defined conditions, could well be attacked. This stimulates the urge to prepare one's own defenses, and the race, as always, is on. Proliferation breeds proliferation.

The nuclear quandary—While seeming, early on, to have obviated the traditional military/industrial model, the injection of nuclear weapons into this broth has greatly increased the temperature. A few decades of talk from the nuclear club members about disarmament, and their actual signing onto it in the 30 year old Nuclear Non-Proliferation Treaty may have slowed the drift of the world into a perpetual arms race. However, the refusal of the US to examine, or even to own up to that commitment in the recently completed five year review of the NPT, along with the lack of effective challenge to that posture by other major powers, was the birth cry of a new arms race. The commitment of the United States to remain armed with nuclear weapons and to upgrade them, and create new types, such as bunker busters now under congressional consideration, has assured a future arms race that will underpin efforts to assure resource supplies and will be limited only by available technologies.

War on Iraq was initiated allegedly to protect the United States from weapons of mass destruction, but as a recently published confidential UK memo makes clear, the President and his immediate advisers knew Iraq did not have such weapons. Threats to Iran, North Korea, or Syria, none of which has threatened the US, add more enemies. Meanwhile, the big challenges are from China and India and others whose aims are to promote, fuel, and protect their own growth and development. Their challenges will be about access to resources, and they will arm to keep from being denied that access. This is the kind of situation that, as former Secretary of Defense Robert S. McNamara said in a recent Foreign Policy article, makes US nuclear weapons policy "immoral, illegal, militarily unnecessary, and dreadfully dangerous."

The role of Israel—Exclusive support for Israel and defense of its repression of the Palestinian people are growing handicaps to American policy effectiveness in the Middle East and, in many respects, worldwide. Israel and its neo-con supporters on the Bush team have made it politically dangerous to buck Zionist plans for a greater Israel. An American politician who tries is likely to be assassinated politically. Past victims include Senator Fulbright, Congressman Findley, and others. Those Zionist plans, and the abominable treatment of the Palestinians that goes with them, were destabilizing the Middle East long before the invasion of Iraq, and the potential impact of Israeli plans and actions on regional stability remains enormous.

Zionist efforts to suppress any criticism of Israeli plans and actions by Americans or American media are widespread, virtually shutting down Middle East studies on American campuses. Those efforts even include attempts to suppress University of California Berkeley publication of a work by one Jewish writer who questions the accuracy of the writings of another Jewish writer. Meanwhile, the noose that conservative Christian and other supporters of Israel have placed around the necks of US policymakers and lawmakers will be the ruin of Israelis and Americans alike if not removed.

The human condition—Poverty, hunger, and disease already create for much of humanity a Hobbsian condition of life that is savage, brutish, and short. Life expectancy in the US, much of Europe, Japan, and China, altogether 35 or so countries, may range from 70-80 years, but in much of Sub-Sahara Africa a life of more than 50 years is uncommon, while in some countries such as Zimbabwe the prospect is less than 40 years.

The US does not lead this pack. In fact, a recently-developed World Health Organization index, the Disability Adjusted Life Expectancy, or DALE chart, places the United States at number 24 in adjusted life expectancy, due to its dietary habits, relatively weak healthcare system, and other factors such as homicide and suicide rates. The index uses a pragmatic combination of mortality plus quality of life indicators.

The global income picture, as painted by the World Bank, has only modest positives. Some 29 or 30 countries have a per capita income of more than $20,000 per year. However, 70 or more countries have per capita incomes of less than $1,000, and 40 of those have incomes of less than $500 per year.

A concerted effort to lift this floor would have quite remarkable effect. It should be no surprise that people who live on the edge of extinction, as many do, may desperately want to have children, but as UN data, and the experience of advanced countries show, birth rates tend to decline as incomes grow.

Two distinct processes of nation state adjustment therefore appear necessary to improving the human condition: Raise the economic floor of the weakest, and lower the economic ceiling of the wealthiest. The present floor under humanity is simply not tolerable, while the ceiling is not sustainable without continuing the great disparities that in part are linked to inequitable distribution of resources. Life style adjustments in the US and other wealthy countries to reduce profligate consumption of limited resources and to make them available to others are as important to future human well being as ridding the planet of poverty and disease. We are not putting nearly enough into the black box to make that happen.

The environment—Assaults on the environment have grown more aggressive and punitive in the past half century. Those assaults are tied strenuously to the way world economies acquire and use resources. It is incredible that major polluters such as the United States refuse to accept the visible evidence that human activities are harming the planet. Rather, as noted in a recent <u>Scientific American</u> article, hoked up industry challenges to serious science are being used by the offenders to preserve bad habits. By failing to join other leading nations in such corrective and preventive efforts as the Kyoto Accords, the United States may, as opponents of the Accords argue, avoid damage to its economy, but even though there are costs, the alleged economic damage is not proven, while the facts of damage to the environment are obvious.

The bad habits of the United States and others unfortunately are linked to political catering to powerful interest groups in energy, finance, manufacturing, and resource extraction. The catering is in turn linked to an acute narrowing of actual control and participation in important decisions by the people. The silencer of complaint from the public may be awareness that income, employment, and life styles depend on the economy as presently run. Our democracy is bifurcated radically, however, between those people who are periodically called upon to elect officials, and that much smaller number who determine what those officials do. The prices we pay for comfort are the continuing degradation of the environment and the growing power over our economic and political lives by political, military, and religious oligarchies.

The outlook—The essays in this book raise many questions about government actions and decisions, but the Bush administration has been less than candid or honest about its plans and intentions. As a result, it has given us a special problem: A failure of trust. Governments can operate successfully in secret when their silence is supported by patterns of conduct that inspire confidence. Under George W. Bush national policy, conduct of the War on Terrorism, the attack and occupation of Iraq, and the unreserved alignment of the administration with Israeli efforts to dispossess the Palestinian people have all revealed patterns of deceit and ideological commitment that make faith in leadership difficult to muster. The resultant patterns of error are cumulative whether the subject is why the United States invaded Iraq, why the US is being globally abusive of prisoners in the War on Terrorism, or why it screws up in hurricane management.

There are enormous global confidence factors that can be perturbed by the patterns of error. The US is deeply in debt. Countries such as China and members of the European Community, Japan, and many others carry US paper on budgetary debt and on the management of trade flows. Threats of oil exporters such as Iran, or Iraq while under Saddam, to change oil price denomination to the euro from the dollar could expose the US to adverse foreign exchange situations that would greatly complicate the US debt management situation and undermine confidence abroad. A run against the dollar and dollar denominated assets could be a disaster.

Our country is not well served by any of this. Our leadership is standing out there in the altogether, trying to brazen it out, while borrowing heavily abroad to keep the neo-con power game going. The Bush team not only is squandering our good name; it is threatening our national survival.

There is much at stake for everybody if this gambit comes a cropper. Other countries would most likely cooperate, therefore, if the US were to show signs of regaining its senses. That means our country starts taking a cooperative and supportive role in world leadership, not a combative and imperial one. Should that occur, may the understanding, goodwill, and enlightened self-interest of mankind pull us back on course.

Made in the USA